"WORDS FROM THE ASHTANGA WORLD"

"In the 30 years I've known Prem he has been a shining example of the benefits of leading a yogic life. I'm so happy he has decided to share his experiences of ashtanga yoga and his knowledge of ayurveda and tantra. to the world."

— **Nancy Gilgoff,**
Senior Ashtanga Yoga Teacher '73

"Prem has poured his heart into the pages of his book. Dive in and enjoy the ride of his life!"

— **David Swenson, Author of**
Ashtanga Yoga Practice Manual

"A light, easy and enjoyable read... Read this book if you're looking for a fun, real world take on the ups and downs of living the yogic lifestyle."

— **Olaf Kalfas,**
Advanced Ashtanga Yoga Practitioner

"The Only Way Out is In" by Antonio *"Prem"* Carlisi is a welcome addition to our Ashtanga World familia. His weaving of Ashtanga Yoga with Ayurveda and Tantra is bravo!"

— **Lino Miele (European Ashtanga Maestro)**

THE ONLY WAY OUT IS IN

THE ONLY WAY OUT IS IN

A MODERN DAY YOGI'S COMMENTARY ON THE SYNERGY OF ASHTANGA YOGA, AYURVEDA AND TANTRA

Anthony "Prem" Carlisi

EDITOR: Thea Petchler
COVER & PAGE DESIGN/LAYOUT: VedicDesign.com
COVER ART: Pieter Welteverde www.santansociety.com
BACK COVER PHOTO: Lisa Seed

First Edition: 2007
Printed in the United States of America
ISBN 978-0-9798698-0-8

Published by:
DREAM WEAVERS INTERNATIONAL
P.O. Box 1341
Hanalei, HI. 96714
www.theonlywayoutisin.com
Printed by Book Masters, Ohio

I dedicate this book to my beloved Osho, whose Grace descended on me through his "living words." Though I never met him in the flesh, he has touched my heart like no other Being. I've had many "teachers" along the way showing me the steps to ascend in life, but Osho is above and beyond any label of teacher, master or guru to me. He gave me wings to fly and the courage to take the leap.

ACKNOWLEDGEMENTS

To my precious daughters Shanti and Mira for their never ending Love.

To Shirin and Kenji who are always there for me, along with my play buddy Sierra; and Roddy, MaMa Manijeh, and Kamron. Plus the rest of my Kauai Family.

Special Thanks to Heather Duplex who assisted throughout the entire process and allowed me to complete this project. Without her help it would not have been possible.

To Len Blank for his help in launching the writing process.

To Cris and Dave Williams for their encouragement to keep going.

There are so many people who have helped me throughout my journey, that I'm sure to leave someone out. But here I go:

To David Williams my Ashtanga brother and Nancy Gilgoff for bringing Guruji to America, Gary Lopedota, Brad Ramsey, Sri K. Pattabhi Jois my beloved Ashtanga Guru, Baba Hari Das, Dr.Vasant Lad, Dr. David Frawley, Ram Dass, Tim Miller, Olaf & Nina, People Forever Immortality Group, Daryl Kohlman, Marta Kohlman, Mark Segars, Maria Curtis, Kelly Prentice, Michael and Jen, Zach, Darci Frankel, Eagle, Sharath, Fred Lewis, Mira, Darine, Big Kahuna Ed, Gwyneth Paltrow and Chris Martin, David Davenport, Greg Jones, Beth Cole, Iris, Elsie, Tara Mala, Luke Chan, Clint, Sayoko, Krishna Prem, Vibhavan, Tara Guber, Ricky, Takeshi, Rupali, Stewart, Bodhi, Cynthia, James, Bhavani, Gabe, Deepika, Lin, Dave Oliver, Enrique, Saskia, Ignacio, Marianna, Richard Rollins, Ellena, Saman family in Sri Lanka,

Tashi, Sarath, Greshon, Sun, Thea, Siva, Charles, Tom Lewis, Sacha, Mom, Dad, Corky, Chuck, Yvonne, Jim and the whole Carlisi clan. To all my students past, present, and future. To all my friends, lovers and teachers…

Thank you all for your continued love and support. Each one of you have played a part in making this book possible.

TABLE OF CONTENTS

ACKNOWLEDGEMENTS   IX

PREFACE   XIV

PART I
My Life's Story

PART II: AYURVEDA
The Science of Life and Living

INTRODUCTION   49

THE FIVE ELEMENTS   59

VATA PITTA KAPHA   67

PRAKRUTI /VIKRUTI   75

SATTVA RAJAS TAMAS   85

SIX TASTES   91

AGNI AND AMA   101

PRANA TEJAS OJAS   115

CLEANSING AND REJUVENATION   121

PART III: ASHTANGA YOGA
The Royal Super Highway

WHAT IS YOGA?   133

ASHTANGA YOGA "SUTRAS" OF PATANJALI   139

ASHTANGA YOGA: A GLIMPSE OF THE EIGHT LIMBS   143

REVELATION OF "THE PYRAMID CODE"   165

THE WIZARD YOGI   173

"MYSORE STYLE": ASHTANGA VINYASA YOGA: THE MOST ANCIENT FORM ?   205

ASHTANGA YOGA AND AYURVEDA   211

PART IV: TANTRA
Divine Ecstasy

INTRODUCTION **219**

PAST AND PRESENT VIEWS OF SEXUALITY **223**

PINEAL GLAND MAGNETISM **233**

SHIVA SHAKTI STORY **239**

BREATHING TECHNIQUES FOR TANTRIC
PRACTICES **243**

TANTRA AND SACRED SEX **253**

EPILOGUE **261**

I wish I could speak like music
I wish I could put the swaying splendor
Of the fields into words
So that you could hold Truth
Against your body
And dance.

I am trying the best I can
With this crude brush, the tongue,
To cover you with light.
I wish I could speak like divine music.

I want to give you the sublime rhythms
of this earth and the sky's limbs
As they joyously spin and surrender, Surrender Against God's
luminous breath.

— Hafiz

PREFACE

his book may surprise some of you who are looking for the typical, linear, step-by-step presentation of Ashtanga Yoga, Ayurveda and Tantra. You won't find that here. I have a hard time taking life too seriously, but I am sincere in my attempt to give you what I feel are the essential aspects of these living arts in their most practical form. My style of writing, like my life, is intense yet frequently full of levity. My language can sometimes be coarse, at other times poetic or humorous, but most of all it is personal. I can speak on these topics much more easily than I write. As you will see right away, I ain't no Bill Shakespeare. I've kept it "raw" on purpose, drawing mostly from my own life experiences. There are an infinite number of synchronistic happenings in and all around us that whisper, or sometimes yell, "Look Here, Go Within!" This book is based on a handful of these kinds of experiences and observations in my own life. See what they parallel in yours. It will then be up to you to explore them more deeply if you so choose.

My main intention in writing this book is to open the discussion on how important Ayurveda, Ashtanga Yoga and Tantra are when they come together as a trilogy. The synergy of the three combine to form a perfect three-sided pyramid, or tetrahedron, giving you one of the most powerful tools available for Consciousness. One without the other two leaves you feeling "shortchanged." You will see this is happening in numerous experiences throughout the book.

To set the stage of this literary journey, I'd like to ask you to visualize yourself as one of the ancient Rishis, enlightened Yogis from India. In your mind, put yourself back in the same jungle or Himalayan mountain peak where they may have gone and isolated themselves in order to uncover the mysteries of life. They observed themselves first and foremost, then nature. These observations became what we now know as the ancient texts of Ashtanga Yoga, Ayurveda and Tantra. Imagine yourself as one of these ancient "Seers," discovering the secrets of these practices without having to endure the austerity of living in a cave, wearing a loin cloth and eating berries. Instead, I will show you how to incorporate these concepts wearing your favorite Calvin Klein yoga attire, having a cappuccino and hangin' out in the comfort of your own living room.

One of our greatest stumbling blocks as human beings is that we've become desensitized to the natural rhythms of life by associating so strongly with our minds, instead of listening to the inherent wisdom of our bodies. Our most profound teacher is reflected all around us in nature, yet in order to recognize and feel her rhythms we must first clear the mirror of our mind. It's important for us "citified folk" to get to the country periodically and undo the effects of the stimulation bombarding us from all directions. I'm sure this is why the Rishis immersed themselves in nature, and it is much more challenging than ever before to find balance.

This book can show you a way out of this dilemma, or perhaps a way In. Sit back and enjoy the ride, as I lay out a road map of what to look for in your own life using my life as an example of mostly "what not to do!" (You can thank me later for saving you hundreds of thousands of dollars and blood, sweat, and buckets of tears!) Having said that, the most important guide you have is your own inner wisdom. Don't hesitate to call on that part of yourself frequently as you read to check in and feel what I am attempting to communicate to you. Does it resonate or not? See for yourself if what I say fits. If not, go back to what you were doing before. I won't take it personally: after all, life is one big experiment!

Truth is expressed in many ways and is repeated over and over throughout time. It is not a matter of learning more, but of recognizing that you already know it. My intention in writing this book is to share with you what I have discovered, to illustrate that the secrets of life are within you. They are merely buried under lifetimes of coverings blocking your vision to truly see. Using the methods of Ashtanga Yoga, Ayurveda and Tantra, you have the opportunity to dissolve the illusion of ever needing anything else but your own guiding light. Clarity is that simple.

One way to accomplish this is to be firmly rooted in the basic principles of these three systems. Let them be your living "compass" keeping you on track as you explore the vast realms within. I'd like to use the image of you as a child again, learning your ABCs, and I'm your kindergarten teacher. This will set the stage to see with "new eyes" as you enter into the deeper aspects of the world of Ashtanga Yoga, Ayurveda and Tantra. Let me say as well, that any of what I share about Ashtanga Yoga can be applied to Hatha Yoga, since I am commenting on the energetic practices which are relevant to all forms. So this is not a book limited to only Ashtangis (practitioners of Ashtanga Yoga),but for the Yoga community at large. We will explore the essence of each of these methods down to its roots, as this is the juice that feeds the whole tree. In this sense we are going back to our own "roots."

As a young child we had to first learn our alphabet in order to comprehend language, before we moved on to reading and then writing. Step-by-step we learned the letters, then created words and sentences. As we became more proficient we then were able to comprehend the concepts and ideas that were represented in those letters and words. Before this time you were a blank slate with no comprehension of any symbols. You simply lived in harmony with "what is," enjoying life using all of your five senses without a care in the world. Slowly your pure, innocent heart and mind were fed with many of the impressions that color your Consciousness. Impressions from your primary caregivers, schools, religions, and friends: these formed your belief systems. I now have the challenge of connecting to an already formed adult mind that has been conditioned to move and behave in a certain way, because that is the nature of the mind.

I do not want you to drop one belief system only to replace it with another, or to mechanically go through the motions. Your perceptions are crowded by multiple layers. Yogic, Ayurvedic and Tantric methods of physical and mental purification allow more space for you to be free in the moment. It is perfectly fine to learn from the past, but not to live in the past; to plan for the future, but not to be attached to the outcome. The essence of the Universe always remains the same. It is your mind that is constantly changes, pulling you from the past and projecting you into the future and then propelling you back again. This constant yo-yo effect keeps us from experiencing anything authentic and genuine. Perhaps the mind should be called "minding," since it is a continuous process going on 24/7, or, as one friend has called it, a "meaning making machine."

Use the experience of reading this book to become more Conscious. Some of what I present will feel quite familiar. This is a good sign that you are on the right track. Proceed with patience. The information I offer can only be a map of the actual path. You must get on the road and see for yourself what is "real" and what is not. Most of what we have been taught serves those in places of power over us. I am reminded of a quote by one of the greatest minds ever, Einstein, who said, "The only thing that interferes with my learning is my education." The teachings I am about to share with you are about reclaiming your birthright as a vibrant, alive, human being, not gathering more information to fill your heads. For it is already something you intuitively have within. Knowing this will enable you to live with these tools in perfect harmony with nature and the magnificent World around you, without getting consumed by it.

As the famous French philosopher Proust observed, "The real journey of discovery consists not in seeking new landscapes, but in having new eyes." Even if you are an experienced practitioner, become a beginner again. As you see with new eyes, it's important to remember that everyone on this planet can be a teacher that helps support your In-volution (going within). Some teachers can only talk the talk, while others will walk the talk. As you read this book, don't confuse the message with the messenger. Ultimately, what matters to your growth is how you apply it. (Whew, that gets me off the hook!!!)

"Life is not a question, it's not a problem to be solved, but a mystery into which one dissolves oneself." This quote is from one of my favorite Indian Mystics, Kabir. After contemplating this insightful statement for years, I have finally embraced its words of wisdom. What a relief it is to experience for the first time that I don't have to figure it all out anymore! I felt for many years I was on this frantic race "to know" when all I had to do was relax and let go. From this peaceful space inside myself, I have finally begun to enjoy the magic of life, without labeling or analyzing it. Of course, my mind pulls me back with its devious ways, but for the most part I have been able to chill out and simply watch the miracle of life unfold.

Why is childhood considered so paradise-like? Because as children, we lived in a world full of wonder. We were in awe of everything. An ordinary flower, clouds floating by, a butterfly in the air. All of life expressed itself through its mysterious ways. We didn't label things or categorize them. We usually remember childhood as our happiest time. Our happiness is in the same proportion to our mystery. Less mystery=less happiness; more mystery=more happiness.

A few days before Einstein died he stated,

"When I started my journey on the scientific path I was certain that the universe can be known, but now I am not so certain. On the contrary, my uncertainty has been growing every day, and I feel that it is impossible to know the existence in its totality. It is a mystery."

All mystic traditions have shared with humanity the dilemma of using whatever method you choose to find your way through this mystery. They emphasize that each method is simply a way to guide you in the right direction, or, as my teacher Osho puts it, "the finger pointing to the moon." Don't get lost in looking at the finger. The methods create the situation for the mind to dissolve, allowing the mystery to reveal itself in its myriad ways through pure passive awareness. The tricky part is that for adults with highly developed intellects it seems too simple, so we go on looking for complicated ways to figure it all out, leaving us No-Where. Initially there is a struggle with the mind in order to go beyond this and be Now-Here. (I love these "secret" word games.)

Living in the moment the mind has no use, so herein lies the struggle. It is the death of the mind, the ego, that is its greatest fear. For if the ego identification is dropped, who are we then? We are left observing life as it is from the source of all that is. Funny thing, if we need the mind we can use it as the tool it was meant to be, otherwise it is constantly getting in the way of us fully living free.

All the mystics say at some point you must drop the method and simply Be. You never know when this will happen, like a gold miner picking away in search of gold. He never knows when he will strike it rich. It's not in our hands. Our "job," so to speak, is to be continually aware of how the mind pulls us away from what is real. The journey is a 180-degree turn in the opposite direction than what we're used to. We're not used to going within to feel what's right for us in each moment. Our minds only confuse the situation by going back into the past or racing ahead into the future. There is a deep rest in coming back "Home" to the space that is available to us all the time in..........Presence.

"Presence is the pure state of being where consciousness is simply observing itself in manifestation."

—Prem

There once was a wise woman traveling in the mountains who found a precious stone in a stream. The next day she encountered a traveler who was very hungry and she opened her bag to share her food. The hungry traveler seeing the precious stone asked if she would give it to him. She did so without hesitation. The traveler left, rejoicing in his good fortune. He knew that the stone was worth enough to give him security for a lifetime. But after only a few days, he returned to give the stone back to the woman. I have been thinking, he said, I know how valuable the stone is, but I am giving it back in the hope that you can give me something even more precious. What would that be? asked the woman. I want you to give me what you have within you that enabled you to give me the stone.

I now invite you to travel with me and experience something you've always had waiting within. It's my intention to share with you, from my heart to yours, the message of Love. I offer you my "Love Story" as a gift to support you on your own personal discovery. My wish is that these words and methods of transformation may somehow touch you as deeply as they have me. The material in this book has come from talks I have given around the world on Ashtanga Yoga, Ayurveda and Tantra.

Are you ready to observe with new eyes?

Enjoy and blessings to you all,

Prem.

PART I

"DAZED AND CONFUSED"
- LED ZEPPELIN

My Life Story

The Only Way Out is In

$\mathcal{I}$'m not a scholar with letters after my name to show vast knowledge of the classic texts. Nor have I studied, memorized or discoursed on their meanings in depth. I'm just a regular guy who happened to be open to new and alternative experiences before it was fashionable to do so. I felt alone at times, but knew I was on to something quite special. This book is a gathering of what fruits I have picked along the way. My expression comes from an array of personal experiences and is my own personal approach to Ashtanga Yoga, Ayurveda and Tantra. I feel fortunate to have had these anchors in my life when the "storms" got rough.

I begin with my own life story to illustrate how all along the way I never gave up; I trusted that ray of truth to always guide me back on the path. Hidden in every "misfortune" was a blessing in disguise. As every story has a beginning, here is mine:

My grandparents came from Sicily in 1908, landing in Ellis Island, New York. I can only imagine how they must have felt seeing the Statue of Liberty and knowing they were about to embark on a completely new life in a place they knew as "the Land of the Free." So I am a third generation Italian-American. My father and mother along with some of their brothers and sisters ended up moving from the East Coast out west to Arizona, the southwestern corner of the good ole U.S. of A. I was the fifth child but the first in my family to be born in Phoenix, in 1955. I had three brothers and a sister all 20 years older than me; one was a brother who died when he was three. His name was Nicolas. I never knew him, but his death influenced my mother's extreme over protectiveness of me.

My father worked his butt off to provide what he thought would make us happy. Unfortunately he ended up dying prematurely from worry, overwork, and poor lifestyle choices. I was seven when his cancer (Leukemia) was discovered, and ten years old when he died, which left my mom to raise me an only child. After my father's untimely death I found myself thrown into the world of being a responsible adult, yet was still a child missing his dad. I distinctly remember one of my "mafia type" uncles at my father's funeral, bending over and placing his hand on my shoulders and saying to me, "Now you're the man of the house, look after your mom." Pretty heavy thing to lay on a ten year-old. I know now he was only trying to make light of a very difficult situation, but having no choice in my impressionable mind, I took on the role. The following eight years of my life meant taking care of Mom, who now depended heavily upon me for her needs. Meanwhile, I was still trying to figure out the complexities of growing up, and was left on my own to do so.

I had a horse, when I was between the ages of 8-10 years old, that my father gave me to buffer the shock of him not being able to play with me. The horse's name was Lucky. Whenever I rode him I imagined I was an Indian boy exploring the vast world of the Arizona desert around me. Tales of Geronimo the famous Apache warrior were told amongst the locals that lived in our area. I would ride Lucky bareback for hours, and shoot my bow and arrow at anything, moving or not! Sometimes I stopped to catch lizards wandering by or would rest under a tree near a washed-out riverbed. My whole world was Lucky and me. Although often I felt alone, his company somehow comforted me within. It was a magical time for me to escape in the wonderland of the barren desert, even as my father slowly disappeared. Those few years with Lucky grounded me in my roots as a gypsy wanderer. I had this "familiar" feeling of somehow being an Indian, growing up in the dry, rugged land connected to everything around me. Those magical feelings faded quickly when my father died, but somehow the mystical seed of those years were planted deep in my heart. I lost interest in everything around me and that included Lucky. We sold him soon thereafter, in a way marking the end of my childhood.

The distress of seeing my father wasting away from cancer began when I was seven. That's when Mom started asking me for help to take care of Dad. This meant sleeping with him at times, helping him to the bathroom, or whatever else was needed for his care at home since she no longer could handle this by herself. My oldest sister Cora and my brothers Chuck and Jim helped out when they could. For three long years, Dad was in and out of the hospital, so when I wasn't sitting in his hospital room doing my homework after school, I was acting as one of his caretakers at home. Prior to his sickness, mom depended on Dad for almost everything, and as he slowly deteriorated and began to lose the strength to take care of his own basic needs, she also became incapable. Being the youngest and still living at home, it was left up to me to do what was needed by both, or so I thought.

Those 3-4 years of basically living at the hospital with him, I witnessed several people lying in the hospital bed next to my father disappear. None of it made sense to me. I would ask, "Where did Mr. Jones or Mrs. Smith go?," only to be told that they had "gone to heaven." I loved my father so much. He was my best friend and I wanted to do anything to help him. I felt the more I could help Dad, the sooner he would get well. After all, everyone assured me that he would get well soon. Unfortunately, this was the lie that was embedded upon my innocent heart, and the intolerable pain of finding out it wasn't true made me feel I didn't want to live anymore. As a young child, I remember feeling depressed and isolated. Afraid to get close to anyone for fear they would disappear as well. In remembering my father, there is almost no recollection of the good times I had with him, only the trying times dealing with his illness. But I know those times must have existed because he was so special to me. The pain of losing someone so important, like my father, was too much to handle. In addition, six months before my father's death, my grandmother, my father's mother, died suddenly. Yet another loss I had to face at such a young age. The pain caused by these two deaths followed me like a shadow well into adulthood.

Watching my father's health deteriorate before my eyes profoundly influenced my life's path and work. Indirectly, I have him to thank for setting me on a course of health and well-being for myself and others. I now realize my father's death was a blessing in disguise, and it helped mold me into who I am. It led me to the connection and commitment to my Yoga practices and study of Ayurveda, which will last forever. More importantly, it changed the way I related to my own children in raising them. It helped to break the genetic code of that way of living. Making conscious lifestyle changes allows us to alter those patterns that have been passed on to us by our parents.

I've observed that most men in modern day society have this drive to amass great wealth and material things, at the expense of their health or the loss of quality time with their family. Maybe not in the way that my father approached it in the 50's, as now we have bigger and better dreams. More now than ever, husbands and wives are both working to make ends meet. Kids are being raised by nannies or child care providers. They get stuck in the "hamster wheel" of life wondering where all the time has gone. Maybe there's money in the bank, but they are bankrupt in their health, and their overall quality of life has diminished.

The realities of my actual journey have been filled with huge swings of the pendulum before I discovered the source of wisdom is within myself. After all, like many of us, I had no living role model to follow but somehow managed to survive through pure grace. My life has been one big experiment as is true for most kids who have lost a parent to some form of emotional and physical separation. If being cast adrift is one of the root sources of all our dysfunctions as a modern culture, the only way back is by turning within. Sometimes we learn by seeing what not to do. I have my father to thank for showing me some of these things. Part of my healing was to acknowledge this, along with forgiving him for dying and forgiving myself for the guilt I carried about not being able to do more for him. I am happy to add that my own kids continue to make healthy life style choices.

The seed of Yoga was planted in my life about four years after my father's death. I was 14 at the time. My best friend John's brother, Mark, was involved with trafficking marijuana across the Arizona border from Mexico and ended up in a very bad situation: life imprisonment without parole. The person with whom he smuggled the ganja shot and killed a DEA (Drug Enforcement Agency) officer who supposedly was their buyer. They were in the car with the agents in the back seat. Once he realized they were dealing with undercover DEA agents, he reached under his seat, grabbed a gun, and to Mark's surprise, shot both of the agents, killing one of them. The other officer miraculously escaped. Soon thereafter Mark turned himself in, but being an accomplice in the killing of a government official, he was given a life sentence.

Yet it was in prison that Mark ended up learning about Yoga and other tools of Consciousness. He began to share them with his brother John. Mark was introduced to all of this through the "Ram Dass Prison Project," which taught inmates about Yoga, meditation, good nutrition, etc. Mark became very actively involved with this project and even became a Yoga teacher while he was "inside." He also was a spokesman for vegetarianism, and got involved with astrology. In fact, he gave me my first astrology reading. Mark shared with his brother John many things about Yoga and living a conscious way of life. John in turn shared all this with me. I remember one day looking at John who was wearing a necklace, that had what appeared to be on the end of it, the

5

number "35." When I asked him why he was wearing "35" around his neck, he said "that's not 35, that's the OM symbol." I said, "The Om symbol, what the hell's that?" He told me it was part of the Yoga tradition his brother was learning about in prison.

Many gems were being instilled in me one by one, by this beautiful being who I only knew indirectly, and who was at that time only 19, and living in the dark world of prison. Basically a naive person who had been in the wrong place at the wrong time, doing the wrong thing and as a result, ended up paying a huge price. It's strange the twists and turns that end up shaping our lives and the people around us.

During this time, there was a huge push in the U.S. to make marijuana out to be a very dangerous drug. In fact, I remember being shown a movie in school not long after all this happened which depicted marijuana as an "evil and demonic" substance. It was called "Reefer Madness." In the movie, the person smoking marijuana looks crazy with deep dark circles under his eyes and then ends up killing someone, implying the dangers of marijuana can even lead to murder. The crime John's brother was involved with was reflected in that movie, and so his crime made headlines throughout the U.S.

Of course all my friends and I were stoned watching this film and laughing at how stupid they made the characters appear. Another lesson in hypocrisy from the adults that wasn't true. They were feeding us this lie and then turning around popping their pharmaceutical drugs for this and that, and boozing it up. It's no different now with the "Just say no to drugs" campaign. Kids see through all this and run in the opposite direction.

I finally got an opportunity to meet Mark in prison after learning so much about him through his brother. One day I went to visit him, accompanied by John, along with his mother and father. I was so excited to finally meet him since so many extraordinary things had been transmitted to me. Things about Consciousness, though unbeknownst to me at the time. I couldn't wait to meet this "boy" of 21 who had already made such a strong influence on my life's course. One of the books that he passed on to me was called, "Be Here Now": my first Yoga book. The author Ram Dass, formally known as Dr. Richard Alpert, a Harvard graduate, also made references to the use of psychedelic drugs, which were very much a part of his spiritual journey, along with that of his Harvard colleague and radical activist, Timothy Leary. I, too, began to experiment with these far-out, mind-altering substances along with John, my best friend. In fact, more than experiment, truthfully, we began to experience them regularly!!! That could be a whole other book....

In visiting Mark in prison, I was deeply touched by the presence of this incredible being. He was instrumental in positively influencing so many people's lives in and out of prison and had an aura that radiated pure love. That day, I remember leaving the prison crying, having experienced something that would deeply impact me for the rest of my life. It just didn't make sense to me. I couldn't fathom why this beautiful soul was locked up and I was free to walk away. A few years later, being the model prisoner he was, he was transferred to a minimum security ward in the same prison. Ironically, about a year later, I got word from my friend John that he had escaped! They never found him. I was secretly thrilled for him. He had assumed a new identity and carried on with his life somewhere in the States, teaching Yoga and working in a vegetarian restaurant. I never spoke to him ever again nor really asked my friend John of his whereabouts, but his influence goes on inside me forever.

In 1974 I was 19. I left my mom in Arizona and went to finish college in California. It was a painful but liberating feeling to finally be on my own. I decided to study marine biology at U.C.S.D. (University of California, San Diego) when in fact I actually just wanted to surf! Although I was raised in the desert of Phoenix, I became a surfer after many trips to the ocean in Mexico and California.

I had always wanted to live by the beach, so this was a dream come true. I found marine biology much too difficult, so I quickly changed my major to Sociology and Psychology. While attending University I was constantly questioning life, and continued to experiment with many drugs and party to keep myself numb from feeling what had happened as a child. One day at school, I met a far-out character named Kenji. He was a student teacher at the University. He was dressed in funky hippie clothing and told me some wild stories of his adventures in India. He planted this book on me called, "The Life and Teachings of the Masters of the Far East" by Baird T. Spalding (a six volume set of which Kenji gave me the first). Reading this book was yet another synchronistic event in my life that reawakened the fire within.

In the summer of 1978 I was faced with, "what am I going to do with the rest of my life?" and at the same time grappling with, "what's the meaning of life?" Somehow, I graduated with a degree in Sociology and gave the diploma to my mom since it was her desire more than mine that I finish college. Yet after graduation I was left feeling empty, and very unsatisfied. It was the wild 70's and I was still hooked on drugs, sex, and rock and roll. There I was, college graduate, and when not stoned wondering where my future was headed. A very troubled time for me. Dazed and confused about what was next, as I saw myself heading for a tragic end if I wasn't careful.

Next thing I knew, two women friends (angels in disguise) came to me excitedly, saying, "You have to come our Yoga class!" "It's so great, you'll love it." In my mind I remembered as a young boy flipping through the TV channels (by hand, since there were only three or 4 channels at that time) and noticing a woman named Lilias Folan doing Yoga. I remember watching the program for less than a minute and quickly changing it thinking, "That's weird!" So when my friends told me to come to their Yoga class, there was no way I was going. My memory of Yoga was of this funny-looking woman with a soft whispering voice and some whiny music in the background. But they swore it was different and it was a style called "Ashtanga Yoga." They told me this particular style was dynamic, flowing, and athletic, and I would surely love it. Curious more than anything, and being an athlete, I figured it'd be an interesting challenge so I agreed to go.

The first class I was told I could only observe, not participate. I arrived in rapt anticipation that morning at a remodeled Christian church converted into a Yoga space, ready to watch. I opened the large wooden door entering a scene I will never forget. Everything was cleared off the ground and there was carpet wall to wall. The ceilings were vaulted, there were stained glass windows with pictures of Christ, and the smell of incense permeated the air. The room had a mystical feeling about it as I walked in, yet having been brought up a Catholic, it also gave me a haunting memory of going to church. What I didn't know at the time was that I was about to enter a world that would eventually become my life.

The class had already begun. I took a seat off to the side and began watching the people practicing. I couldn't believe my eyes. Everyone looked so amazing, so beautiful. At that time 80% of the class were women (which by the way is still true today). My mouth gaped wide with amazement at the grace and beauty flowing in the room, but also because a lot of those beautiful women were doing their practice in barely any clothing! This got my lustful attention. I was 21 years old with hormones raging. At that time there were no "Yoga clothes." No designer Yoga paraphernalia to be seen anywhere. Everyone was basically practicing in their underwear. I was watching all these gorgeous, tanned southern California gods and goddesses practicing what I now know to be one of the most poetic forms of movement on the planet.

For hours I sat and watched people going through a particular sequence of asanas or yogic postures. Everyone seemed to know what they were doing as if they were in their own world. There were 25 people in the room moving silently, yet all that could be heard was the deep resonant sound of their breath. There was a stillness in the room I had never experienced before. The teachers at the time walked around the room giving both verbal and physical adjustments to different practitioners. By physically moving their bodies in a particular way they assisted them in going deeper into the postures. Watching them touch these beautiful, sensuous female bodies led me also to fantasize one day of becoming an Ashtanga Yoga teacher! Anyway... I continued to watch as the instructors glided around the room intuitively flowing from one person to the next whenever they felt the need to give some kind of instruction.

After class, one of the instructors moved slowly over to me and asked if I would like to begin. I said yes, and he told me that to join the class, I would have to commit for the month, which meant I had to pay $75.00 up front. That was the fee at that time for coming to class six days a week, but taking off Saturdays, as well as full and new moon days. I agreed, not really knowing what I was getting myself into. In all honesty it sounded a bit strange, but I was intrigued nonetheless. I was instructed to show up the next morning at 7 a.m. This was the beginning of my Yoga journey.

I showed up every day, practicing diligently, and was loving every minute of it. Being an eager student, I couldn't get enough of this practice but the teachers kept my desires in check. The method was start off slowly and learn it thoroughly in order to become proficient at it. The idea is that you become efficient enough to be able to practice on your own without being dependent on the teacher. You know, "teach 'em how to fish," instead of just giving it to them. The method is still taught today and is called "Mysore style."

After about three months of practice, I began to gain flexibility and strength but not before some very unexpected things happened. Remember, I was just off the street coming from hotdog and hamburger land, drugs, etc. and jumped right into regular Yoga practice and vegetarianism. So my body began to purge like crazy! Stuff began to come out of every orifice, even from openings I didn't know existed!

My nose was running, I had terrible diarrhea, my skin was breaking out and I was getting regular "Yoga" fevers. I was told these were all "good" symptoms. Apparently I needed to rid my body of all the toxins that had accumulated over years of neglectful eating and poor lifestyle habits. I was being put through the fire, cleansed and purified like molten gold. This was a different kind of cleansing, a deep purging of internal tissues and organs, unlike any other form of exercise. The sweat that came out of my body was profuse. I was sweating like a horse during practice. After three months of this, I was sore as hell! Sometimes, in the morning walking to class (as I lived only a block away), I could barely walk. I often thought, "oh my god, is this really good for me? "

One day, not long after I started, I heard a buzz in the room about a man coming from India who they called "Guruji." I said, "What's a Guruji?" Guruji is a term of respect that they use in India for your teacher, similar to the way a martial artist would say "Sensei" to his instructor. The literal translation of Guru is, "one who shines light where there is darkness" and Ji on the end of a name is a term of reverence. It's also a cosmic, comedic acronym for G. U. R. U. = "Gee, You, Are, You."

I heard through the "grapevine" that Guruji, also known as Sri K. Pattabhi Jois, was next in line to guide this ancient Yoga tradition of Ashtanga which had been going on for hundreds of years. He was coming from Mysore, India to teach at our center for several months. "The living embodiment of the source of this tradition was coming to us. How cool is that?" I thought. What good fortune since India seemed light years away from Southern California.

Students from around the world came to be with him in Encinitas, California, at the "church" where I was learning Ashtanga Yoga. Our modest group of 20-25 people soon swelled to 45 or 50 people. The majority of the people who came to study with him came from Maui, Hawaii, David Williams and Nancy Gilgoff from Maui were instrumental in launching Ashtanga Yoga in the West. My teachers Brad Ramsey and Gary Lopedota studied under them. The students who arrived from around the world were all experienced Ashtanga Yoga practitioners. Some of them were the most far-out looking people I'd ever met: long-haired freaks who looked like they came out of the jungle- and some of them actually had! Yet they blew me away with their yogic abilities, moving beautiful, lean, sculpted bodies, with grace and suppleness, like poetry in motion. Some of them were 50 years old at the time(which I am now). I thought, "these guys are really old but they don't look it". Funny, huh?

Guruji showed up a fully animated 62-year-old. Today he is past 92 and still teaching. He was literally bouncing around the room, going from person to person, and doing so with boundless energy pouring out of every cell of his body. My teachers warned me about him, but nothing could have prepared me for what I experienced in his presence. What I remember most about what they said was to trust and surrender to Guruji's direction; otherwise you could get hurt since he gave very strong physical adjustments. My teachers told me to just breathe and go with whatever he was helping me in. The first class he adjusted me. He came up to me while I was sitting on the floor with my feet folded inward and legs out (Baddha Konasana). I was just about to finish the pose, when he came without notice, and pushed my knees to the floor with a foot on each of my legs while pushing my head to the floor with his hands. After he released my knees they immediately sprang back up, like some kind of cartoon character. Day after day for months this went on, him helping each of us dig a little deeper inside ourselves, pushing what we thought was impossible to do. He always seemed to come and adjust you in the pose you hated the most. From all the intense adjustments and pushing myself over those months of being with him , some heavy duty soreness kicked in, and my body began to feel a kind of "sweet pain" that I experienced to the bone. My body was transforming before my eyes, along with waves of emotions coming from who knows where. Somehow I knew that all these things, inside and out, needed to come to the surface to be released.

Guruji stayed around for about four or five months on this visit. On particular days during those months there were sessions or "conferences," where we all had opportunities to ask any questions we had about Yoga. All of us listened with rapt attention to him going off on ancient Sanskrit slokas or verses. His grasp of English was limited so we had to pay close attention to every word as he translated these ancient texts. We regularly- met as a group on Saturdays for potlucks and bhajans (chanting). I had this great connection with this man who continued to share his wisdom and experience with all of us. My love for this practice grew stronger and stronger. I felt a part of a family, the Ashtanga family. At the end of his stay Guruji invited everyone who had become his students to come to India, but only seven of us decided to go: me, Gary, Brad, Sherry, Lynne, Hans and Pistachio. We were the first "group" (prior to this students had only shown up individually, not in groups) of western students to land in Mysore, India, the home and Yoga Shala (school) of Guruji.

The following year, 1979, when we actually arrived, he was so happy to greet us. All seven of us arrived excited to immerse ourselves at the feet of our Guru. We all ended up hanging out doing Yoga daily and living there for three months. My practice soared as I made tremendous progress being with him. We met for asana practice in the morning and then in the afternoons we would meet and practice the traditional Ashtanga pranayama or hold informal discussions on life and Yoga.

There were some very funny incidents during that first trip. One was when he was teaching us "sutra neti." This is a yogic cleansing practice using a rubber tubing with a string on the end of it which is then inserted into the nose and out through the mouth. You could call it "nasal flossing," if you like. It was quite humorous what followed. All of us showed up by his request one

Saturday morning, since we were not practicing asanas on that day, for a demonstration of this technique. He told us that we were going to learn this method of clearing our nostrils for better pranayama, yogic breathing. He sat us down one by one and shoved this tube in one nostril; out it came through the mouth. He grabbed hold of it once it came out of the mouth and proceeded to pull it back and forth to ream the nasal passage clear. We cringed and grimaced as we watched Guruji perform this on his first victim. Oh, did I say that he used the same neti string for all of us? Yeah, that's right, it was washed out in the sink and then was down the next person's nose. When we saw him washing it out and then call "Next!" we were laughing like hell and fighting to be next. It was quite comical. Ah those were the days...

Sometimes we simply showed up to have coffee and Indian sweets with him, Amma his wife, and Saraswati his daughter. Sharath, Guruji's grandson, and Saraswati's son, was six at that time. He would be playing cricket on the street in front of their house/Yoga shala in the Lakshmi Puram area of Mysore. He has been groomed since the age of twelve to take on the role of the Ashtanga Yoga Research Institute (AYRI). Sharmila, Saraswati's daughter, was there as well, helping out in the kitchen or playing. It was a rare treat to be in such close contact with this family. In retrospect, I am very thankful for those months of being able to go deeper and deeper in such an intimate setting with a living master of this ancient form of Yoga. I knew deep in my gut that this particular style of Yoga was going to take off in the West, because I felt so damn good. I thought to myself, "Who wouldn't want to feel like this?" It was just a matter of time. Now every major city around the globe has an Ashtanga center and thousands around the world are practicing Ashtanga daily.

After three months, everyone left, but I stayed on. I decided to experience India on my own, so I traveled north to Agra, home of the Taj Mahal. I was awestruck at the majesty of this beautiful structure. The first time I saw it was early dawn just as the sun was rising. There was a mist in the morning air. It looked like it was floating on a cloud in the heavens.

Not knowing anyone, I connected with a bicycle rickshaw driver. He spoke no English, yet we had a wonderful communication through sign language. We joked continuously with one another, and became instant brothers. I put him in the back of the rickshaw so that I could pull him around as well! All the locals got a kick out of that, including him.

The following day my rickshaw driver friend invited me to his home for a meal, which I immediately accepted. We traveled to his village where I quickly became a "star." Everyone wanted to meet me since I was probably the first Westerner to visit. The village consisted of many mud huts and obviously people there had very little, but as is typical in India, whatever little one has is shared. You see, most Indians are Hindus, and they see everyone as an incarnation of God, so when God walks into your home, you naturally feed them. I walked carefully, bending my six foot two inch frame into his little hut, which was only about four feet by six feet. In the middle of the room sat his wife with their two kids in her lap. She prepared lunch for me. She was squatting on the ground facing a fire fueled by dry cow dung, over which was a can which served as a pot containing the dahl (Indian lentils). Next to the can was a pile of chapatis and hungry flies hovering above, looking to land at any opportunity. As she stirred the dahl, she swatted endlessly at these ever-present vermin. I was becoming quite concerned about eating this food, but I knew I couldn't refuse these people who were giving me all they had. In addition, standing behind me, peering in curiously, were about 20 faces watching my every move from the doorway. We all sat on the dirt floor when the dahl and chapatis were served. It was now time to eat. I said a prayer for my well-being and proceeded. I ate only a small amount and then told them I was full.

After the meal, my friend biked me back to my hotel and then to the train station where I took an overnight coach to Benares, also known as Varanasi. Benaras is the best-known holy city along the sacred Ganges River, where people go for spiritual pil-grimage. To Indians, this city is a very auspicious place. They be-lieve that at death if the body is burned and the ashes are thrown into the Ganges, the individual will receive another human re-birth. Dead bodies are continuously being burned day and night on the banks of the river. Benaras is famous for its burning ghats. Ironically, I didn't know that at the time.

As my friend was bicycling me to the train station, I heard rumblings from my belly, and my stomach began to move and sound like a washing machine. "Oh no!" I thought, "This is not good!!!" I hurriedly got on the train and began shitting my brains out after having fought off people to get to the one toilet in the overcrowded car I was traveling in. If I didn't have a good Mula Bandha (contracted muscles that hold the anus closed), I would have shit in my pants! The overnight journey was a living hell and by the time I reached Benares, I was physically and emotion-ally spent. By now I couldn't keep anything down in my gut.

I somehow made my way to the river and ended up staying on a houseboat with no toilet, where all I could do was lean my butt over the side of the boat and continue to purge. Having little energy from purging and dehydration, I could hardly stand up. I looked out into the distance and all I could see were fires consum-ing dead bodies on either side of me. Nightmarishly, I began to imagine if I passed out, I could end up on one of those pyres, hav-ing my ashes thrown into the Ganges. I realized I could actually die if I didn't do something soon. But my experience with India had taught me it might be a good idea to stay away from Indian hospitals. I imagined that if I ventured into one I might be given a rusty or used needle, which would result in something even worse than what I was experiencing at that moment. Scared and delirious, my only hope was to go back to Guruji, thousands of miles away in Mysore, since he was the only person I knew in In-dia. I summoned enough energy to get on a plane and showed up on his doorstep. Upon arrival, there was barely a spark of energy left in my body. Having lost 10 kilos and looking like death warmed over, I knocked on his door.

Guruji was shocked as he helped me into his home. He called me "Raghava", an endearing Sanskrit name he gave me on that trip. It is another name for the famous Indian King Rama, out of the epic tale called the Ramayana. He still uses it today to address me. "Oh Raghava...Why?!" Guruji said, shocked, as he looked at me. He and his wife Amma took me into their house and cared for me until I had enough strength to then travel back to America. For those few weeks with them, I experienced so much love and compassion. A bond was created between us that will never be broken. I am forever grateful to Guruji and his devoted wife (who is now deceased) for all they did for me during this life-threatening time.

For a year my intestines were completely screwed up. What I had going on was amoebic dysentery, a horrible disease caused by parasites that lodge in the intestines. I had to take a series of antibiotics and other treatments to rid my body of the parasites. Surprisingly, even ten years later, after a medical examination, I discovered that my body still had parasites in my intestines. The doctor gave me an ultra sound test for my liver to see if any had gone there. He also mentioned that they can go into the brain. (Maybe that's what's wrong with me?)

On my return to America in 1980, I experienced "reverse culture shock." I had become very comfortable living in India and found it hard to adjust back to the Western lifestyle I tried to recreate the hippie, yogi lifestyle I had been living in India. Since Guruji spoke very little English, no one was satisfying my deep hunger to know what this was all about. Voraciously reading and studying everything about Yoga I could get my hands on, delving into the texts known as the Vedas and Upanishads that are said to be thousands of years old, I continued my exploration of what I had learned thus far with Guruji, drawing on books I had brought back from India and similar resources I found in the States. I took some of this new information quite literally.

One was the concept of "brahmacharya," which I misinterpreted to mean "celibate." Yeah, I actually tried to implement this as a young American guy. Crazy, huh? Here I was, a 25 year old highly sensual, sexual male who wanted so desperately to become a "yogi" that I made a commitment to do whatever it took to be "enlightened". I didn't realize it at the time that I was building a sexual inferno. As a result, in every waking and sleeping moment, I was fantasizing about sex. It was driving me nuts! Everywhere I looked I saw sexuality because I was repressing my natural sexual urges. Conversely, my Yoga practice was stimulating and intensifying my sexual feelings. I felt like a volcano ready to erupt!!! Now I realize I was doing the same thing thousands of priests and monks have done in the name of "religion" and being "spiritual."

I wanted desperately to return to India and now see that one of the reasons I wanted to go back was to buffer or suppress all of the sexual frustration that was raging inside me. I didn't have to directly face my sexuality there like I did in America: India was a great place to hide since all the women were covered up. So I worked my ass off to get the money as quickly as possible to return. I decided to sell whatever stuff of value I had, and before long I was back in India with Guruji. Every day I studied, going deeper and deeper, learning everything I could. I was then practicing "Advanced A" Series (now called Third and Fourth Series) a highly challenging sequence of poses that built internal energy and vitality by doing postures that created amazing flexibility along with incredible strength. I was also practicing an extensive 45 minute Pranayama requiring you to sit in Padmasana (Lotus pose) the entire time. This was more challenging than the actual physical asana practice itself since it required "laser focus." I was holding my breath for long periods of time up to one minute per hold and creating an intense pressure cooker effect in my body, purifying more deeply than ever before. All the pathways had been cleared from the Advanced "A" series of asanas and I was now able to handle the "high voltage" of energy coursing through my channels (nadis). It's like hooking up a 220 volt charge through 110 wiring. If the wiring is not correct there will be a severe blowout somewhere along the circuitry. My body and mind were being conditioned like a warrior, a "spiritual warrior."

I was so fortunate at that time because I was able to get Guruji's full attention, which is no longer possible. Now, 30 years later, hundreds of people from around the world flock to be in his presence. It was an incredible time in my life, learning from Guruji directly things I could only dream were possible. I was so open and available to any and all of the teachings. Most importantly, for the first time in my life, I was learning how to create balance- or so I thought.

I came back to America, made some cash, and again quickly returned to Guruji. On that trip in 1981 I ventured out into India on my own to explore some more of the country and see what else was out there. There I found many Yogis or Sadhus along the way who shared with me their experiences. I sat and smoked Ganja with some of them as they openly shared their insights. I traveled for many months connecting and searching Mother India for any kind of verification that I was on the "right" path and what was next in this seemingly endless journey.

A fellow traveler told me about one Yoga institute located in Lonavla near Pune. There was a Center there called Kaivaladhama where they did extensive research studying, in depth, the effects of doing Asana, Pranayama, Meditation and the Shat Kriyas or the Six cleansing practices of Yoga. At this center some amazing research had been done since the early 1900's. With the advent of technology they were able to monitor various states of consciousness during the advanced Yogis practicing postures, pranayamas, meditational states using EKG machines and other devices that measured significant data on the body/mind. For instance: blood pressure, heart rate, nerve impulses, to name a few. This scientifically verified information that the ancient texts have been saying for thousands of years.

I talked at length with various Yogis and Yoga Research Scientists during the few months that I lived there. The Shat Kriyas or Yogic Cleansing practices captured my attention right away since they seemed to be quite "freaky." I already mentioned to you earlier that I learned one of them called sutra neti the "nasal flossing" with Guruji. I will mention some of the other ones so you can judge for yourself if they are bizarre or not. There were ways to clean every orifice of the body. One was swallowing about seven meters of very thin Muslim cloth that was three fingers wide into the stomach and then "bottle brushing" the inside lining of the stomach by performing another cleansing practice called "Nauli Kriya," rolling the abdominal muscles side to side massaging the internal organs. It was like having a big ball of cloth in your stomach. The cloth massaged the lining of the stomach clearing mucous and bile. It was a highly effective technique to alleviate asthma. Learning to swallow the cloth taught them to relax the gag reflex in their throat which in turn helped them to alleviate the onset of an asthma attack. I used this method several times over the years to help asthma patients instead of them having to use an inhaler with cortisone steroids in it to open the air passage. It really worked. Another was sucking water up the anus into the colon filling it completely, giving themselves a yogic colonic. (Knowing me by now you can see how I would love this stuff. I thought, "I have got to learn this one. If nothing else they would be great stories to tell or excellent party tricks!") I learned all six of them (I won't mention all of them but you can look them up in the text called the Hatha Yoga Pradipika). They were actually all quite profound in their effect inside and out.

I actually did learn the sucking water up the colon trick. I stuck a bamboo reed about the size of my little finger in diameter and four inches long up my anus, leaving two inches out. I got in a bath tub full of water and squatted down inside it. In India they performed this in rivers or streams. I then performed Nauli, a process of isolating the rectus muscles of the abdomen creating what appears to be a long line from the pubic bone to the front of the ribs. Squatting with this bamboo reed up my ass, I sucked water into my colon through the anus by performing nauli. My colon filled with water over several rounds of sucking the water up the bamboo reed. I then stood up, pulled the reed out and performed several rounds of nauli kriya. Then squatted on the toilet and had a complete evacuation. This is called Yoga Basti, or a Yogic Colonic. (Kids, don't try this at home without adult supervision!)

My life began to revolve around many new and rather bizarre ways of supposedly vibrant health. Some worked and some didn't. Some included using medicinal herbs and other substances, putting them up every orifice: my nose, in my ears and eyes, down my throat, up my butt, wherever I was told they should go. I learned Iridology from a teacher in America, so I was able to determine what was going on in every part of the body through examining and reading the Iris (colored part of the eye). I also learned that not only the eyes but the feet, hands, ears, tongue and face were all mirrors that reflected what was going on in various tissues and organs of the internal body. Unbelievable worlds were being exposed to me on a daily basis. Learning all this was very interesting, yet also very confusing at times. I was having to ask a lot of questions, but also getting a lot of contradictory answers. I didn't know who or what to believe most of the time.

The only thing left for me to do was to continue experimenting on myself and learn what worked and what didn't. I found myself going to every possible workshop or retreat, going to libraries and reading books on raw food, macrobiotic, herbs, and cleansing, and purchasing and consuming anything that related to the body or the mind, in order to discover how this miraculous mechanism worked. I gave up on that whole trip for a while since I was experiencing some serious physical and mental mood swings. I was doing everything that all these books and people were telling me to do. Trusting it was "correct." It wasn't until a few years later that I came across Ayurveda which saved me from irreparable damage.

Before long I was on to the next adventure. While in the States I visited an astrologer who gave me a reading about what was next in the stars for me. At his house I noticed this guy's picture hanging on the wall. He looked kind of cool. He wore a turban, had a long white beard, and looked very spiritual and quite god-like.

I asked the astrologer who he was and he said we could talk about him later but all I could think about while he was doing my chart was this man in the picture. Finally he revealed the story of the person in the photo, named Charan Singh, who lived in North India at the foothills of the Himalayas in an area known as the Punjab. He gave me a book to read called the "Path of the Masters." After reading this I was hooked. I started listening to taped talks that Charan Singh gave on how to be a "spiritual devotee," and all that it entails. It was another quantum leap for me.

I found myself leaving once again for India. After seeing Guruji and practicing again for about three months, I headed up north to meet this meditation teacher. I stayed with him for several months. Charan Singh was only into deep meditation, not the physical form of Hatha Yoga that I had been practicing already. Every morning from 3- 6 am I practiced a three hour sitting meditation.   After that, I did my three hour Ashtanga and Pranayama practice. Sitting for that length of time was made easier because I had developed such a strong asana practice which gave me a firm, steady, and healthy body. There I was practicing Ashtanga Yoga on a roof top by myself........ until word got out in the Ashram that I was doing this. Soon many others from the ashram wanted to join my class. This is how I began my teaching of Ashtanga Yoga, up on a roof top at the foothills of the Himalayas, incognito.

Because my body was healthy and strong I appreciated the challenge of sitting for long periods without moving. I noticed that people whose bodies were weaker had a more difficult time sitting. When you have a weak body/mind you'll struggle with attempting to sit in meditation, because your focus will go right to where your body hurts. A healthy body is one that you don't feel. You're free in your body to do whatever you want, whereas a unhealthy person is consumed by the pain which always draws their attention. This is a very important point to remember, and a seeming paradox. In a healthy individual all the organs, tissues and systems are well nourished creating a strong immune system. All the ancient texts say this is the main reason for all the austerities or "tapas" to purify the body, to make it fit for meditation. Through this process of not moving I was discovering how to look inside myself with more awareness and understanding, and I was getting super high doing it.

When I first started practicing Ashtanga Yoga, some drug use which included smoking ganja (marijuana) was prevalent in the community. I continued to smoke a joint, or would hit the bong after class, thinking it was cool and enjoyed the feeling of shifting my reality, but soon I began to notice that smoking and doing a practice didn't mix very well. I felt so much better without the drugs, and realized through this Yoga experience and meditation I could get just as high or higher. So I naturally began to let it go. Charan Singh also advocated that in order to do a meditation practice, it was necessary to take four specific vows. The first was, you had to become a pure vegetarian. That is no fish, meat or eggs. Secondly, no sex unless you were married. Thirdly, meditation was necessary three hours a day, and last, no drugs or alcohol. Believe it or not, I lived that way for about eight years up until he left his body in 1990. (Well, I did have a little sex along the way!)

Staying in India with Charan Singh proved to be beneficial for me not only spiritually but financially as well, as he didn't charge any money for food or rooms for those staying with him in the ashram. Unfortunately there was a three month maximum period. After that they requested you leave, but I secretly stayed on. I lived in a shed in a nearby village. It was basically a garage with a cement floor and a roll up metal door. This became my "home away from home." A cardboard box was my bed. This was all done in secret since I was not supposed to be at the ashram anymore. I would go early in the morning, sit in the audience of thousands of Indian initiates in silence, and listen to Charan Singh speak in Punjabi. A few times when there was a special ceremony, there would be over 100,000 people gathered in anticipation waiting for him to come with rarely a sound.

After the morning "satsang" (group meeting or being in the presence of truth) I would hang out, read and meditate most of the day. In the evening he gave an English discourse to about 300 westerners. After the evening meeting, I'd grab some dinner, then bicycle back to my "penthouse" late at night and do it all over again the next day. I felt so high, so light, from just being around Charan Singh and meditating for sometimes 6-8 hours a day. I was literally soaring inside myself. I became quite clairvoyant and telepathic. This was my first encounter with consistently living an "otherworldly" life. I imagined this was what it was like to be an apostle of Jesus Christ. Hanging out with him and receiving his words of wisdom and grace and flyin' high!!! There were times during Satsang or seeing Charan Singh driving or walking by I would catch a glimpse of Charan Singh's eyes looking back at me and it would set me off into oblivion. My eyes would be open but all I could see was light. I know it doesn't make sense, but that's what I experienced. I felt bathed in light. Sometimes I did not come back for several minutes; a few times I went in for hours.

Eventually, Charan Singh summoned me to his room. He started off lovingly telling me that I needed to leave. I pleaded, saying I would do anything to stay. He was a bit angry with me for overstaying, and for secretly teaching Yoga at the ashram as well. It got to a point where he became vehement. Again, I interjected but he would not hear of it and again said, "You go back to your country." I was crushed. I didn't have a clue what to do next. Did he know something that I didn't? In retrospect, I now know he saw through my guise of wanting to be a monk and out of compassion was doing me a favor. Plus my karma was elsewhere as I'm sure he was able to see.

After leaving Charan Singh in North India, I decided I wasn't ready to go straight back to America and re-enter the "civilized world." So I went to Mysore and found myself once again with Guruji and family. It was the fall of '82. While with Guruji one day, I had an urgent feeling to contact my mom right then and there. But I knew I couldn't just pick up the phone and call home. Back then in India it wasn't that easy: you had to "book a call" 24 hours in advance. So I did. The next morning the phone rang in my room at the Kaveri Lodge. It was ringing through to America. I sat and waited. It was my sister-in-law who picked up on the other end. Right away, I knew something was off. She answered in a frantic voice, "Hello?" I said Hello back....and she quickly replied after recognizing my voice, "Tony, where are you?! I was just sitting here going through all the letters you have written, looking for a way to contact you. Mom just died yesterday." Then I realized that the moment she died was the exact same time I felt the urge to call her. I immediately asked, "How did she die?" To which Yvonne, my sister-in-law replied, "She was in Vegas with a group of her friends, and Corky (my sister). She was in a restaurant, laughing and having a great time. She stood up to go to the bathroom and said "Oh my god, I'm dizzy", and fell to her death on the floor." I thought to myself, what a great way to go laughing and enjoying herself. I told my sister-in-law "I don't feel to rush home for a funeral." (From my early experiences of funerals as a child, I resolved in myself that I would never go to another one again). "Please give my regards to the family, I will get home when I can." Our conversation ended soon afterwards. Hanging up the phone, I sat quietly on the bed as a wave of emotion washed over me, as tears welled up in my eyes. An overwhelming sense of freedom flooded my body as her presence filled the room comforting me.

A week went by, with beautiful memories appearing to me at various times during the day and night. One morning after practice Guruji called me into his office and said, "Raghava, I have one letter for you," shaking his head from side to side in the "In-

25

dian nod." Right at that moment my heart sunk. I knew no one else was writing me. It had to be from my mom. I took the letter, walked outside, immediately opened it and began bawling my eyes out. The floodgates had finally opened. I was able to grieve. Her letter was like no other, as if she knew it was her last letter to me. It was filled with so much love for her "baby boy."

I finally made it back to America, with the sense of the "umbilical cord" having been cut. I went directly to my mom's house in Arizona, the house I grew up in. Many experiences growing up came to mind as I walked around the house peering into each room. I also made the trip to the gravesite where my mother and father were buried next to each other, for a final clearing with them, having not made it to the funeral.

America now had become even more foreign to me this time around. I was back in the USA and feeling quite lost and adrift. One day I picked up a copy of Yoga Journal magazine, and noticed there was an advertisement for Mount Madonna Center, a Yoga and meditation retreat center. It read, "one month teacher training." I thought, "that sounds interesting, a one month Yoga program practicing Ashtanga Yoga." I showed up at Mount Madonna Center which overlooked the beautiful Santa Cruz mountains, of Northern California. There were a couple hundred people living in residence at the community on 300 acres of lushly forested land. The community revolved around this Yogi named Baba Hari Das. He was a Yogi that chose to not speak. Quite a powerful being in his own right. The most fascinating thing about him was that he felt it was a waste of vital energy to "blah,blah,blah" all day. So he hadn't spoken for some 30 years when I met him. He did however communicate by writing on a very small chalk board these one liner, Zen zingers. I thought it was kind of cool at the time. But I also remember thinking it was a bit strange not to talk for so long. All of this stuff made sense on one level, but on another I was still a bit skeptical. But for where I was in my life, the place felt perfect. I signed up for this Teacher

Training course which focused on the traditional path of Ashtanga Yoga of Patanjali and I tried out the silence trip as well.

I was starting to find out slowly there were a lot of paths out there that talk about various methods and techniques sharing the same name but are not really related when closely inspected. This was a perfect example when I landed at Mount Madonna. Hari Dass was sharing with people about Ashtanga Yoga but not the version I knew. He taught his interpretation of the ancient text and called it Ashtanga Yoga. The Asana and Pranayama part of the practice was definitely not the same. This was one of those incidents in my life when I was faced with, what is authentic and what is not? I was trusting all these "masters" to be genuine and true. I was quite naive in my journey, a real neophyte.

It was there that I met Dr. Vasant Lad, who is regarded today as the foremost authority of Ayurveda in the West. Dr. Lad was teaching Ayurveda as part of the teacher training program I was in. This excited me because I had already been introduced to Ayurveda in India and knew it existed but never got into it in depth. I eagerly wanted to study it further. Now my opportunity had come to learn it from a genuine practitioner of this science. After his introductory course in the training it made me want to explore it even more. Dr. Lad was very enthusiastic and invited all the students from the teacher training to come to Albuquerque, New Mexico where he had an Ayurvedic school. I figured "why not?" · The problem was I didn't have any money. A man named Lenny Blank, Dr. Lad's manager at the time, knew about my financial position, and generously offered me a scholarship, if I would be responsible for video taping all of Dr. Lad's lectures. "Great," I said, so I moved to Albuquerque and started studying with Dr. Lad. I ended up studying with him from 1983-87.

During that time I learned everything an Ayurvedic medical doctor would learn along with an extensive clinical program that included treating patients with Dr. Lad. I learned a tremendous amount being closely associated with Dr. Lad over those three years. I became quite proficient in being able to read what was going on with an individual and recommend what was an appropriate tack to take for them. I saw that the Ashtanga Yoga practice I was doing was perfect for everyone if approached in the light of Ayurveda, otherwise it could throw you into further imbalance. Over time I modified my practice to fit what I was learning with Ayurveda. (This is what I will go over later in the Ayurveda section of the book.)

In the meantime, there was this woman named Cynthia who was interested in me, and I was this celibate yogi guy. But when Charan Singh told me to go back to America, one of the thoughts that quickly flashed through my mind was "maybe I needed to be a householder?" I began to explore a relationship with her "long distance" as she lived in Encinitas, California where I originally met her. She began to express an interest to join me in Albuquerque. At first I hesitated to invite her, but she was eager to join me and although I was attracted to her, I was not really ready for a long term relationship. She was cute, an amazing cook, into health and healing, and also the thought crossed my mind that "she will be a good mother," which she was and still is. I also had this feeling of the spirit of a child hovering around me, whose name came to me as "Shanti" (my now 21 year old daughter). I finally agreed and we began to share a house together. She was very supportive at the time. One day, feeling very romantic, I asked her to marry me by writing it on my little chalk board that I had gotten at Mt. Madonna. She said "yes" in uncontrolled excitement!!! (not on her chalk board).   Dr. Lad married us in an Indian ceremony, but we didn't live "happily ever after." She lost control of her temper frequently and was often violent, which became unbearable to live with. At the time, I didn't see my contribution to the madness. In order to deal with her behavior, I would disappear and escape into my room to "MEDITATE" ....what a joke!!! I blamed her for her uncontrollable rage which I ignited by ignoring her. Like throwing gasoline on a fire! I finally asked her to leave, which she did, and she went to live with her sister in California.

Once she was gone, of course I felt great again, being by myself in my "perfect world" doing my meditation and Yoga practices daily. I was now able to go deeper into my self feeling at peace once again (funny what I considered spiritual back then). I have observed that others like myself would either isolate or keep themselves busy, in order to not look at the root cause of their suffering. If you approach life this way, the same theme will continue to appear, haunting you until you face it.

One day the phone rang while I was in this very receptive loving space and guess who? It was Cynthia. She cried and begged me for forgiveness and to please take her back. I said, "Okay, come on home."

That night she came back, we made "love", and my daughter Shanti was conceived. Now she was pregnant, and the crazy behavior that I ran from before began again. I thought to myself "Oh no, now what do I do? There's a baby coming......" Shanti was born and she was so beautiful! She smoothed some of the energy out between us with her radiance and love, so I knew I had to do everything I could to make this marriage work. I was struggling financially to keep the family together, and finding work was not easy. Yoga was not popular in those days, but somehow we managed.   The problem was, we never fully addressed the root cause of our discontent since we were caught in the everyday drama of surviving. Then Cynthia got pregnant again with my second beautiful daughter, Mira. The three and a half years we spent in Albuquerque consisted of working during the day, Ayurveda classes at night, and any free time I had playing with the kids. We decided after I finished my formal training with Dr. Lad, and with another baby on the way, to move back to Arizona where we both had families.

Ayurveda and Yoga were still not in the mainstream yet, so I still had to find odd jobs to support the family as I didn't want Cynthia to work. This included everything from washing windows, waiting tables, and construction jobs, to substitute teaching in elementary and high schools. We bought a house, yet life continued to be a struggle. We tried seeking all kinds professional help but nothing fundamentally changed in our relationship since we were so caught up in trying to figure it out on the outside. Despite seven years of trying to make it work, and two beautiful daughters, I decided it was time to end this relationship. I realized if I continued in this direction any longer, in five years I could be a candidate for cancer (like my father) or a heart attack. I felt at the time it would healthier for all of us if we separated but co-parented, creating some sense of space to breathe again. It was a desperate move out of not knowing what else to do.

The separation was not easy for me, or any of us for that matter, as Cynthia decided to move three hours away from where I lived to raise the kids in a small rural town of 800 people in southern Arizona, called Patagonia. My children were very important to me and now I could only see them on weekends. I continued to live in Phoenix, where I was born. Phoenix was becoming a booming metropolis. There I could generate enough money to pay for myself and the kids. But being a weekend dad sucked. I would go there, have a great time, then drive home crying terribly, missing my kids. Then for years we would meet at a half way point where I would pick up the kids and afterwards drop them off at the end of the weekend. I would cry the entire way home. The grieving I felt in leaving my children each weekend was like having a loved-one die over and over again. It was horrible! I saw in their precious eyes, they were not happy with this as well. I remember them asking me when I was going to live with them again. But I just didn't have the courage or the strength to get to the other side of this. I now see I mostly blamed Cynthia for what was going on and she did the same instead of claiming full responsibility for all that we were creating individually in our situation. A simple solution but not always easy to see in the cloud of confusing, emotional, mind tripping.

During this time I got involved with a network marketing business which sold a health product that I found very beneficial for my own body. It was a micro algae that feeds the body and

the mind, a "super food" very rich in nutrients. I'm still distributing it after 20 years; an amazing product. I got all my Yoga
friends involved with it and then the interest in this product ex-
ploded. I was making $12,000 a month, which was a lot of money
for a poor yogi! I thought, like my father had, that money would
solve all my problems, but it only made them more complicated.

Around the same time, I met someone in my business who
was part of a group who believed in "physical immortality," that
is, people living in their body forever. The concept intrigued me: I
had read about how scientists discovered that it was possible to
prolong life and that immortality from a scientific viewpoint was
a possibility as well. The body was inherently not supposed to die
if given everything it needed inside and out. I also remembered
reading references in stories and Yogic texts to beings who were
living in the Himalayas, hundreds of years old. The Bible as well
told stories of people living to be hundreds of years old. So this
was not a new revelation to me.

I was invited by my business partner to a meeting where 200
in attendance were talking and "living immortality." The group
was called "People Forever." The people involved in this movement from all over the World were very generous and supportive
of one another, like a family. Being around them created a feeling
of togetherness, that each individual was a significant part of the
whole. In order to make this unimaginable idea of immortality
happen, we had to do it together. Although I had never pursued
this before, this group made me feel it was a living possibility. In
our coming together we discovered that a genetic happening was
taking place within the cells of our bodies that directly affected
how we lived. In changing a core belief anything was possible.
Most of the people in the group understood this.

There was going to be a gathering of 1200 of these immortalists from around the world in Scottsdale, Arizona that year. I
wanted to go, but before this gathering took place, I decided to
take a trip to California on my Harley Davidson motorcycle. A
friend and I did the "Easy Rider" thing from Arizona to Califor-

nia with the sleeping bag on the back of our bikes. We cruised up the coast of California and landed in Big Sur amidst the Redwood Forest where the biggest trees in the world grow. I had rounded up some psychedelic mushrooms to take on our trip, and thought it would be great to take them in the middle of the redwoods.

I was very confident taking mushrooms since I had grown up with them. I also had had several vision quest experiences with Shamans in Arizona. As a young person I wanted to find God and thought taking these substances was a way to achieve that. It definitely opened some doors but it quickly closed them once I came down. They never allowed me to access from within like I have experienced with Yoga and Meditation.

We met up with a husband and wife team, "Jack and Jill" from up the hill, who were friends I knew from the "Big Sur" area of northern California. I felt like a Shaman distributing the mushrooms to my friends. Together we all took the mushrooms except "Jack," who realized there should be someone responsible to watch over us. He was an experienced tripper—and I agreed, thinking this was a great idea. We all took the mushrooms, but the others were a little hesitant about taking the full amount I had doled out. So I decided to take the leftover mushrooms along with my share. That was a big mistake!!! The mushrooms were powerful and after some time, I began to "trip" on some birds flying above. We were near a cliff and as I watched the birds soaring over these cliffs I wanted to join them. I was about to take off when "Jack" realized what I was about to do, grabbed me and said, "you're not a bird!" Luckily, he kept me on the ground!

The next hallucinogenic experience was triggered as we entered a dark forested valley in the redwoods. Massive giant trees surrounded me. Having recently been to a "People Forever" immortality meeting, I was wearing a tee shirt which said "Death Sucks" on the front and on the back was a tombstone over which was drawn a circle with a line across it indicating "no death." Tripping out of my fucking mind, I was faced with the image of the Grim Reaper. Death was swirling around me, and I saw black figures hovering above. I screamed "NO!!!!!!!!!!" as I took off my shirt and pushed it into the demons' faces yelling again, "Death Sucks!" Fortunately "Jack" grabbed me once again, held me back and consoled me that everything would be all right.

My experience with taking drugs has shown me, they only bring out what is already inside you. They simply bring all that is dormant to the surface. They didn't create my reality, they reflected it. My own "inner demons" were being confronted. On a positive note, this one hellish experience was followed by beautiful ones the rest of the day. Mind expansion, watching butterflies and flowers become "live" works of art........... and of course laughing hysterically at silly things. Everyone came down from the effects of the mushrooms, but I continued tripping since I had taken a dose for two or three. My mind and body were still disconnected, even as my friend and I left the following day, for Reno, Nevada.

I hadn't slept at all yet. When we arrived in Reno, Nevada's second biggest casino city, we got a hotel room, cleaned up and hit the streets looking for some action. We met up with some "showgirls" who just got off from their performance and were ready to party. They kindly gave us some cocaine laced with speed, or something like it, to catch us up to their pace. I was reluctant to take it, but my friend egged me on, and I figured "why not? I'm already high...what's a little more?" Whatever it was, it spun me out even more. I ended up passing out at their house.

When I finally woke up, I was completely disoriented and alone. No one was around. All of sudden my friend appeared and took me back to the hotel where we were staying. I woke up later confused and disjointed even further. I looked everywhere for my friend....................He was gone???!!! The damn guy left and went back to Arizona without me!!! Now my brain was scrambled and I had no idea what to do. I couldn't decipher even the color or meaning of a traffic light, not to mention the direction I needed to go in order to get back home to Arizona hundreds of miles away. It was summertime, and the temperature in the desert was outrageously hot, about 120 degrees Fahrenheit or 48 degrees Celsius!!! The wind as I was driving felt like the "breath from hell." Somehow I managed to find the interstate highway. Driving in circles, caught in a circular "hamster wheel maze" on the highway, I started seeing the same road signs over and over and over again. I had no idea what direction I needed to go. I pulled over several times crying, my mind completely disoriented and not knowing what was going on. I somehow found a hotel to rest and then when it was cooler I started driving again. I managed to make it back to the Arizona border, and was soon after pulled over by a cop. Not knowing why he was pulling me over, I got off my bike and squatted on the ground thoroughly confused thinking, "he knows I'm stoned and I'm going to jail." I gave him what I thought was my driver's license when in fact it was a credit card. He looked at me like, "what the hell are you doing, boy" and he handed me a pink piece of paper and drove off (I had a tail light out). Luck was on my side. I put the paper into my wallet, not knowing at the time what it was, got up shook my head, and said to myself, "what just happened?........a glitch in the Matrix?" I climbed on my bike and hit the road again.

When I arrived home some friends caught wind that I was back. They came and nursed me back to a place where I could make some sense of my life again. Needless to say, I was whipped. The convergence of the "People Forever" immortalist group was supposed to happen in a few days. My friends brought me to this gathering, as they felt it would help me snap out of it. It did, as I was in the middle of this powerful energy. I began to wake up from my drug experience. Deepak Chopra was the Keynote Speaker on the opening day. He had just released "Ageless Body, Timeless Mind." The energy at this conference was electric, as you can imagine, being around 1200 enthusiastic immortalists from around the globe.

At the meeting, there was a woman who caught my attention. She was strikingly beautiful, and I began checking her out. Later that week at a party, I was watching her dancing seductively with this guy who never seemed to leave her side. I thought they must be together, so I let it go. Several days later I gave a talk on Ayurveda at this event, and the same woman showed up with this same guy. She stayed and asked questions along with others at the end of the talk, but I only focused my attention on her. Everyone else eventually left, but she and I. I had managed to blank everyone else out so of course they all disappeared. I invited her to walk with me and immediately asked her if she was involved with this man I always saw her with. She said, "Oh, he's just a friend," "Cool," I thought, "this is my opening."

Before long we were in the lobby of the hotel talking and laughing. Soon she was sitting so close I could smell here sweet scent and feel her skin against mine as we caressed each other playfully for hours. I leaned in and whispered in her ear if she wanted to come up to my room. In no time, we were shagging like two insatiable monks right out of the monastery. Nonstop sex like crazy for three days!!! Taking breaks to order room service and tend to whatever other bodily needs we had to carry on with our "new found lust" for each other. On the third day, I asked her to marry me. Logical right??? As I shared the news with my immortalist friends, most felt I was totally nuts. "You just came off a crazy drug trip and you're marrying a woman you met three days ago? You're out of your fuckin' mind! Don't do it!" (In retrospect I wish one of them grabbed by the shirt and slapped me saying, "Wake up man, you're still tripping!") Of course my very spiritual friends thought that it was so romantic, and of course we looked so good together. "It will be perfect," I thought, why not just do it? So I did!!!

She was from Berlin, Germany and although I could make some wisecracks about it being the Headquarters for Hitler's Third Reich, I'll refrain. After the convergence we married at a "wedding chapel," Las Vegas style, along with a couple of friends, champagne and a bubble gum ring. A few days after we got married, we both flew to Berlin. She was there to pick up her things before she moved to America permanently with me, where by the way, she always wanted to live. She could get her "Green Card" (Immigration papers) quickly now to live and work in America. I was making alot of money at that time, so I was this great catch, her perfect ticket to come to the USA. When I got to see her in her "real" life at home in Berlin, she was a completely different person. She was not a pretty picture anymore. She treated me like a servant. Ordering me around, yelling and screaming, not the happy go lucky person I remembered in America on vacation. "What is going on here?" I thought. What also came to mind was, "This may be the quickest marriage and divorce in history." I somehow was able to rationalize this woman's horrible behavior by telling myself she's stressed, I was strong, she was beautiful and we would get over this. Obviously, I was afraid to leave or to be left, and too embarrassed to admit I had made a horrible mistake. I made up excuses for her "demon" like behavior and my own insecurity.

She came to America and nothing changed. She met my kids and didn't like them. She wanted her own kids. Eventually I could not even bring my kids over to the house as she would belittle them constantly in front of me. I had to basically hang out with them in parks, movies, anywhere but home. I'll spare you the gory details that transpired over that long "one year sentence." I hung in there, but looking back I don't know how. We bought a $400,000 house that she filled up with all kinds of stuff and we owned two expensive cars plus a Harley Davidson motorcycle.

I seemingly had everything you could possibly want on the outside but inside I was feeling absolutely horrible. The guilt was killing me about not being able to be with my kids. After a year I told my second wife, "this isn't working and I want a divorce." Her response was, "If you're going to divorce me I'm going take everything you've got."

I left, got an apartment and was soon served with papers from her lawyer. I immediately hired a lawyer who said, "This woman's an extremely vindictive person, and she'll take you to court, string out the proceedings for years, and it will probably cost you thousands of dollars in legal fees. Therefore, I suggest you settle with her. Give her the house, all the stuff in it, as well as the car, and pay her off in cash. Then you can walk away." After thinking about the consequences of having to struggle with this for years, I agreed. She wanted more of course, but we negotiated and finally came up with a viable settlement.

This left me with nothing financially and another failed marriage. The worst part was that I had distanced myself from my children. I felt so empty, an utter failure and completely bankrupt as a human being. My Yoga practice also went to hell during this time. In retrospect, I recognized what I had done going from a confused, struggling, and college student to thinking I had found all the answers through Yoga. Problem was I didn't properly integrate it all. The energy I had pent up as a "Yoga neophyte" came out with the Immortalists. It's no wonder that I flip flopped from Yogi to "Playboy" when I finally had the opportunity to release some steam.

I avoided going home to my apartment at night because I found no peace there. My income also took a dramatic nose dive during this time. I was disgusted with my life, and what I had done with it. One lonely night feeling desperately low, I jumped on my motorcycle and decided to end this suffering. I didn't want to live anymore. In the desert where I was living a two lane highway stretched for miles. It was in the middle of the night. As I was flying down the highway I began to weep. My eyes were clouding over. Looking up, I saw two headlights coming towards me. I could care less about anyone in the other vehicle. I just wanted to end my life. As the car approached, I started to take my hands off the handlebars, but quickly re-grabbed them just before impact. I began to shake and tremble uncontrollably, realizing what I had almost done. Driving back home was difficult. I felt washed out and empty. My eyes were swollen and my head was pounding. I barely made it back.

37

Returning to my apartment, I went into the bedroom, sat in the middle of my bed and started yelling to God at the top of my lungs, "If you don't show yourself right now, if you don't give me some kind of sign, I'm gonna kill myself!" I was weeping with snot pouring out of my nose as I screamed desperately to be heard. This went on for about 15 minutes, until, out of nowhere there was complete stillness and silence. The whole room was flooded with light. I stopped crying, sat straight up, and continued to sit immobile for three hours. A deep tranquility came over me that night like a wave sweeping through me washing me clean. Never before in my life had I ever experienced anything like this. I felt beautiful, innocent and pure, like a new born baby, as if everything I had ever done in the past was gone, completely absolved. I was flying high. It reminded me of being on a psychedelic drug trip, but I was fully lucid and aware. I was not so "awake," not tired at all, nor did I want to go to sleep for fear of losing this exquisite feeling. I was afraid if I slept I would wake up and it would all be gone. I definitely had delusions of grandeur. I felt that I was somehow......... enlightened???

For several months I didn't sleep other then taking catnaps. When I did lay down, out of physical exhaustion, sleep would overtake me. After a few minutes I would wake up and check to see if that feeling was still there. Relieved when I realized the high was still there, I would carry on with my day. Meditating was interspersed with taking care of the body by showering it, feeding it, toilet duties etc. When I picked up a book I was able to read it within minutes. This included numerous books on Yoga and Ayurveda, the chakras, diet, herbs, massage, and the Bible........ in minutes!!! I would merely scan them and flip the pages as fast I could. My entire library, which was quite extensive at the time, was devoured in weeks. And I was constantly journaling about this inner experience.

It was a period of amazing introspection and discovery. I had access to information that previously I had only read about. I knew when things were going to happen before they occurred. I was so lit up I was reading people's minds, if I happened to see them, since I spent most of my time in my modern-day cave. I did teach a few Yoga classes here and there, plus went out for food or shopping. I put on a "good face" and did my best to not shock anyone with my "wild ideas" and experiences. I loved interacting with people but was a bit scared as well that I didn't fit in anymore.

So much continued to flood into my consciousness, but I couldn't assimilate and process it all. I had no spiritual mentor on the outside to make sense out of what I was experiencing and I didn't realize the best one was inside me. I asked a few "close friends" and they laughed and said "Right.......you're doing what?" I saw early on that divulging any inner experiences to people who are not in the position to clearly hear them means they will condemn you or laugh derisively at what you had to say. Yet I had more compassion for everyone still living in the illusion as I had been not long before. Everything was on the right track and I only needed to integrate it all a little more, but that didn't happen. Slowly, over the next few months, my energy dissipated into everyday life.

I came out into the world again and guess what? That's right, I met another "beautiful" woman. She was gorgeous, taught Yoga and Ayurveda. The best part was that she loved my kids and they loved her too. She was perfect, or so I thought. New to town, she had just moved from Florida to Arizona. Feeling generous and open, I gave her everything. All the energy I felt inside went to her, and she accepted it. I helped her become successful, giving her my well established Yoga classes and business connections, and I got her struggling Ayurveda practice going too. Don't get me wrong here, It wasn't all one sided. I am magnifying this to emphasize wrong judgment on my part. We had some fabulous times, some of the best with any woman to date. It was unfortunately imbalanced as I gave her all the juice I had without keeping some for myself. I got lost in the outside once more. From the very beginning there were "red flags," as she was always flirting with other men right before my eyes. It was inevitable that she met someone while I was away for two weeks. I was slapped in the face once more.

I was alone again and feeling depressed. Looking back I see that it all worked out perfectly. I finally learned my lesson of how to be with a woman without giving away my power and becoming a victim, losing myself. I was blessed by an angel named Shirin, who helped me through this critical breakthrough experience. She is a Shaman (Mystic Healer of the Native American Tradition) who lives on the magical island of the Kauai, where I live part of the time. She guided me to look within and helped clear many of my dysfunctional patterns of relating with women in an intimate way. Very powerful rituals were performed as I released and let go in sacred ceremonies using fire as a tool to burn the seeds. In deep prayer I burned the pictures and names of all the women I had been with over the years, throwing the ashes into the sea and cutting all the psychic ties I had with each one. I then "baptized" myself by swimming in the ocean as well. From that point on it was my conscious choice how I interacted with the women in my life. I was still the fun, adventurous person that I was before, but wiped clean of the many patterns that forced me back over and over again into destructive relationships.

I feel it's important to say here that I take full responsibility for everything that happened to me with every relationship that went wrong. After all, "wrong" is a relative term and let's face it, I did co-create it. They were invaluable lessons along my journey. I'm sure I was no picnic to live with, as I allowed myself to be either an untouchable spiritual person or just a plain old victim. I realize all the painful experiences I've ever had over the years were actually blessings in disguise. Being aware of the patterns now allows me to consciously pull which ones I don't want and instill what qualities serve my higher purpose. I finally have the tools in hand to create what I want, and I am!

THE GUEST HOUSE

This being human is the guest house.
Every morning a new arrival.
A joy, a depression, a meanness,
A momentary awareness comes
As an unexpected visitor.
Welcome and entertain them all!

Even if they're a crowd of sorrows
Who violently sweep your house
Empty of its furniture.
Still, treat each guest honorably.
He may be clearing you out
For some new delight.

The dark thought, the shame, the malice.
Meet them at the door laughing
And invite them in.
Be grateful for whoever comes
Because each guest has been sent
As a guide from beyond.

— Rumi

In 2001, on one of my annual trips to be with Guruji (Pattabhi Jois) in Mysore, I met people who knew I'd been practicing Ashtanga Yoga and Ayurveda for decades. They figured I knew something with all the time I put in. They began to invite me to their centers in various locations all over Europe and Asia. Little did they know of my untamed and checkered past! Nevertheless, I started to put together teaching tours under the name Ashtanga World.Com, which is what I have been doing these past seven years. During this time I was told by Sharath, Guruji's grandson, "you should be certified, you are very old student."

I said jokingly "yes, you're right I am very old!" We went to Guruji and of course he agreed I was (very old), and yes I should have a Certificate. Guruji is a man of few words and his presenting me the Advanced Certificate to teach Ashtanga Yoga was a momentous step in my calling as a teacher. The timing was perfect since I had had the opportunity many times in the past but realized that if I had accepted it years ago it would have been only a piece of paper to me. It was now time for me to accept the acknowledgment of all that I had done for the past thirty years. This certificate is an honor as it enables me to pass on this tradition to you, with confidence from my Guru.

Around the same time, I connected with my beloved Osho, an enlightened master from India. He is no longer in the flesh but his spirit lives on. Although I knew about him in the late seventies I wasn't ready to connect with him then. I actually thought he was "evil" when I first heard about him from many of the "spiritual do gooders" of that time. I learned from that experience to believe no one without checking it out for myself. So several years later I was more open and began to read his books and listen to some of his tapes. I then realized what a special Being he was. I regret not listening to my heart, instead of my righteous mind. I had the opportunity to meet him in the body, in 1979 in India. I now realize he is still "alive'" in his hundreds of discourses that he gave on Yoga, Christianity, Buddhism, and Zen all available through transcribed books and live audio and video tapes. His message touched me deeply and has influenced my outlook on all the subjects I am going to share with you. He even said himself that, "I was never born and will never die." His words were filled with eternal truths. No one being to date has had such an impact on my life.

Author Tom Robbins said this about him:

I recognize the emerald breeze when it rattles my shutters. And Osho is like a hard, sweet wind, circling the planet, blowing the beanies off of rabbis and popes, scattering the lies on the desks of the bureaucrats, stampeding the jackasses in the stables of the powerful, lifting the skirts of the pathologically prudish and tickling the spiritually dead back to life.

Jesus had his parables, Buddha his sutras, Mohammed his fantasies of the Arabian night. Osho has something more appropriate for a species crippled by greed, fear, ignorance and superstition: he has cosmic comedy.

What Osho is out to do, it seems to me, is pierce our disguises, shatter our illusions, cure our addictions and demonstrate the self-limiting and often tragic folly of taking ourselves too seriously.

So what to say of Osho? The ultimate deconstructionist? A visionary who becomes the vision? Certainly a proposal to existence - that it is everyone's birthright to enjoy that same oceanic experience of true individuality. For that, Osho says, "There is only one path, which goes inwards, where you will not find a single human being, where you will only find silence, peace."

I ended up finally going to his Ashram in Pune, India. I wanted to experience the place where he delivered his talks and communed with thousands of devotees. I also knew there had to be other brothers and sisters into him as well. I wanted to meet my other "tribe" besides the one I found with Ashtanga Yoga. I did, and enjoyed a month there meditating, dancing and celebrating life with everyone there.

On January 16th, 2003 I was initiated and given the name "Prem," which means Love. It was a shift that needed to happen to get out of the old patterns of being called "Anthony," my family name, and all the energy that went along with it. By embracing this name I feel the courage and the insight to speak from my heart and share with you what I have experienced. It's another tool that reminds me of my divinity, and it's actually quite beautiful being called "Love" all the time. "Hey Prem (love), how are you? or Prem (love) have you........." The timing couldn't have been any better, receiving the certificate to teach and forging my deep connection to Osho. I am forever grateful for Osho's consistent inspiration and guidance from within.

I am an intense person, a "Scorpio." I'm all about transformation in whatever form it looks like. Scorpio is represented as the "Phoenix" rising out of the ashes. A mythical bird that never dies, the Phoenix flies far ahead to the front, always scanning the landscape and distant space. It represents our capacity for vision, for collecting sensory impressions of our environment and the events unfolding within it. It was also in early Christianity a sign of Christ's resurrection from the "dead," symbolic of not a physical death but a rebirth into the light. (Interesting how I was born in the city named Phoenix!!!) As you have read in my life story, I go full on into most everything I do. So it is no wonder that I attracted what I did. Even though I had all the tools from Ashtanga Yoga, Ayurveda and Tantra right in front of me, I still had a very strong momentum in my mind pulling me towards the illusion of needing something outside of myself.

Looking back on my life, I see how the dramatic pendulum swings were necessary. For if you go so far in one direction you will swing back to the other with just as much force. It's a law of nature. I was like many people whom I know and have observed who went headlong into this manic-depressive pattern of life, chasing what they thought would make them happy or fulfilled only to wake up with another "unfortunate" relationship, job, or other life situation. The high gives a sense of Presence, that momentary glimpse of bliss, and the low creates a sense of futility, "a what's the use, life is meaningless" attitude. Swinging back and forth over and over again leaves you exhausted. Do this enough times and you will find yourself either on the verge of suicide or awakened with a new lease on life. There's nowhere else to go, either up or out. Hence the name of this book, "The Only Way Out is In."

There is no need to leave the world. The world is a perfectly good place, as a fire test. What is needed is to go In, not to go somewhere out. Once and for all it should be clear that the future of religion cannot depend on the escapists. The authentic religious man will live in the world without being disturbed by all kinds of disturbances. He will be simply a watcher, unperturbed. In fact the world is a good place because it gives you an opportunity to test your silence, your meditativeness, your watchfulness. Be in the world but don't be of it. Be in the world but don't let the world be in you.

— OSHO

Now that you know my own journey, I welcome you to journey within, using the guiding lights of Ashtanga Yoga, Ayurveda and Tantra. These are anchors to the world of Presence, vast dimensions where connection to oneself is possible and lasting. I say possible because connection is not a done deal once you begin the process, as you have seen with me. None of us know when the final veil will be lifted. In other words, "it ain't over till it's over." You can use these tools for years, as I have, without shifting your core beliefs and programs until you are fully Present. This is your wake up call to look more closely at who you really are. If you don't wake up now, then when? The exciting part about this whole game is that you never know when that moment will come. Our effort polishes the internal mirror. The clearer the mirror, the sooner you recognize where you are at. Effort on our part is "showing up" in everything we do, walking, talking, eating.... trusting that all will be revealed when we are ready. We always get exactly as much as we can handle in any given moment. If everything was revealed to us all at once we couldn't handle the intensity.

Each of us has his or her own script to play out. The essential answers to all our questions live inside of us; outside circumstances are irrelevant in spiritual matters. You don't have to become a "Yoga Teacher" to realize this. In fact that might make things even more difficult as it can give you the illusion of being

45

spiritual, as it did with me, when in fact you are just like everyone else. There is only one direction for each of us and that is within. All the clichés that I and many other people have thrown around (Be Here Now, Presence, Living in the Moment) are all hollow words until you have tasted the silence within. Having access to this at will is our only solution.

Let's begin our adventure with Ayurveda, since this is where it all begins, in the womb of what the ancients call "The Mother of all Healing Systems." One thing I can definitely say about my life is I've never been a "fence sitter." So I encourage you to jump in with both feet. The rewards are literally "out of this world."

PART II

AYURVEDA

The Science of Life and Living

1

INTRODUCTION

$\mathcal{I}$ begin with Ayurveda, because as a system, it is the birthplace of all life principles, spoken and written. It creates clarity for each individual to make decisions based on what will bring balance to their everyday life. Ayurveda is a system filled with ancient secrets of living as applicable today as they were thousands of years ago. Embrace its principles and you will have a solid base for radiant health. In my experience I have found it invaluable for anyone, especially practitioners of Yoga, to understand Ayurveda first, since it is the foundation for all of Life.

Before I learned about Ayurveda, I had studied many other natural healing methods: Shiatsu, Acupuncture, Chi Gung, medicinal herbs, raw foods, massage, macrobiotics, fasting, and iridology, just to name a few. All of these methods ultimately came from Ayurveda since it is the "mother" of all healing systems. Although these systems mentioned are valid for some individuals, I have found that Ayurveda has been consistently successful across the board with all people no matter who they are. There are no generalizations made about individuals, since each individual is seen as unique and treated that way.

Understanding Ayurveda first and foremost allowed me to walk through this "Jungle of Life," as a medicine man or "jungle physician" with wisdom. Once the principles became an integral part of my life, I saw they fit perfectly with everything I had already learned in Yoga. Knowing that Ayurveda was sister-science with Yoga made perfect sense to me as I became more familiar with it. Essentially, it is a "blueprint" for perfect health.

WHAT IS AYURVEDA?

Ayurveda is a Sanskrit word which means, "The Science or Wisdom of Life and Living." Most of the time Ayurveda is translated as "the Science of Life," but to me the word "life" is dead without the added word "living." Living means movement, actively participating in life. It's wet and wild, not dull and dry. The word life is either about the dead past or about the projected future. Living is in the Now. It's fresh and new in the moment. It's not talking about something, but fully participating in it. Stop sitting on the fence. Most people make the mistake of approaching their life from living in their head. NO!!! Life's a vibrant "happening" when you are connected to your source. Approach Ayurveda with these eyes and it will come alive. If you only look at it as more information to fill your head with, then it's useless. Entertaining at best, but basically useless. In other words, integrate Ayurveda into your living or go back to watching the Discovery channel on TV. Look at all the "reality shows," travel channels and magazines, novels and movies about someone else's adventure or love story. Our modern life has become watching or reading about other people's lives rather than fully engaging in our own. Ayurveda is your invitation to live again with the enthusiasm of a child.

WHERE DID AYURVEDA COME FROM?

More than 10,000 years ago, enlightened yogis known as Rishis lived in India. They were great observers of life, which is the literal translation of the word Rishi. In deep meditative states they explored themselves first. Then and only then, from this place of wisdom they were they able to see nature clearly. These Rishis were full of compassion for humanity, so they were constantly observing how life could be understood in its most practical, basic form. They came down out of the mountains or jungles to share this information so that everyone could benefit and live in harmony within themselves and their surroundings.

They saw human beings as a microcosm of nature and the Universe as the macrocosm. Whatever exists in nature is also found in humans: they mirror each other. Throughout this book you will read about many examples of this relationship not only to physical mirrors but to mental, psychic, and astral reflections inside of and everywhere around you. This entire universe is full of "signs" along the journey, inviting you to wake up and explore the deeper realms of your being in this mysterious world of energy.

These Rishis knew that everything came out of Consciousness. I would like to define Consciousness as, "Existence observing itself in Manifestation." In other words, Existence or Divine Presence, observing itself in Everything that exists, seen and unseen. These Rishis saw Consciousness as a perfectly balanced state of Being, where no separation exists. These ancient seers observed that unconscious humanity experienced itself in a dualistic way because of its association with the mind. This duality creates a split of self and other. Their challenge was to find a way to help humanity come back into equanimity and recognize we are "All" (meaning everyone and everything) in this together. There can be no difference between self and other. Divine Presence is alive in consciousness and unconsciousness. When Divine Precense is awakened, then there is Absolute Consciousness. It was out of this desire, to "wake people up" to this reality, that Ayurveda was born and communicated. This concept of duality permeates all mystic traditions and is hidden in many texts including the Bible. In the Old Testament book of Genesis, there is mention of the, "Tree of Knowledge of Good and Evil" (the mind). It was this tree in the middle of the Garden of Eden from which God directly forbade Adam and Eve to eat. The other tree in the middle of the Garden was the "Tree of Life" (Consciousness). God allowed them to eat any fruit from any tree in the Garden, which included both trees. After Adam and Eve ate from the forbidden fruit of the "Tree of Knowledge," being tempted by a serpent (the devil, an agent of the mind- "thoughts and feelings"), it was then they became aware of their nakedness, and were banished from the Garden (Paradise- that we now live in!).

Its branches reach up to the sky; its roots go deep into the earth. The "Tree of Life" is experienced in all three worlds — heaven, earth, and the underworld; uniting above and below. It's both a feminine symbol of sustenance and a masculine, phallic symbol of virility; another "union" represented in nature. In the mystic traditions of all world religions, sacred texts are read for metaphorical content concerning the relationship between states of the mind and the external experience of reality. "The Tree of Life" represents the state of Eternal Aliveness or Presence, not merely the immortality of the body or soul. Once the ego/ mind experienced shame after eating from the "Tree of Knowledge of Good and Evil," it believed in the myth of duality. This belief prevented us from living eternally in Paradise. Therefore, when we relinquish our association with our mind, which is the source of duality, then we too can live in Paradise here on Earth. Mystics in all religious discourses attempt to guide us back to the journey of Self and Unity, based on committed effort. The practices vary between individuals, religions and cultures, but they are All saying the same thing!!!

2

ATTRIBUTES

$\mathcal{T}$he Rishis first realized it was necessary to pay attention to what the senses, the "antennae" of the body, registered. What they observed was that the senses provided very specific information, known as Attributes. Attributes are defined in Ayurveda as the ten pairs of opposite qualities that express and reveal all of life's physical and emotional states into a workable form. There are many other pairs that can be used, but Ayurveda chose to use these ten as its basic platform to describe all of life and living. The mind works by dividing everything into these ten fun-da-mental (fun comes before da mental) opposite qualities in order to make sense of the world.

The Attributes are: hot/cold, light/heavy, sharp/dull, clear/cloudy, smooth/rough, dispersing/dense, fast/slow, soft/hard, moist/dry, and mobile/static. These 10 pairs of opposite qualities define life's multifaceted expressions of existence into a system that brings balance. The mind jumps back and forth between these 10 pairs and uses the 5 sense organs as it's "feelers." It then categorizes basically everything into these attributes. It does so unconsciously. For instance, when we look at a sunset, the mind wants to compare it with one that it saw somewhere else, to one that was similar or more spectacular. Or the mind races into the future, wanting to go on to the "next event." Rarely do we fully experience what is happening, in each moment. This is why we hunger for new experiences. When we are truly Present, it's our moment of bliss, a touch of spirit. A sense of oneness with that object. We are in Awe and Wonder. For instance, when we see the ocean for the first time, we experience that blissful connection, but then we forget it the next time we see it, out of our automatic reaction to compare. Through Presence everything is transformed into being fresh and new for in reality it is, if YOU are FRESH and NEW, otherwise you're taking things for granted e.g. your wife, husband, kids, health, surroundings…

The mind is like a "hungry monster." It needs to eat continuously; thoughts and feelings are its food. It needs to be chewing on something all the time, it's never satisfied unless it's eating. If we are not constantly preoccupied with something to "do," we are bored. I have a friend who said "if you're bored, you're boring." I agree! This is the main reason we jump from relationship to relationship, job to job, town to town. Once this underlying principle is understood, then you can observe how it carries from one thing to another. When you truly get this, then you know your mind will always move this way due to its restless nature, and you watch it without being sucked into its drama, thriller, comedy, romance....

You can simply observe whatever is happening like a movie, and enjoy the ride.

Ayurveda, Yoga and Tantra take you one step further and guide you to go "beyond the mind," beyond duality, to a place of Pure Passive Awareness or Presence. In being this, we create a state of witnessing the experience instead of living in the world of thought about the experience. The mind wants to group everything according to the Attributes, but in reality, things are, just as they are. Our minds categorize everything according to past programs. This is the source of Illusion in the world and the root cause of all our suffering. In Yoga it is called, "Maya."

Animals simply live life instinctually. They are great teachers of living in the moment. Have you ever really watched an animal run or fly? It does so without hesitation. It just moves. I can't even imagine a dog, cat, horse or bird having a conversation about doing something. They don't discuss it or mull over it in their heads. "Is this the right grass to eat or should I eat the low fat grass?" or "I'm going to fly to Florida, uh No, maybe I'll go to Hawaii this year for the winter." They just do it! They are free from having a mind that filters everything. They are also not in a position to be conscious of their life and yet look at how vibrant and healthy animals are in the wild.

This is our blessing and our curse as humans. Blessed with the ability to transcend the dualistic mind with pure Consciousness and cursed with a relentless filter clouding everything we experience. The animal world can be great teachers of Presence and health, but we can't teach animals how to be more Conscious. That's why we are considered in Indian philosophy to be the highest form of creation in the cycle of Reincarnation and it is considered a great boon to be in a Human form. We have a choice: we can ascend to the Gods or hang out like animals. There is a catch, though, in this "Free Will" concept, which I will discuss further in the Yoga section. For in order to be FREE, you must first be free of the mind, otherwise we are no different than our animal brothers reacting unconsciously to the mundane world of eating, sleeping, sex, etc.

This information about the way the mind functions is a valuable instrument from a health and well-being standpoint, but useless in a spiritual context. This is a very important distinction to get: if we are functioning in the world we need our mind to communicate one way or another. It is a gift of God, if used correctly. The analogy of the utility of a knife is a good one. You can use a knife to carve a beautiful statue or to kill someone. Is it the fault of the knife? You can't blame God or anyone else if you're not using it correctly. The mind is part of God as well, so don't ever fight with it. It can be used to the benefit of all. So it goes into everyday living events like operating a moving vehicle, talking on the phone, using your computer, or balancing your checkbook. Otherwise it's not necessary, "Spiritually" speaking. It becomes a futile attempt to solve the Mystery. There is no way to make sense out of Life. It is a Mystery to be Lived. We need words to convey concepts to each other on one level, head to head, but they tend to distort the real essence of something. This is why words are so awkward in transmitting the truth.

And here I am attempting to do just that!!!

Trying to control life in any way doesn't work, as you know... or do you? To use control you are simply using your mind to control the mind. For example: when we make a promise to ourselves never to do something again, who is making the promise to whom? It never works! It's one thing to observe the natural flow of something and quite another to try and control it. Once you realize this, you can then step outside the loop and have better health, work, and relationships. Then you can drop the tools, "the rules of Ayurveda" and just Live them. You become less mechanical and more intuitive, which is what Ayurveda, Yoga and Tantra are essentially all about. Put on the training wheels at first, then take them off and soar!

LIKE INCREASES LIKE/OPPOSITES BALANCE

The next set of principles the Rishis observed was "Like Increases Like" and "Opposites Balance." "Like increases like," means that you are attracted to things that are similar in nature or appealing to you. For instance, if you are attracted to movement of any kind, especially fast-moving things, you will be drawn to: fast cars, traveling, exciting things and people. If you are an intellectual, you will be drawn to things or people that stimulate or challenge your mind such as: people who read voraciously or go after a PhD. If you are more inclined to being sedentary then you will watch other people being active on T.V. while sitting and eating on the couch.

Knowing that "Like increases Like," then the next principle, "Opposites Balance," makes sense. Let's take this same individual who likes to move fast. What will balance them is to slow down or to stop and "smell the roses." This will help to balance their energy. Other examples of this are, if you are feeling hot, eat cooling foods. If you're feeling dry inside or out, use oil on your skin, or add more oil to your diet. Observe how you can stop the cycle in its tracks by avoiding these things in the first place. For instance, if you are hot and you know that you tend to get overheated easily, two things you might want to do is avoid hot spicy foods and stay out of the sun. If your natural tendency is to be dry, avoid eating dry foods like chips, popcorn, or dried fruits. You see, it's actually quite simple by using the attributes to bring balance. This will make even more sense as we go further into the principles of Ayurveda.

SANSKRIT, THE ANCIENT LANGUAGE

Sanskrit is the language of the Gods. It is a based on vibration, and all language is said to have come out of Sanskrit via the Rishis. All Ayurvedic texts, as well as those of Yoga and Tantra, were written in Sanskrit. All the words I was familiar with in Yoga, came up again in Ayurveda: Prana, Chakras, Mantras, Ojas, Tejas, etc. This made my integration of Ayurveda user-friendly, as I was already used to them in my study of Yoga. It also made sense for learning a system about health with Yoga terminology since the two are "sister sciences." It's best to keep it in the same language, as opposed to using Chinese terms like Yin and Yang, Chi, or Meridians. It keeps it from getting too confusing. Yoga and Ayurveda are speaking the same language so let's keep it that way. Keep in mind, I am going from Sanskrit to English, which doesn't always work because sometimes there are words that can't be translated straight across the board, even if you're a Sanskrit scholar. The Rishis were in profound states of Consciousness when developing these systems of Ayurveda, Yoga, and Tantra, so we have to be careful not to take the literal translation to be the final word. They were coming from an expansive place.

Before I begin to explain the five elements, I want to first bring out the concept of "Sutras." All the literature of Ayurveda, Yoga and Tantra are made up of "Sanskrit sutras." Sutra literally means, a rope or thread that holds things together, and more metaphorically refers to an aphorism (formula), or a collection of such aphorisms in the form of a manual. They served and continue to act as grand treatises on various ancient Vedic texts. They elaborate in succinct, sometimes esoteric verse on metaphysics, the human condition, liberation, and how to maintain a blissful life, in a cosmic spin of karma, reincarnation, and desire.

3

THE FIVE ELEMENTS

*E*verything *that exists in the external universe, exists also in the internal universe of the human body, mind and consciousness."* This sutra comprises the theory of the Five Elements. According to the Rishis, all of life is made up of five basic elements: Earth, Water, Fire, Air and Ether or Space. You recognize the five elements through your five senses.

EARTH

The Earth element is experienced through your sense of smell, since that's your most primal sense organ. Have you noticed how animals use smell to interact with their environment? I'm sure you've seen dogs use scent to track prey or how dogs sniff out a mate. As humans we use our sense of smell to choose a mate in a more subconscious way: we're not walking around sniffing each others asses! The nature of the Earth element is structure, solidity and stability, expressed in the world as form.

WATER

The Water element is perceived through your tongue as your sense of taste. It is impossible to taste when your tongue is dry. Remember when you last had a cold, your nose got plugged up and you were only able to breathe through your mouth? As a result, your mouth got dry and you couldn't taste your food. Do this experiment. With a piece of cloth dry your tongue and put a few grains of sugar on it. That's right, you'll see it's hard to taste the sweetness, because your tongue is dry. You need a moist tongue to taste. Taste is also very important when chewing your food; your brain then knows how to prepare the body to digest whatever it has eaten. If you just bite and swallow, which I sometimes do when I am in a hurry, you miss out on a very important part of the digestive process. As soon as you start chewing your food, information is passed from the brain to the mouth, stomach, liver, and pancreas. Various digestive enzymes are mixed with the food itself before moving on to the next phase. Many people can solve their problem of digestion by simple chewing their food more thoroughly. Ayurveda says to chew your food until it liquefies.

FIRE

The Fire element is perceived through your eyes, which are known as the "windows of the soul." If you have a good internal fire, your eyes will be clear and bright. Your eyes are constantly receiving images and relaying information to the brain where it is then turned into a thought or feeling. It is said that 80% of your energy goes out through your eyes. The other 20% is divided amongst the remaining four senses. The fire element also represents the "fire" of perception, which means being able to clearly see beyond the mind's made-up meaning of something. The nature of the Fire Element is to create heat. It transforms one state of existence to another.

AIR

Air is the next element, which is perceived through your skin. You feel the air element through touch. The skin is considered our largest sense organ because of its expansive network via the nervous system. Notice the sensation on your skin as a breeze goes by. When the wind moves across the extensive surface of your skin, the Air element is in effect. Air is movement in Space, and thus responsible for all movements within you and around you. It's responsible for the blinking of your eyes and the beating of your heart. It is the energy that initiates all actions. It can be as gentle as a summer breeze or as forceful as a tornado.

SPACE

The last element, Space, is perceived through your ears. Sound is the most subtle of the five. This is why music and sound vibrations like Mantras are so powerful. The nature of Space is that it's everywhere and ever present. Out of it, the other elements manifest. In Physics, it's described as the field in which everything takes place. It's the container, and an infinite one at that! Space can be described as the distance that separates matter. Look up into the night sky. For every grain of sand on all the beaches of the planet, there is an equivalent number of stars. And between all the stars is infinite Space. Space occupies most of what is around you and inside you. It's unbelievable, mind boggling. Wherever you are right now, look around and feel the existence of space, or when you get a chance, stare up into the sky. You lose yourself in it.

The five elements are represented on your fingers (or toes), which makes them easy to remember. I am going to give examples using the fingers: the little finger represents the Earth element, your rooted nature. The "ring" finger is the water finger, symbolizing the emotional body. Isn't this the finger you wear a marriage or engagement ring to show the world you are in love with that person? The middle finger denotes fire, especially when pointed up in the air with the other fingers down, expressing the "f—-you" gesture when you're angry. (You've probably never used that one, now have you? But I'm sure you've seen it flying around somewhere?) The index finger, the one that you point with, represents the Air element. Finally, the thumb stands for the Space element, as used to hitch a ride or give a "thumbs up" to show you're feeling good.

SYMBIOTIC RELATIONSHIP

In a symbiotic relationship the components work in unison. With all the elements, a symbiotic relationship is happening between your internal and external environments. In the body, the Earth element is represented as bones, teeth, skin, hair, nails, and all other bodily structures. When you digest food, you receive the Earth element from the plants or animals you eat and by what they have taken in from the earth. The body is made up of minerals. When you die, if the body is cremated, what's left is minerals in the form of ash.

The Water element in the external universe is the oceans, rivers, lakes, and streams. In your internal universe it is the plasma, blood, sweat, tears, urine, digestive juices and mucus. The planet is made of 70% water, as is the body. Is this just a coincidence? Think of how good it feels to quench your thirst by drinking a tall glass of water. You feel refreshed and more alive. Having sufficient water in the body keeps us "flowing" in relationship to the water element. You know the expression, "swimming up stream?" This is what it feels like when we don't go with the flow. Look at how animals move with such beauty and grace.

The Fire outside of us is the Sun; inside of us is the digestive fire, called, Jathar Agni. It's responsible for digestion and circulation. The overall key to health and well-being of the body is Agni. It applies to the mind as well. If your central fire is not burning bright you will have mental as well as physical indigestion. Have you ever built a campfire?

If you have, you know you must start with twigs. Gradually you add larger pieces of wood, which create a strong, burning flame. Your metabolism is like this too. A good appetite usually signifies it's time to eat, and eating when you're not hungry turns food to poison. These toxins are called "ama." (Interesting to note here that the acronym A.M.A. stands for the American Medical Association......not surprising!) Even if the food is beautifully prepared and you're using organic ingredients, when Agni is weak it will become ama. The movement of air within and without the body animates all life. Weather patterns change as air strokes the earth with its "hands." Air scatters the seeds of trees. It is the earth's breath. Without it everything would be stagnant. The air inside you is represented by any kind of movement: breathing, first and foremost; muscle movement; blinking and heartbeats; food's passage through the digestive tract; and also thoughts or feelings.

The last element is Space, or Ether. It is the infinite container for all else — Earth, Fire, Water, and Air. It is the field in which all matter moves and flows. Science has shown that 99.9999% of the human cell is space, not matter. Despite being made up of trillions of cells, we are mostly space!!! In fact, we are barely here!

We need space everywhere in the body in order for the many systems to function properly. This includes the nervous system, arteries, veins, heart, and lungs, down to the most minute capillaries. Plus all the subtle channels that the Rishi's referred to as Nadis, which are energetic pathways in the physical body as well as the "etheric body," like meridians.

* * * * *

There are numerous stories throughout the Ancient Texts of superhuman Beings or Yogi's being able to transport themselves from one place to another. This is where modern day "mythical characters" such as Superman, Spider Man, and Wonder Woman are not so far off. Most of us live in the limited reality of our five senses so we've lost the "magic" that we had as children. But what seems like a dream of flying through space may well happen in reality. Stick around long enough and mark my words, it will happen. I mean, look at what Science has created at the turn of this last century by only scratching the surface: electricity, cell phones, cars, flying machines like airplanes and rocket ships, computers, laser surgery, artificial insemination, DNA cloning. Pretty amazing stuff! I can foresee in the near future we will be able to dissolve our bodies through some machine and reassemble them somewhere. Why not?

* * * * *

Any kind of pain in the body signifies a blockage or constriction of space. When pain appears, most of us find something to cover it up. Drugs are good for this. Staying busy is another escape mechanism. However, if you don't deal with the root cause, space gets congested. Thus the pain comes back. Then you become addicted to the drugs in order to get relief or preoccupied in activity to divert your attention. Once I was attuned to the element of Space in my life, I became cognizant at its effect on virtually everything. The quieter you become inside, the more space is automatically created. This is the beauty of Yoga and Meditation when done "correctly."

The more energy given to a thought or feeling the more likely it is to go round and round in your head. If you allow more space to exist around your thoughts, their effect on your life diminishes. This is the beauty of pure Presence. Simply witnessing or watching the movement of the mind without getting caught up in it. Let thoughts and feelings move as they will, without giving them energy. Mind is movement. (It should be called "minding.") Creating space in your mind allows for more creativity to flow. You are available to receive an abundance of vital life force all around you. The cosmic source of intelligence is at your fingertips.

To show you how we are already experiencing these factors in our everyday lives, here are some common English expressions that relate to the five elements. I'm sure there are similar ones in whatever language you speak.

- Space: "Give me some space" or "He's spaced out"
- Earth: "I slept like a log" or "I feel more   grounded after that"
- Fire: "I feel burned out "or "She's on fire!"
- Water: "Go with the flow" or "It's just water under the bridge"
- Air: "He's an airhead" or "did you just pass wind?"

A HARD DECREE

Last night God posted on a tavern wall
A hard decree for all of love's inmates
Which read:
If your heart cannot find a joyful work
the jaws of this world will probably
Grab hold of your sweet ass.

— Hafiz

4

VATA PITTA KAPHA
— *The Basic Energies Of Life*

$\mathcal{H}$aving looked at the five elements, let's see how they relate to the three basic energies of life, Kapha, Pitta and Vata. These three distinct energies appear everywhere in life, as they are a combination of the five elements. Through Kapha, Pitta, and Vata, the ancient Rishis could communicate how these elements interact in life and living.

KAPHA

Let's start with the foundation, Kapha. Kapha is a result of Earth and Water elements combined together. The attributes of Kapha are heavy, cool, dull, slow, cloudy, smooth, dense, gross, soft, moist, and static.

In your physical body, the main sight or "home" of Kapha is the stomach. Other sites are the lungs, the synovial fluid of the joints, the mouth and nose, all secretions, plasma (lymphatic system), and lymph glands. The basic principle of Kapha is expressed through form, stamina, and any physical structure (bones, teeth, hair, nails, organs, tissues etc.).

It is also responsible for all the lubrication in the body. The mucous lining of the entire digestive tract is Kapha, which is extremely important for proper movement of bodily nutrients and efficient absorption. Synovial fluid is a liquid that lines all joints as a protective layering. What it comes down to is this: Kapha's main function is protection and cohesiveness.

These are the factors that increase Kapha: late winter and early spring, exposure to moist cold, eating too much sweet, meat, fats, cheese, milk, yogurt, fried foods, excessive use of salt. Drinking too much cold water, eating after satisfaction, naps after meals, not moving or exercising, under use of the senses, oversleeping, being sedentary, all build up excess Kapha.

When Kapha is high from these factors, some symptoms may be: nasal or lung congestion, excess weight, water retention, bloating, feeling heavy, dull aching pains, lethargy and sluggishness in all systems. Emotional symptoms include: depression, apathy, possessiveness, greed, attachment and lust.

The positive quality of Kapha is nurturing. It will create a feeling of being nourished and secure. When it's balanced physically, it's expressed as having more strength, stamina and endurance which are signs of a strong immune system. When you have healthy Kapha you experience more love and compassion, and feel centered, grounded and content. Other qualities are patience and forgiveness.

PITTA

The next energy is called Pitta. It is the combination of the Fire and Water elements. The attributes of Pitta are light, hot, sharp, clear, smooth, dispersing, subtle, soft, moist and mobile. Pitta is the principle of transformation. Fire transforms things, even your thoughts. It gives clarity of perception.

Pitta's main location is the small intestine. Other sites are the stomach, liver, gall bladder, spleen, pancreas, blood, sweat, eyes, and endocrine glands. At the juncture of the stomach and small intestine is where the digestive juices pour in. This is where the main internal fire (Pitta), Jathar Agni, resides. Pitta is responsible for digestion. When the digestive fire is strong, proper assimilation and absorption of food takes place. Pitta transforms any kind of "food" whether it be mental food (thoughts, feelings, ideas) or physical food that you eat. It has the ability to take anything in the external environment and make it part of you. Pitta is expressed in the body not only as digestive enzymes, but as whole enzyme systems. Enzyme systems are the catalysts for every function in the body from cell division, to tissue repair, to immune system functions.

The factors that increase Pitta are: late spring and summer, exposure to heat and sun, eating too much red meat, salt, spicy or sour (acid) foods, alcohol, too much intellectual work and thinking, getting overheated in exercise(yoga), "over intense" competition, deadlines for work.

When these factors are present, Pitta is increased or imbalanced. These symptoms may occur: burning sensations in the stomach (heartburn or acid reflex), diarrhea, jaundice or any liver complaints, ulcers, toxic blood, eye or vision problems, skin rashes, boils, acne, strong body odor, profuse sweating or excess urination from overheating, any kind of infections, extreme hunger. (You know the friend you go to lunch with who's always eyeing your plate and asking, "are you going to finish that?" Pitta for sure!) Emotions associated with high Pitta are: anger, rage, jealousy, frustration, impatience, perfectionism (anger at one's self), arrogance, and being overly intense.

When Pitta is balanced physically, the body responds by having good digestion. Good digestion is processing and eliminating the food easily as it moves throughout the entire digestive tract. Food choices are important, but not as important as how you digest. This means no discomfort will be felt from mouth to anus.

Other signs of balanced Pitta are clear eyes, radiant skin, good muscle tone, sharp intellect, and healthy sex drive. Energetically it will express itself as passion, courage, confidence, and clear thinking.

VATA

The last energy is Vata, which is Air and Space combined. The attributes of Vata are cold, light, sharp, fast, clear, rough, dispersing, subtle, hard, dry, and mobile. Vata is changeable and unpredictable. It can be a summer breeze or a devastating hurricane. It is the principle of movement, which is responsible for all expression in life, enthusiasm, and prana (life force energy). It is inhale and exhale. When you're born your first breath is inhale and when you die your last is exhale. Every breath in between is energy spent on ascending or descending. The main site of Vata is the colon. Other sites are the pelvic cavity, lower back, joints, ears, skin, nervous system and anywhere space resides.

Vata is responsible for any kind of movement physical or mental. It directly affects the nervous system. In our modern world stress is a major problem. It over stimulates the nervous system, aggravating Vata. Vata moves everything including Pitta and Kapha. Pitta and Kapha are left immobile without Vata to circulate them. It's essential that you monitor the condition of Vata at all times. It is the initiator of all activities. Here are some examples: it moves food through the digestive tract, it circulates blood through all the blood vessels. It regulates breathing and moves all the muscles in the body. It is also responsible for our cell dividing and multiplying.

Factors which increase Vata are: fall and early winter, exposure to dry cold, no routine in your life, eating too much dry, frozen, or leftover food, or foods with bitter and astringent tastes, not enough oil in the diet, prolonged fasting, too much traveling, too much or inappropriate exercise(running, jogging, yoga, etc.), misuse or overuse of senses, too much sex, suppressing natural urges (yawning, belching, sneezing, farting, pooping, peeing, sex, sleep, hunger, thirst), stimulants and other drugs, staying up late, and overuse of colonics, enemas or laxative herbs.

When Vata is high or imbalanced, constipation is the main symptom. This is important to watch because if the bowels are not moving, the toxins in the colon begin to back up and will poison your body. The toxins (ama) then go to a weak site in the body eventually manifesting into a chronic problem. Bloating and gas will be another symptom of constipation. (Ever notice how women handle the passing of Vata from their colon differently? Men will be proud of their farts and women will wait until there is an opportunity to release. You know when your father would ask you to pull his finger and then let one rip!)

In addition high Vata will cause the joints to dry out, creating lots of popping and cracking sounds. This may be a precursor to Arthritic conditions. Also there is a tendency to nervous "fidgeting" which results in self-adjusting the spine, knuckle cracking, tapping the fingers or feet, eye twitching, stuttering and nail biting. Since Vata is also responsible for circulation, if it is out of balance, it may express itself as cold hands and feet. Extreme weight loss may happen. You'll walk fast, talk fast, eat fast, drive fast.....everything that you do will be at a rapid pace. Sleeping becomes an issue when Vata is increased because of excess movement in the mind and body. Look up "erratic" in the dictionary and every synonym expresses Vata. Appetite and thirst will be up and down, the heart will beat irregularly, and relationships will change quickly. Most everything is inconsistent and unpredictable.

Mental and energetic imbalances are as follows: constant and incessant thinking, worry, fear, anxiety, forgetfulness, insecurity and ungroundedness. When Vata gets dispersed, an emptiness results. Panic attacks, paranoia and insomnia, are severe Vata nervous system imbalances.

When Vata is physically balanced, peristaltic movement of the colon/ large intestines is working properly. This means no effort is required to push fecal matter out. The nervous system will be relaxed, unaffected by excess stimuli. Heartbeat will be at a regular rhythm. Circulation will flow efficiently throughout the body. Little or no joint popping will occur.

Energetically when Vata is balanced there will be a flow of creativity, joy, enthusiasm, vitality and artistic expression. A calm tranquil mind will also be predominant. There will be a sense of freedom to direct your energy in whatever way you choose.

VATA, PITTA, KAPHA IN RELATION TO TIME

THE 24 HOUR DAY

In a twenty-four hour period Vata, Pitta, Kapha change every four hours. The hours from 2 to 6 in the morning and afternoon are Vata time. This is the most auspicious time of the day for Meditation and Yoga practices. Especially the "nectar hours;" the transition of darkness to light just before dawn. The hours 6 to 10 in the morning and evening are Kapha time. That's why if you sleep into the later morning you feel heavy, because you're accumulating Kapha. It's also a good time to rest for high Vata since Kapha is available at that time. Pitta reigns from 10 to 2 in the morning and at night. From 10 am to 2 pm is the hottest time of day and the most intense Pitta time. Since Pitta is the highest at this time, it is the best time to eat your heaviest meal. Also notice that if you're up past 10 p.m. you might begin to feel a second wind of energy for activity and perhaps some hunger as Pitta is enlivened again during these hours. If you want to create a healthy lifestyle you may want to consider living according to these cycles, which are in sync with the natural rhythms of nature. Not adhering to them is, "going against the flow."

SEASONS

The seasons change, and each season is related to either Vata, Pitta or Kapha. Summer is Pitta, the most vibrant and radiant season. The energy on the planet is most intense at this time. Climate-wise it is the warmest season. It is a time of growth and expansion. Remember the attributes of Pitta are hot, light, sharp, intense, etc. Vata is the autumn season. It's a time of harvest. Leaves are beginning to dry out and fall, that's why they call it fall! There is more wind in the air. It's starting to get cooler. Can you see the attributes of Vata are well expressed in this season? Dry, light, cold, dispersing, etc. Kapha season is in the winter. Winter is a time for hibernation. The temperature is getting colder and there's more moisture in the air. It's darker this time of year. The attributes of cold, moist, heavy, and slow predominate. Spring is a combination of Kapha and Pitta. The early part of spring is when Kapha begins to liquify. Spring brings with it new life. Energy begins to escalate as late spring kicks in. It's a time of renewal and rejuvenation, then full bloom kicks in for summer.

Paying attention to the change of seasons is very important, as there is a natural accumulation of any one particular dosha by the end of their respective season. For instance: Vata will be highest at the end of fall so you need to be sure to eliminate it before it expresses itself in the form of some Vata imbalances. Pitta is at the end of summer, Kapha is the end of winter. The beginning of spring is Kapha and Pitta starts accumulating as spring moves into summer.

The way Ayurveda recommends to handle this natural phenomenon is to fast at the junction of the seasons or to do what is called Pancha Karma, a cleansing and rejuvenation program. (See page 121) Moving in harmony with your external environment is critical for vibrant health. Another aspect to this is changing your diet appropriately to the season at hand. An example of this: summer is a time of fresh seasonal fruits and veggies. You can only get certain things at that time. As fall comes and then winter, the available produce changes. Yet the delivery system of the modern day grocery store means we can get whatever we want, whenever we want. This is not always what's best for our bodies at that time. It's better that we flow with our natural surroundings otherwise we are out of balance. So it's best to buy what grows locally. That doesn't mean that we can't have something out of "season" here and there, but to eat the same thing throughout the year is a major reason for allergies. We must always see where we can work in harmony with nature or else there is a drain on our immune system struggling against natural cycles.

AGE

Your chronological age also has a direct relationship to Vata, Pitta, Kapha. From birth to puberty is Kapha time, when you're body is growing more rapidly than any other time in your life. From the end of puberty to about fifty is Pitta time, which is the time you are most ambitious and prolific in your personal and professional life. You're out there expressing yourself in a fiery way. After fifty is Vata time. It is a time of reaping what you've sown. Have you gathered your energies (financial, mental, physical, spiritual) wisely? If you have amassed great wealth but not health, then are you living a balanced life? This time reveals your inner wisdom and shows what you've been cultivating over the past fifty years. If you're not living a healthy, balanced life by the time you reach fifty, you're probably full of aches and pains, which is defined as "getting old." Western medicine has supposedly increased our life span, but not the quality of our life. Ayurveda is about adding life to your years, along with years to your life.

—§—

5

PRAKRUTI /VIKRUTI

et's look at another important Ayurvedic sutra:
"Your individual constitution, your basic overall physical and mental makeup, is determined at the moment of conception and remains the same throughout your whole life."

It's your genetic code, your "blueprint." In Ayurveda this is called Prakruti. This is a Sanskrit word which means, "first creation." Everyone on the planet is completely unique. Your Prakruti is as unique as your fingerprint, or your individual hair and eye color, bone structure, teeth, and skin. Being that it remains the same throughout your entire life, it is similar to your Astrological chart. You were born at a particular time and you can't complain and say, "Hey I'm not real happy being a Scorpio, can I trade it in for, say, Capricorn?" These are the cards you've been dealt this time around. It's all in how you play them.

Vikruti is your imbalance showing up in the moment as high Vata, Pitta or Kapha. This can be confusing since Vata, Pitta, Kapha can change on a regular basis inside and out. Many factors affect these three including the ones I mentioned: time of day, seasons, your age, weather, food, relationships, work, stress, and other events in one's life. Dr. Lad, the Ayurvedic doctor that I studied with used to say, "Keeping Vata, Pitta and Kapha in balance is like a juggling act. You have to keep all three balls in the air at once."

I will use myself as an example to explain Vikruti. First thing in the morning, I check in with my Vata, since I am Vata predominant. I ask myself, How was my sleep? Am I energized and clear? Do I feel constipated?" Any signs or symptoms of feeling off? How I answer any of these questions will determine how I go about my day. If I am feeling good, I've slept well, bowels have moved freely, and I feel clear, then I'm balanced. If not, then I need to address Vata. This will involve avoiding foods and other things that have Vata attributes such as: dry, light, subtle, or dispersing. In order to balance this out I must choose their opposite qualities which are heavier, grounding foods: grains, breads, root vegetables, soups, or stews.

The way I move through my day will also dictate how whether my Vata is high or low. Am I moving, walking, or talking fast? If so, I need to consciously walk more slowly and feel my steps, and watch my thoughts; be clear before blurting something out of my mouth. I need to create routines and schedules. If I feel constipated I must eat appropriately according to where I am living at the time, the season, the climate, etc. Sometimes I will take herbs to accelerate balance. Maybe even have a day of fasting with juices that will help relieve my bowels. I need to make sure I'm practicing Yoga regularly. If I've been traveling a lot then maybe my practice isn't as long as usual, but that's alright; consistency is most important, since Vata is irregular and inconsistent. You can have the same approach for Pitta and Kapha if you feel they're high. Do what I just did using the attributes of either Pitta or Kapha to balance them with the appropriate opposite qualities.

DOSHAS

Vata, Pitta, Kapha are known as "doshas" in Ayurveda. The word dosha means "fault," or that which is likely to go out of balance. Dosha refers to your Vikruti, not your Prakruti. Your Vikruti as I have shown above will most likely be the same as your Prakruti because your imbalance is more prone to go with natural tendencies and energies.

It demonstrates the principle "like attracts like." As I said earlier, the doshas change on a moment- by-moment basis, seasonally and through the stages of your life. You can see the mirror of microcosm and macrocosm, as life consistently ebbs and flows. You know the expression "the only thing you can rely on is change."

DETERMINING YOUR CONSTITUTION (PRAKRUTI)

Prakruti means "first creation." It's your own personal "recipe" of Vata, Pitta, Kapha. I want to share with you now what you're probably all curious about; how to determine your own constitution. Keep in mind what's most important here is that when I mention a characteristic, look at it in relation to your entire life, not just the recent past. Another very important point to keep in mind is that in determining each characteristic, you look at it from the perspective of your tendency to be a certain way rather than absolute. In fact, in doing this exercise you're not determining what label, Vata, Pitta, Kapha, you'll wear on your forehead, but rather recognizing that you have a strong tendency in your nature that you have to be aware of, since this is where you most likely will go out of balance.

I'm going to go through various characteristics starting with the body frame. I'll mention different qualities of each group relating to VPK. Put a tick mark next to the characteristics you've had since birth. Sometimes, the choice you make may not ade quately express that bodily characteristic, and it might be necessary to answer with two ticks for the same one. That's okay. At the end of the list, add up the number of ticks in Vata, Pitta, Kapha, and the column with the greatest number will be your basic constitution, your Prakruti. The column with the second largest number of ticks is your secondary characteristic. Don't forget that each aspect of VPK exists in all bodies, just in different degrees. Once you understand what your Prakruti is, then you can determine what kind of lifestyle will best suit your nature. This includes work, relationships, exercise, places to live, seasons, foods to eat, colors to wear, or anything else you need to do in order to live in balance with your Prakruti and the outside world. The following list will give you a general idea of what your Prakruti is. There are more extensive lists in other Ayurvedic books and if you want a more thorough examination, seek out a qualified Ayurvedic Practitioner.

DETERMINING YOUR PRAKRUTI

	VATA	PITTA	KAPHA
Body frame	Short or tall thin frame, small bones	Medium build, muscular, athletic	Fleshy, more weight, large bones
Skin	Dry, darker, tans easily, cool	Reddish or yellow color, freckled,acne	Moist, cool, oily, lighter color, soft
Hair	Thin, dry, curly/kinky, brittle, dark	Red or blonde, grey, men balding	Thick, oily, wavy, lighter color
Eyes	Dark color,fidgety,small	Intense, bright, sharp, gray, green	Big, blue, soft, calm
Teeth	Irregular, thin gums, cavities	Yellowish color, tender gums	Big,white, few cavities, strong gums
Circulation	Poor, cold hands and feet	Great!	Good, not great
Thirst	Variable	Extreme	Moderate
Sweat	Scanty	Profuse	Moderate
Stool	Constipated, gas, dry, bloating	Loose and plentiful	Thick, oily, sluggish

	VATA	PITTA	KAPHA
Urination	Variable and scanty	Frequent and yellow color	Moderate and cloudy
Sensitivity	To cold and dry	To heat or extreme sunlight	To cold and damp
Activity	Very active, multi-tasker	Focused and intense	Passive, voyeur
Stamina	Low	Good	Great
Sleep	Restless, light interrupted	Moderate	Sound
Speech	Fast, very talkative	Sharp, cutting and direct	Slow and steady
Sex	Variable	Strong, easily aroused	Steady desire

Now add up the ticks to see which is predominant. The one you checked the most will be your primary nature. The second highest will be your secondary nature. For instance: Vata (predominant) and Pitta (secondary) = a Vata/ Pitta type (like me; Pitta (predominant) and Vata (secondary) = a Pitta/Vata type. There are ten different body/mind types that Ayurveda recognizes. They are: V, P, K, VP, VK, PV, KV, PK, KP, and VPK. Keep in mind that hair, eyes, and skin may be the same for one particular race but will vary in shades.

A predominant Vata type person will have the qualities I mentioned earlier. The main theme for equilibrium is warming and calming. A balanced Vata will be: creative, a strong communicator, artistic, adaptable, alert, emotionally sensitive, enthusiastic, imaginative, spontaneous, intuitive and charismatic.

An imbalanced Vata will be overly active mentally and physically, extremely sensitive to people and environments, have sleep problems (insomnia, "restless leg syndrome"), spend money rapidly, lack confidence, and be quick to judge or make decisions, grasp things quickly but forget them just as fast, be disorganized and, moody.

A predominant Pitta type who is balanced will be: highly intelligent, confident, willful and determined, ambitious, funny, articulate, organized, and perceptive. The main theme for equanimity here is cooling and soothing. If imbalanced, a Pitta will be: overly intense, manipulative, stubborn, arrogant, jealous, materialistic, loud and aggressive, controlling of others, egotistical, critical and judgmental, and demanding center of attention.

Kapha predominant in the constitution will reflect balance by being: patient, sweet, forgiving, gentle, and emotionally stable; they love helping people, are loyal, nurturing; they are homebodies who love to feed and entertain; they are community-oriented, good listeners, and deeply satisfied with life. The main thing to prevent Kapha from settling in and stagnating is keep life stimulating and exhilarating.

If imbalanced , Kapha will be: greedy, attached to people and things, easily depressed, introverted, complacent, unable to say no, easily taken advantage of, fearful of letting go, and likely to accumulates things and weight.

LIFE STYLE FOR BALANCED VPK

So once you have determined your constitution, then what? Keep in mind that your constitution is your tendency for that particular dosha to go high (vikruti). For instance, since I am VP with Vata predominant, the tendency is to have my Vata go high. My Pitta will go high as well if I don't watch it closely, especially during summer, living in hot climates, or taking in too much Pitta energy through my lifestyle choices. My main challenge is always Vata, as it's the one most likely to go high. What I am doing in my life will determine if it goes up or not. Staying up too late at night watching a movie; traveling too much; talking too much; being overactive through the day; taking on too many "projects." Lacking routine so that I eat irregularly and consume high vata foods (foods that are dry, light, subtle, dispersing), get up at various times in the morning, or do my Yoga practice erratically........... All of these will for sure disturb my Vata and then I will feel uneasy and unstable inside and out. I will get constipated, my skin will dry out, I will feel nervous, anxious, and insecure. I won't be able to sleep at night.

If you understand who you are from this standpoint then you can make "intelligent" decisions regarding your lifestyle: diet, relationships, work, where you live, colors you wear, scents you put on, things you drink, music you listen to, movies you watch, books you read. It doesn't mean that you have to avoid the things that are similar to your Prakruti for the rest of your life. It's to be aware of what you are taking in via your five senses. Do they serve you or not? If you are Kapha predominant or Pitta predominant, Vata symptoms are less likely to occur, but over time you could also end up with high Vata.

More and more people living in "modern" society are having increased Vata problems due to the intense speed and movement of daily life in this "fast paced" world. The lesson here is to address what's high with the doshas/vikruti. If everything is balanced (no symptoms of high VPK), go with what your prakruti (constitution) is. That is, follow a regime that supports who you are inherently. Then you adjust accordingly with what season it is, where you live, the kind of work you are doing (physical or mental), etc.

{*An extensive list of foods are available in "Eat, Taste, Heal- An Ayurvedic Cookbook for Modern Living," by Yarema, Rhoda, and Brannegan, Five Elements Press, 2006 }

COMMUNICATION AND VPK

Your tendency to learn and communicate is in one of three ways or a combination of the three, to lesser degrees. These ways are hearing, seeing, and touching. Even Western science recognizes them as fundamental to learning and communication. The spoken word is essential for Vata.

A visual has to be shown for Pitta, and some action or experience has to take place for Kapha. Vata people experience and learn predominantly through hearing all kind of sounds (especially verbal). They communicate and express mostly through talking. This sense relates to the ear and to the elements Air and Ether, which make up Vata. Most musicians are Vata since their sense of hearing is so refined.

Pitta people tend to express themselves through visual means. They learn best by using their sense of sight, and easiest through reading the printed word and seeing something done. They love to read, study, and analyze things. Their visual expression shows up in the colors of the clothes they wear, their jewelry, design of their homes, etc. They make fabulous visual artists.

Kapha learns best through contact, by doing things with their hands. They accomplish things well on a physical level and learn by physically touching something so they have an experience of it. Tasting (water element) and smelling (earth element) are Kapha as well, as they tend to use these to experience the world. Some of the best chefs in the world are Kapha, along with "body workers."

Always take these factors into account when presenting anything to a predominant Vata, Pitta, or Kapha person. You will then have an easier time getting what you want across. Being aware of this for your own growth and development is equally important. This allows you to pursue those things that resonate with you and thus you will feel at ease in understanding them. Don't run away from or deny who you are; instead, embrace it. Become more natural and listen to the wisdom of your body's innate intelligence. This will bring radiant health. Even if you know nothing about Ayurveda, tuning into nature will connect you to its essential principles. After all, Ayurveda is called, "the Mother of all Healing Systems," and nature is referred to as "Mother Nature." So you have to ask yourself, "have you been listening to your Mother lately?"

6

SATTVA RAJAS TAMAS

QUALITIES OF MIND

H umans are unique. We have access to the subtle aspects of Vata, Pitta, Kapha through having a mind. Being blessed or cursed with a mind is what sets us aside from the animals. We can soar to great heights like Einstein or to the bottomless pit like Hitler. There are three subtle energetic qualities of Vata, Pitta, Kapha, called Tamas, Rajas, and Sattva. Tamas is a thick, heavy, dull energy similar to imbalanced Kapha. Rajas is the opposite of Tamas and similar to high Vata. It expresses lots of activity and erraticness and is dispersing. Sattva represents balance and equanimity and is associated with Pitta. Sattva is symbolic of fire. It is clarity and perception and is piercing. Fire is transformation in action.

There are Tamasic, Rajasic and Sattvic lifestyles. If you're living a Tamasic lifestyle, you're consuming lots of red meat, alcohol, leftovers, microwaved or overcooked foods, and basically doing things that create heaviness and dullness in your life, which increases Kapha. It's the classic "couch potato" syndrome or the apathetic, "just getting by" attitude.

A Rajasic lifestyle reflects excessive energy: hot spicy foods, drinking too much coffee, smoking cigarettes, taking drugs, and engaging in other over stimulating activities. This lifestyle creates nervousness and anxiety, scatters your energy, and increases Vata. It's the classic "busy person" syndrome, always having to do something to stay occupied, even when on vacation. Tamasic and Rajasic are two extremes of the same pole.

Sattvic is in the middle, living a more balanced and "spiritual life." Buddha's path was known as the "middle way." That's not the same as the expression, "middle of the road," which gives a feeling of playing it safe. Rather it is to live consciously, choosing what serves the "highest good." Sattvic foods are fresh, pure, vibrant and are natural and organic. It is practicing Yoga, Meditation, eating vegetarian foods, or anything considered "wholesome" and virtuous in your living. Finding the balance of activity and rest is the key to a Sattvic life.

I want to point out there have been spiritual traditions like the Native American Indians who ate meat but expressed a reverence for what they killed. They are thankful for the animal giving up its life so they may be nourished. (Hitler was a Vegetarian, so don't be too righteous about a particular way of life. It doesn't always equate to being spiritual). If you know a certain choice will create a lot of nervous energy, why go there?

If you eat a piece of meat you know you'll feel heavy, lethargic and maybe even aggressive. Again, it's being conscious of what you want out of life. This yogi friend of mine called Swami Beyond Ananda has an interesting take on it all. He says, *"I'm a Humanitarian, not a Vegetarian. I eat people, and only the highest Beings, because as you know, you are what you eat."*

AYURVEDA AND NOURISHMENT

The foods you eat are an important part of your Ayurvedic regime, because you consume food at least three times a day. Ayurveda says about 60% of your nourishment comes from the foods you eat and the other 40% comes from your breath. Nourishment in Ayurveda is said to come from Prana. Prana is your

Life Force energy. That is why breathing in Yoga is so vital. It is like a meal. In Asana or Pranayama (breathing exercise) class I will say out loud, "Savor each breath like a delicious meal," for it directly nourishes you each moment. Another source of nourishment is the sun, which we absorb through our skin. After all, we are "solar powered." That's why in countries where the sun doesn't shine much, there are higher incidences of depression and suicides. The less sun the body gets the less melatonin it produces. This is the hormone that regulates the Pineal gland, the master gland and psychic channel. The Pineal gland is responsible for altering your moods.

Our nourishment is vital on the spiritual path otherwise we do not have enough juice to pursue this Himalayan feat of ascending within. Again it's not only physical food; carrots, potatoes, beets, that can nourish you. You get "fed" by the colors you wear, the people you're with, the kind of books you read, music you listen to, the movies you watch and so on. All of these are either nourishing you or not. These "foods," have different energies about them. Like you, some "foods" are more Vata, Pitta or Kapha than others. Each one has attributes, either increasing Vata, Pitta or Kapha or decreasing them. Think about many of the other aspects of your life that have these qualities and contribute to you either being balanced or unbalanced. Notice that, "one man's poison is another man's medicine."

If you constantly observe this in your life, you eventually become more "natural" with your choices. Your intuitiveness guides you to the most vibrant ways of living possible. Here is a small example to give you ideas of things to choose in your life that increase or decrease VPK.

NOURISHMENT FOR VPK

	Nourishment for VATA (Anything increasing kapha)	Nourishment for PITTA (Anything cooling and calming)	Nourishment for KAPHA (Anything increasing Vata)
Scents	Lavender, cinnamon	Sandalwood, rose	Eucalyptus, cedar, myrrh
Colors	Earth tones, warming colors	Blues, white	Red, orange, violet
Textures	Smooth, soft	Smooth, soft	Rough, dry
Music	Classical, mellow, slow, soft	Ambient, "chill out," jazz	Rock and roll

Good for all three: plenty of rest, sunshine, spend time in nature, playing, and most of all laughing!

Mulla Nasrudin and his wife were sitting on a bench in the park one evening just at dusk. Without knowing that they were close by, a young man and his girlfriend sat down at a bench on the other side of a hedge. Almost immediately, the young man began to talk in the most loving manner imaginable. "He does not know we are sitting here,"Mulla's wife whispered to her husband.
"It sounds like he is going to propose to her. I think you should cough or something and warn him."
"Why should I warn him?" asked Mulla.
"Nobody warned me!"

7

SIX TASTES

This will help you better understand the foods you eat. There are six distinct and separate tastes that Ayurveda recognizes. They are Sweet, Sour, Salty, Pungent, Bitter and Astringent. All foods have predominantly one of these six tastes. That's very important because as a result of each taste a food will either increase or decrease Vata, Pitta, or Kapha.

In the Ayurvedic system, sweet is considered the heaviest taste, anabolic (building/nourishing), and the most Kapha. Therefore Ayurveda recommends starting a meal with this taste and ending with Bitter, the lightest taste, which is catabolic (breaking down/cleansing), the most Vata. What do we do in the West? The exact opposite! We eat dessert last and salad first! This wreaks havoc on digestion. Be aware that when Ayurveda speaks of sweet that refers mostly to grains or complex carbohydrates, not just simple carbs like refined sugars, flours, candy, sodas, etc. When selecting tastes of food we want to include all six tastes to our main meals. Sour, salty and pungent tastes stimulate the body to secrete digestive juices that break down carbohydrates, fats, proteins and fiber.

The chart below demonstrates the various qualities of these six tastes and how they affect VPK. You should emphasize the taste which best suits your needs. For instance, more Sweet increases Kapha, more Bitter increases Vata.

THE SIX TASTES AND VPK

TASTE • Examples • What are its Elements?	What are its Qualities?	• Cooling or Heating? • Nourishing or cleansing?	Effect on VPK
SWEET Whole grains, breads Earth and Water	Cold, heavy, soft, static, moist, slow, gross, dull, mobile, dry, fast, subtle, sharp, cloudy, dense	COOLING NOURISHING	Vata Decreased Pitta Decreased Kapha Increased
PUNGENT Hot chiles, black pepper Fire and Air	Hot, light, hard, clear, dispersing	HEATING CLEANSING	*Vata Dec./Inc. Pitta Increased KaphaDecreased
SOUR Lemons, yoghurt Earth and Fire	Hot, heavy, soft, static, hard, gross, sharp, subtle	HEATING NOURISHING	Vata Decreased Pitta Increased Kapha Increased
BITTER Green leafy vegetables Air and Ether	Cold, light, clear, dispersing	COOLING CLEANSING	Vata Increased Pitta Decreased KaphaDecreased
SALTY Seaweed, rock-salt	Salty, hot, heavy, hard, static, moist,	HEATING NOURISHING	Vata Decreased Pitta Increased Kapha Increased

Fire and Water	slow, gross, sharp, cloudy		
ASTRINGENT (dry taste in the mouth) Pomegranate, unripe banana, legumes Air and Earth	Dense, cold, light, hard, mobile	COOLING CLEANSING	Vata Increased Pitta Decreased KaphaDecreased

*Vata is at first lowered, but increases with prolonged use due to drying action

Here is the diet recommended for each type:

For Vata (increases Kapha):
50% whole grain cooked cereals, breads
20% protein: eggs, high quality dairy products, poultry, seafood, beef, tofu, black and red lentils*
20-30% fresh cooked vegetables with minimal raw
10% for fresh fruits

For Pitta:
50% whole grain breads
10-20% protein: beans, tofu, tempeh, cottage cheese, ricotta cheese, raw milk, egg white, chicken and turkey (white meat), shrimp, rabbit, venison
20-30% vegetables with an optional
10% for fresh fruits

For Kapha (increase Vata):
30-40% whole grains: rye crackers, dry cereals, and cooked grains

20% protein: chicken, turkey, rabbit, boiled and poached eggs, small amount of goats milk, and most beans (including garbanzos, adukis, pintos, black beans, red lentils, navy and white beans, split peas)
40-50% fresh vegetables, raw or cooked
10% (optional) fresh or dried fruits. A daily salad is good.

Notice that Ayurveda gives "meat" selections for all three as they have benefits for each one physically. Most Yogic texts will only maintain a strict Vegetarian diet. I eat a small amount of fish because I live on the coast of Sri Lanka and Hawaii nine months or more of the year. I feel healthier eating a small amount of it here and there, but that's me. Plus, I figure Jesus must have eaten some fish, since he was hanging out with a bunch of fishermen. He wasn't too bad of a guy, now was he?

It's very important to taste your food. All the six tastes in Ayurveda give information to the body so it knows what to do. If you just bite and gulp, there's nothing being communicated to the digestive system. The information from the six tastes is extremely valuable to your physiology and mind. Again, this is how the attributes can contribute to your wellbeing. What do you want to create, balance or random chaos in your life? The body/mind receives both physical nutrients and energetic qualities. The more Conscious you are about the food you eat and the nourishment you get from many other "foods" — people, jobs, life situations — then the closer you'll be to being whole and complete. Otherwise, the actual food you eat doesn't get digested and become part of you. Rather, it becomes ama, toxins that get lodged in the deeper bodily tissues and organs, which when built up over time create minor and then major diseases.

INTEGRATION OF KAPHA , PITTA, VATA IN NATURE

The integration of Kapha, Pitta and Vata is demonstrated in nature in numerous ways that we are all familiar with. Here are a few. Imagine yourself gazing at the ocean (kapha) and the sun (pitta) is beating down on the water. The heat created by the sun causes the ocean's water to evaporate as gaseous molecules (vata) release into the atmosphere. The gaseous water molecules collect and form a "sponge" that becomes a cloud (kapha). When the cloud is full of water it bursts, creating rain falling back into the ocean.

Another example is a cycle that we have in our bodies; blood circulation. A man weighing 68 kilos (150 pounds) will contain about five and a half litres (6 quarts) of blood. The same five and a half liters are circulated via the heart/blood vessel matrix throughout the whole body. Some 7,500 liters (2,000 gallons) a day are circulated over and over again! The earth has a fixed quantity of saline water that it cycles over and over, like the blood in our circulatory system.

Once again the microcosm/macrocosm is mirrored between nature and man. This is why it is important to be conscious of what we put into our bodies and the waste we dump on our planet, as these are "closed loop" energy systems. I will be so bold (like I haven't been already) as to make the assumption that how we treat our bodies is the way we treat our earth. It is no wonder the planet is in the state it's in from unconscious living, inside and out. Once more the finger is pointing back at each of us saying, "Look within for the solution to what is happening outside." If we truly want to have harmony on the planet, we must start with ourselves first. This is a constant theme throughout all of the ancient wisdom sciences. You start with yourself; centered from there, naturally you will treat everything and everyone outside of you with Love and Compassion. After all, when you connect with your own heart you recognize you are "One with Everything."

I heard about this enlightened vegetarian hot dog stand guy in New York City who when people found out he was "awakened" would go up to him and say, "make me one with everything." When they would pay him with large bills he never gave back any change. He said, "change comes from within."

DIGESTION AND THE MIND

You now see that the main home of Kapha, Pitta, and Vata is the digestive tract. That's why digestion is so important in Ayurveda, and the key to vibrant health. This part of the anatomy is so critical. The base of all health problems is based on weak digestive fire or Agni, which creates ama. The root is digestion, but what feeds it is your reactive mind. The state of your vitality is rooted in your mind. The body is simply a mirror of what is happening mentally and emotionally. Ayurveda states that, "95% of all disease is based on unconscious mind choices." When we are struggling mentally or emotionally it directly impacts the digestive process. Think back to the last time you ate something when you were emotionally distressed. The food you ate probably didn't get digested very well. There are two ways in which people emotionally eat. One way, is the way that I react: when I get upset emotionally, I don't eat. I have no appetite, my fire has completely gone out. The other way of emotional eating is eating to fill the void.

The mind always pulls you one way or another on food choices. Picking foods that are "healthy" and nourishing for you can only come from having a clear mind. This is where Yoga assists in the remedy of the restless mind. Restlessness creates uneasiness, or "dis-ease." We must address this first and foremost. Once the mind is at rest, you become more conscious of making beneficial choices. Always listen to the needs of the body. Otherwise you make decisions from an emotional place, based on past memories.

What is a true craving? The body will direct you to what is most beneficial. The mind will steer you to pick what I call "comfort foods," foods that feel familiar or have an association with a past pleasurable experience. For example, craving pasta is not necessarily healthy for me, but it reminds me of "what mama use to make(please read this in an italian accent!)."These choices are fine, if recognized for what they are. Enjoy your pasta, white sugar or flour, wine, whatever it may be, occasionally, but be careful not to get in the habit of blindly reaching for things that don't nourish you thoroughly in the long run. As you can see, most all "health problems" are based in the mind. That's why Ayurveda can make such a bold statement as, "95% of all disease is rooted in our unconscious mind." When we make decisions from a mechanical place, that is the result. Cancer, heart disease, diabetes, and arthritis, are not things you "catch" by someone sneezing on you. You've earned them, so to speak. A life-long pattern of choosing things that are "unhealthy" becomes a slow suicide. I'm not just talking about food that you put in your mouth. And remember, "food" doesn't just come from what you eat.

I know it may sound crazy, but it's true. How can I relate eating sugar with suicide? Well it seems benign enough at first, but reaching for unhealthy food over and over again to satisfy some other need will catch up with you. That is how people create Diabetes. It's all relative, of course.

Having something periodically is alright, and the degree to which food or lifestyle affects you depends on what you choose. Eating red meat constantly may cause heart disease. It's a well-known fact in Western medical science. Yet look at how much meat is consumed in the world, especially America. How about cigarettes? Again, it is a scientific fact that smoking causes lung cancer, but look at how many millions of people continue to smoke. How soon someone dies from this is individual. Some people have a stronger immune system than others. We all have genetic predispositions to certain ailments. These predispositions come from not only physical habits, but also mental habits we "inherit" from our family, passed from one generation to the next. To fully claim your "perfect health" you must choose to live in a way that totally transforms you from your past genetic coding. It is the messages we decide to give our cells today that create the bodies of tomorrow. Ayurveda speaks of a force most basic to nature, a force that underlies everything. This force is called, "universal cosmic intelligence." This is the vast power that lies silently inside our cells. I'd like to call it "cellular intelligence," the true mind of the cell, which knows no limit. The secret of life at this level is that anything in your body can be changed with the flick of an intention. We tend to see our bodies as fixed material objects, when in truth they are more like rivers, flowing patterns of intelligence that are constantly changing.

Every five days you acquire a new stomach lining. Your skin is renewed every five weeks. Your skeleton, which seems so solid and fixed is entirely new every three months. Every seven years the total number of the cells in your body are replaced; you are a completely new person cellularly. Someone who dies of a heart attack or develops arthritis has had innumerable opportunities to build new arteries, or to make healthy joints. The trick is, to change the printout of the body, you must learn to rewrite the software of you mind. Otherwise you end up with the same body for the next seven years!!!

Life is immensely flexible and the forces that cause it to endure are at least as strong as those that cause it to decay. There is an impulse in all of us to grow and change. We must be sensitive to this impulse, and feed it with our intention and awareness. Before disease can exist physically, it must be triggered at a deeper mental and emotional level. Rather than talking about the breakdown of the DNA's self-repairing mechanism, or the actions of carcinogens in our food, Ayurveda says that illness results from distortion in the pattern of universal cosmic intelligence. The individual cosmic intelligence therefore needs to align with the universal cosmic intelligence by accessing what is available through methods of Yoga, meditation, Presence.......in other words going beyond the mind.

Nature is like a radio band with an infinite number of stations. The reality you are now experiencing is only one station on the band. This can be completely convincing as long as you stay tuned to it, but it is masking the unlimited number of choices that lie on either side. We can all learn to live a vital existence by fully taking on the certainty that life and living vibrantly is our truth, and that sickness and disease are horrible lies. Human beings have, thus far, given only to sickness and disease. This perpetuates from generation to generation in our genetic code. Since what we give ourselves (our cells) to has profound and lasting effects, we can create a new reality together. We are a "new species" walking this earth, recognizing the inherent coding of the DNA that says, "Life is endless if we choose to be."

YOU'RE IT

God disguised as a myriad of things and playing a game of tag
has kissed you and said "You're it.......I mean, you're really IT !!!
Now it doesn't matter what you believe or feel for something
Wonderful Major league wonderful is someday going to happen.
— Hafiz

8

AGNI AND AMA

gni is the fire that burns within and transforms the food that we eat. This is the central fire or Jathar Agni, located in the lower part of the stomach and beginning of the small intestine. This is where various acids and enzymes are secreted for the main digestive process. In an earlier section I discussed how agni works and how ama (toxins) are created. In it I mentioned that if you put something heavy on top of your fire it will put out the flame. Well, "heavy" is relative to taste. Remember, sweet taste is considered the heaviest taste. Eating this taste predominantly puts out our digestive fire, which creates toxins (ama).

It's important to select foods from all six tastes in proportion to what suits you. Taking the time to check where your agni is at, is important. The way you check in is to ask yourself if there is "real hunger" or not. If there is, then your agni is ready to receive food. If not, then ama will be created no matter what you choose. This is a perfect example of listening to the needs of the body. Let's further explore the aspects of the sweet taste.

In Ayurveda it is said that the sweet taste is the taste of love. Love provides a feeling of nourishment, therefore the sweet taste is one that nurtures the body. When there is a lack of love in your life you tend to reach for the sweet taste more than any other taste. Being the heaviest taste, sweet pacifies Vata. The outside world can be overwhelming at times. Sweet foods build flesh and fat in the body, which can be a protective buffer from the outside the world. We reach for something that will bring comfort, but it gives a false sense of security and love. Overeating sugars and carbs has created the modern-day problem of obesity in the US. Another example of the connection between love and sweets is how people give each other the gift of chocolate every year on Valentine's Day. We also use endearing terms like, "honey," "sugar," "sweetie," to call our loved ones.

What is it that attracts us to this sweet taste more than any other? Well it is the first taste we experience right out of the "chute." We go from the womb to the breast. Do you have any idea how sweet breast milk is? Well I do. I remember when my first daughter Shanti was born and her mother was engorged with milk. "Please take some of this milk from my breast," Shanti's mother asked me, "it's too much for just Shanti and I'm ready to explode." I said, "Are you serious?", thinking this was a bit strange, but what the heck, I always wanted to taste it again. So I began sucking on one tit while Shanti was sucking on the other. She looked over at me and got the biggest grin on her face and pushed my head off of the nipple. As if she was saying, "what do you think you're doing? That's mine!!" And oh, did I mention, it was sweeeeeet!

There are many signs of weak agni, creating ama. Feeling heavy, unclear thinking, dull eyes, aches and pains, poor circulation, joint inflammation, bloating, gas, skin blemishes, fever, lack of energy, stickiness of stools, phlegm or excess mucous, cloudy urine. Also, foul smells of: urine, sweat, stools, phlegm, lack of appetite, tired after eating, catch a "cold" easily, thick white coating on tongue…Nasty list, yeah?

Bad combinations of food create ama. Here are a few guidelines: no milk with eggs, fish, meat, yoghurt. No eating cooked with raw foods as raw is harder to digest; not having been "pre-digested" from the cooking process. Fruits alone are best since fruit get digested first.

How you eat can have a critical impact on digestion. Eat in a quiet place, wait until your previous meal is digested before putting more food in, don't over eat nor under eat, eat only about 3/4's of what you could eat — or a better way to put it is eat to a point of comfort, not stuffing yourself! Postpone eating if you are upset, sit down when you eat, rest after each meal or you can have a slow walk about 10 minutes after the meal, avoid cold or carbonated drinks, and don't drink large quantities of anything before, during or after meals. Lastly, always acknowledge the food with gratitude before eating it, this alone will create good digestion.

There are many reasons why people eat when they're not hungry. Feeling stressed out from work or home, people eat out of a desire for "comfort" and crave foods that make them feel good. This refers back to what I was talking about earlier: imbalance is based in the mind. People are looking to fill the void of emotional emptiness, not an actual physical need. They eat out of boredom and want to feed the "hungry monster," or the restless mind. Since in the West you can get anything you want, whenever you want, wherever you want, weight problems are rampant.

People also eat out of convenience. How many of you eat lunch or dinner at a certain time? Or reach for a snack between meals? Not necessarily because you're hungry, but that it's 12 o'clock -lunch time, or 6 o'clock -dinner time. It's not natural to eat this way. If you don't "listen to nature" you pay the price. It comes down to this. Weak agni and ama are created by simply not listening to the inherent needs of who you are. If you become a slave to your mind you are bound to create dis-ease. A great example of this is the way people treat their pets. They feed their pets as if they are feeding themselves. Domesticated pets have the same disorders as their owners. You never see this taking place with animals living in the wild. Have you ever seen an over weight coyote? Probably not, but your neighbor's German Shepard is breaking out of it's skin!

A healthy agni is also associated with a healthy appetite for life. Centurions, people who live to be over one hundred years old, say without a doubt a passion for life has been their secret to longevity. They are excited about living and see life as one big adventure. They remain young at heart and their body matches their enthusiasm. Some could have possibly extended their life even longer if they incorporated Yoga, and made healthier food and lifestyle choices. But the main factor for them living this long was their attitude of gratitude and having fun.

FOUR TYPES OF AGNI

There are four types of Agni, or digestive fire. Vishama Agni is variable and associated with Vata. Tikshna Agni is sharp and intense, and relates to Pitta. Manda Agni is slow and connected to Kapha. The fourth is beyond the other three. It is Sama, which means perfectly balanced.

Vishama Agni has no pattern and the appetite goes up and down with no apparent reason. It is a very sensitive digestive system that requires constant vigilance. Symptoms of this Agni may appear as a nervous stomach and intestines with a lot of bloating and gas. Tikshna Agni is extreme hunger. There is a need to eat all the time, if not, anger will be there. It's a good idea to have food around for these types, otherwise look out! People tend to be jealous of this type because they can eat anything and never gain weight. Manda Agni gains weight easily because of low fire. There is not really much hunger and whatever is eaten turns to fat.

Sama Agni is what we all want. Sama is the result of a balanced mind and body. When you are happy and content your agni burns strong. You will have a "healthy" appetite for life. Your choices will be clear. You will naturally choose what is right for you. Agni is built from the inside out, so if you are happy, your agni will be too. Getting stuck in following regimes or popping pills or going on diets has no beneficial effect. When you're not content, it won't matter how organic or pure the food that you eat is. It still will not nourish you. I have to say from experience that the most important factor for strong agni is a healthy enthusiasm for life. This includes playing, laughing and enjoying life's many pleasures. So when you really want that piece of chocolate cake , eat it and fully enjoy it!!!

CIRCULATION OF NUTRIENTS AND THE TRANSFORMATION OF THE SEVEN DHATUS

In Ayurveda the distribution of nutrients through the whole body happens by an intricate set of processes called the seven Dhatu cycle. These seven tissues are nourished first by a strong digestive fire, or Jathar Agni. When the food is fully digested by a strong agni, it is then able to proceed to the first tissue or Dhatu, Rasa. Each Dhatu does its thing by feeding the next one in line, until all seven are completely nourished. There is an agni at each tissue which plays a major role in this refinement process as well. This agni has to be strong in order to adequately nourish the tissue that follows. The end product is the essence of all seven, called Ojas.

Once the food you eat has been properly digested it makes its way to the first tissue, Rasa-Plasma/Lymph, then onto Rakta-Blood , Mamsa-Muscle , Meda-Fat, Ashti-Bone, Majja-Nerve and Shukra/Artava-Reproductive tissue. These are the seven stages of nourishment that happen in the body/mind. These seven tissues can be seen as "factories." Once each factory has sufficiently completed its job, it passes its "raw" material to the next factory for more refinement, similar to an assembly line. It's good to begin by selecting high "pranic" or sattvic foods. Foods rich in vibrant energy and aliveness, not over cooked or processed, if possible organic. Otherwise the end product is not of the highest quality.

The first bodily tissue is called Rasa. Its energy is "prinana," meaning nourished; another meaning is romantic Love. When the body is hungry each of its cells are hungry, and just as a withering plant begins to wake up immediately when watered, each cell perks up when fed. Rasa in itself is not sufficient to nourish the whole organism, but it's a taste of what's coming. The body feels loved. It gives the body/mind a feeling of confidence. You know that feeling when you are in love, you feel like you're on top of the world.

Rasa is the Plasma/Lymph system. Your body has two circulatory systems, one for blood and another for lymph. Blood plasma is a yellow-colored liquid in which the blood cells are suspended. It is the largest single component of blood, making up about 55% of total blood volume. Mainly composed of water, blood proteins, and inorganic electrolytes, it serves as a transport medium for glucose, lipids, amino acids, hormones, etc. The remaining 45% of the blood is made up of red blood cells, white blood cells, and platelets. The Lymph system moves blood plasma and distributes nutrients to all parts of the body. There are twice as many lymph vessels as blood vessels and the volume of lymph in the body is twice that of blood.

The circulation of the lymph system results from pressure applied by muscle contractions near the vessels. That's why it's important that you move your body, especially a conscious movement like Yoga, which gets the nutrients to deeper tissue levels beyond normal "exercise." This is how the agni at the Plasma /Rasa level is stoked. When nourished, there is a sense of fullness to the tissues and pleasure in the mind. The whole body/mind experiences a deep rest from knowing there is plenty of juice for living life without reservation.

The next tissue is called Rakta, or blood tissue. Its action is called "Jivana," which means passion or invigoration. One whose Rakta is nourished has a passion for Life. Remember Pitta is asso-

106

ciated with blood, so if Pitta is high, you're said to be "hot blooded." Blood is a highly specialized circulating tissue consisting of several types of cells suspended in a fluid medium known as plasma or Rasa. Red blood cells (erythrocytes), carry oxygen from the lungs to the tissues. Blood is a red color because it contains hemoglobin (an iron-containing protein that binds oxygen in the lungs and transports it to tissues of the body).

Here are yet some more symbiotic relationships we have with Nature. Blue Green Algae (the algae that comes from Klamath Lake) is another way to oxygenate the blood through food. This algae is rich in nutrients, specifically chlorophyll, which has an indirect relationship on the oxygenation of the blood. Chlorophyll is the substance that makes plants green and allows them to use the energy of the sun to create their food. Remarkably, green plants (especially algae) create oxygen for us to live, while we, on the other hand, put out carbon dioxide for them to breathe. Did you know that 70% to 80% of all the oxygen we breathe comes from algae?! I mentioned earlier that the oceans cover about 70% of this planet and land is only 30%. If we assume that every square mile of the ocean produces as much oxygen as every square mile of land, then this makes sense.

Chlorophyll has exactly the same molecular structure as Hemoglobin, except it has a magnesium atom in the center. The life blood of us humans is paralleled by the life blood of our fellow plants, except for that atom in the center of their molecules. The molecular affinity these two have for each other could explain why eating Blue Green Algae, one of the richest sources of chlorophyll and iron available, has been found to boost hemoglobin production, generally improving oxygenation in our bodies and helping with iron deficiencies. With good Rakta, or blood tissue, you experience more passion for life and feel overwhelming excitement to contribute and participate without fear of exhaustion. You are literally inspired and inspiring to others when this tissue is nourished.

107

Mamsa, the third dhatu, is muscle tissue. Its energy is one of plastering, called "lepana." It provides a barrier between you and the outside world and gives you a sense of security. Muscle tissue is classified as skeletal, cardiac, or smooth, and its function is to produce motion, either locomotion or movement within internal organs. Much of the muscle contraction occurs without conscious thought and is necessary for survival, like the contraction of the heart, or peristalsis (which pushes food through the digestive system). Because it is linked to the Autonomic Nervous System, I will go into more detail about involuntary muscles when speaking of breathing exercises, or Pranayamas, in the Ashtanga section.

Voluntary muscle contraction is used to move the body and can be finely controlled, like movements of the eye, or gross movements like the quadricep muscles of the thigh. There are approximately 639 skeletal muscles in the human body! Muscular activity accounts for much of the body's energy consumption. Mamsa is also represented as all the connective tissue in the body. This matrix of tissues plasters together the whole bodily structure between muscles. With strong Mamsa, you feel a sense of courage and confidence. When you exercise and build muscle tissue, don't you feel better about yourself? Yet overdoing "body building" by lifting weights is usually a sign of insecurity and increasing the Mamsa to an unhealthy proportion. Also when you've had the flu, your mamsa deteriorates through inactivity, leaving you feeling weak and susceptible to everyone's influences. If there's no juice from rakta in the muscle tissue, then vitality of movement is impossible.

The next Dhatu is called Medas, or fat tissue. Its energy is "Sneha," which means affection or Love, like that of a mother and child. Just as a mother holds you and cuddles you when in need of love and warmth, so too does Medas. This tissue is being fed by Mamsa, which depends on the strength of agni in the muscle tissue for its nourishment. Healthy mamsa keeps the medas from over accumulating and turning to adipose tissue or fat. Fat accumulates in the deepest level; the subcutaneous layer, providing insulation from heat and cold. Around organs, it provides protective padding. It also functions as a reserve of nutrients.

Medas provides a lubrication inside for proper flow and protection of organs, tissues and joints. Sweat is the waste product of Medas and it serves as the insulator to protect us from the cold. Fat creates a feeling of warmth and comfort, as if you had your favorite down comforter on your bed. Hence, my aversion to cold weather, since I have little or no fat, and why I live in the tropics most of the time. Having this "buffer" also allows the body a reserve to draw from when its resources are low. This is another dilemma I have in needing to eat constantly or I will lose weight.

It drives women crazy since I can eat whatever I want when I want and not gain an ounce. If this tissue is nourished well you will have "healthy" fat, if not you will have excess fat or Medas and may have problems with obesity. Healthy Medas will in turn feed the next tissue which is Asthi.

Asthi is bone tissue, which creates Dharana, strong foundation and support. It gives form to the shape of the body. If we had no bones, then we would be a mass of flesh sitting on the floor. Bone gives support for muscles, organs, and soft tissues. It protects the internal organs ("rib cage"-lungs/heart) and brain (skull). They assist in leverage and movement. Healthy Asthi gives you a sense of stability and security. When this tissue is weak, you will feel internally insecure and unstable. Indirectly, the bones are responsible for Hemopoisis, the formation of blood cells (more precisely this is performed by the marrow interspersed within the spongy interior of bone and is linked more with Majja, the next tissue). Bones are porous, not solid, giving lightness and fluidity to the body. They are the last things to disintegrate when the body is decaying.

If the body is cremated, bones turn to ash (minerals); from "dust unto dust." Strong hair, nails and teeth are signs of good Ashti.

Mineral absorption happens in the colon, where macro-minerals (calcium, magnesium, phosphorus, sodium, potassium, sulfur, chloride) as well as micro nutrients (cobalt, zinc, copper, iron, selenium, etc.....) are found. The mineral calcium phosphate builds bone, neutralizes acidity, clears toxins, and helps the blood stream. Micro-nutrients catalyze many functions in the body: healthy tissue repair, immune system support, protein metabolism and so on. There is a direct relationship between good colon health and the vitality of other tissues requiring minerals. You should make sure you have macro-minerals in your diet. Blue Green Algae is another great source of trace elements that are missing in our corporate farmed food chain. These trace elements are also found in fresh, organic produce from your local farmers. Another reason to buy organic food is to ensure you are not taking in all the contaminants such as pesticides and herbicides that the body then has to deal with on top of everything else it does.

Ayurveda states that Ashti's nourishment comes from the colon. When proper assimilation and absorption of minerals (calcium and phosphorus) take place in the colon, then the bones are nourished. Another very interesting nourishment happens via the colon, which is Prana absorption. Prana comes from two sources. The first source is through our lungs in breathing, the second is through our food via the colon. This is one more integral relationship happening that Western medical science does not recognize. It's quite amazing to note that when the lungs are congested, the colon has to work harder to extract Prana or vice versa; when the colon is stagnated the lungs must work harder.

Another example of an integral relationship are the kidneys and skin. When the kidneys are not working efficiently our skin picks up the slack. Conversely, if your not sweating properly then the kidneys have to work harder.

The sixth layer or Majja is called "Purana," or filling of space. It is connected to the fatty yellow bone marrow and the blood forming red bone marrow. This is related to the formation of red blood cells, platelets, stem cells and the white blood cells of our immune system. It also applies to the nervous system; the "electrical wiring" of the body, including the brain and spinal cord. We are considered a bio-electrical organism with a network of "wiring" that when laid out end to end on the ground, goes on for miles. It is spread through every fiber of our being, from the tips of our toes to the top of our head. The main channel of this current is the electrical energy that flows up and down the spine acting as the central nervous system. The function of the nervous tissue is communication between all parts of the body. A strong and healthy nervous system buffers us from the ever-present array of energies attempting to get our attention, especially in this modern day and age. Majja when fully nourished overflows to feed the next tissue.

The seventh tissue is Shukra (male) and Artava (female). These are the reproductive tissues called "Garbha Utpadana," which means embryo production. Shukra is mostly related to sperm and Artava, the ovum or egg. If you're not procreating, this energy is directed to other creative outlets: art, poetry, music, dance. Many people in modern society disperse it into the world through their work, creating money. If this tissue is weak, then there is no juice to produce anything worthwhile.

Each month, endometrial tissue grows and thickens in preparation to receive a fertilized egg. Menstruation occurs when this tissue is not used, disintegrates, and passes out through the vagina. It is also directly related to your creative energy, your life force juice. As you can see, reproductive tissue is the culmination of all tissues.

After food is first broken down in the mouth and stomach by Jathar Agni, then it will take about five days to create each bodily tissue. For instance, when you cut yourself, since it is the first tissue, it will take about five to days to heal. When you break a bone, which is the fifth bodily tissue, it takes about twenty five days to heal. When you pull a muscle, the third tissue, it takes about fifteen days. It's important to note that when a healthy body is healing, it passes through each layer at a rate of 3-5 days.

However, in a body that has lost its vitality or has a compromised immune system, it may take 5-10 days or more to heal the same problem. It takes the longest time to create reproductive tissue, approximately thirty-five days.   When a man constantly eliminates his vital fluid, Shukra, through ejaculation, he diminishes his vitality and weakens his immune system. A man can learn how to have an orgasm without ejaculating! This vital energy lost through "coming" can be redirected to build the immune system along with nourishing other organs and the previous six vital tissues. "Coming" should actually be called "going." Wouldn't you agree ladies? (I will go over this more in the Tantra section.)

For a woman, how she experiences her menstrual cycle is directly related to this essential fluid. This "blood" that would have been used in the uterus to feed a newly forming embryo is shed during menstruation. So this precious fluid is important to regulate in creating a healthy cycle.

A woman can do this through good diet choices as well as particular herbs according to her Prakruti or Vikruti. The cycle should not be longer than a few days or excess bleeding, otherwise many nutrients are lost every month. This repetitive cycle, month after month, can weaken the immune system and all the tissues. It is healthy for women to bleed every month as it is a cleansing and revitalizing process but excess bleeding is debilitating. In women, signs of poorly nourished Artava show up as, irregular and painful menstruation as well as fertility and uterus issues.

*   *   *   *   *

Conscious movement like Yoga is the thread that weaves together vibrant health. It plays a major role in keeping the Agni burning strong at each tissue level allowing complete nourishment to take place. Any exercise is good but Yoga Asana, in my opinion, is by far the best. It feeds not only the gross physical level: cells, tissues, organs, but also the subtle pathways, the nadis, thus creating the most efficient and thorough way to keep the body/mind beaming with vitality.

9

PRANA TEJAS OJAS

*T*he end product that is created from this healthy set of dhatus being fully nourished, is called Ojas. It is your body's true essence. Tejas and Prana are an essential part of this dynamic trio. Ojas is typically the only one spoken of, but the other two are key as well. Ojas is your creative "juice." It fuels the latent artist within to create whatever you choose, whether that be a conscious business venture, art, music, spiritual quest, or even parenting, gardening- whatever your heart desires.

Let's look at the bigger picture of how Ojas works in conjunction with Tejas and Prana. Without Tejas or Prana, Ojas is immobile. Prana is the movement of Ojas, and Tejas is the effulgent light of it. These three energies are actually Vata, Pitta and Kapha refined. Prana is refined Vata, Tejas, refined Pitta, and Ojas, refined Kapha. Transforming Vata, Pitta and Kapha into their essence, is achieved by spiritual disciplines and lifestyle practices that support being more Conscious.

When you increase Vata, Pitta and Kapha, imbalance or Vikruti is created. In order to transform VPK into Ojas, Tejas and Prana, we must first make sure VPK is balanced according to your Prakruti, then we can transmute it into its true essence, OTP. If not, then the body has to expend a tremendous amount of energy constantly working to bring it back into equilibrium. With strong Ojas, your immune system becomes strong, and you develop a radiant aura surrounding you. It is the subtle form of attraction that we feel towards people. People with bright auras have high Ojas, Tejas and Prana. You feel drawn to be in their company. People with low OTP have a dim aura and a "draining" effect around them. Your natural response is to avoid hanging out with them. If you are sensitive enough, you can see auras. In all the pictures you see of Christ or Buddha, a golden halo surrounds their head, which is symbolic of their aura. Their Ojas, Tejas and Prana are radiant from living a spirit filled life.

Let me give you an example of OTP using the analogy of a "camp fire." The wood that fuels the flame is Ojas, the radiance of the flame is Tejas and the wind that fans the flame making it brighter, is Prana. They all work in harmony together. If you have one without the other, the fire can not exist.

The body is a living miracle. If you give it whatever it needs and get "out of the way," it knows what to do. Provide it with little or no blockages and nourish it with vital essential nutrients and it will reward you with radiant health. With strong Ojas, your breath is sweet, the body has a pleasant smell, voice is melodic, you feel centered and grounded, your immune response is efficient, and your flesh is full, not fat. An interesting sign of good "Oj-Ass" is a firm, full, well rounded butt, as opposed to a "Med-Ass" or "fat ass" (Medas-Fat tissue). People with low Ojas have little or no buttocks and actually, if the "cheeks" on your face are sunken, this is also a sign of low Ojas.

With strong Tejas, your skin glows, your eyes glimmer, you'll feel more passion for life, your intuition and perception is heightened, and your intellect and speech are sharper. You are clearer as the fire inside burns bright, causing a strong, piercing, radiant, heat likened to the purification of gold. When you have a lot of Tejas you become more courageous, adventurous and fearless.

116

You are able to transform things in your life. With clear vision, you begin to see what's good for you because you have more clarity. You make appropriate choices as they show up in the moment as a Response, not a Reaction.

With nourished Prana, you have more enthusiasm, creativity, and inspiration. You move with grace and ease. Without properly nourished Ojas, there will be no juice for Prana or Tejas, thus no enthusiasm or clear perception. Prana is the life force within that gives you energy. When you practice Yoga and Meditation and live a balanced lifestyle, more Prana naturally floods in. You can then express its myriad of forms to your hearts' desire. With abundant Ojas, Tejas and Prana, you live a much fuller life without feeling obligated or depleted. It is overflowing Joy.

KAPHA VS. OJAS

There's a bit of confusion amongst the Ayurvedic/Yogic community who have studied Ayurveda but have not grasped the distinction between Kapha and Ojas. Understandably, since the qualities of Kapha can resemble Ojas. If you have a solid Yoga practice and are living a balanced life according to your Prakruti, you will experience more Ojas. Your memory improves and you experience more love and compassion, patience, confidence, stamina, and endurance- all the positive qualities you associate with balanced Kapha. Your immune system is strengthened, which means you're not getting sick any more.

Why I bring this out is because individuals tell me they are "Kapha" Prakruti, when in fact they have just increased their Ojas due to the practices of meditation, Yoga, etc. Anyone can cultivate more Ojas, but you cannot change your constitution no matter how hard you try, as it stays the same throughout your life. This is why it's confusing as Vata, Pitta, Kapha are constantly changing everyday. Just remember this simple rule: Increased VPK is not beneficial. Increased Ojas, Tejas and Prana is!

DECREASED OJAS- TEJAS- PRANA

Things that diminish Ojas, Tejas and Prana are unconscious lifestyle, which includes stress, losing too much "shukra" during sex, overworking, excess traveling/eating/talking, or overdoing anything, which is high Vata. Have you noticed in yourself or in others that reaching the age of thirty is a pivotal point in your health and well-being? You are given a certain amount of Ojas at birth and then if you are not replenishing it throughout the years, at around thirty or so you will begin to feel the adverse effects of aging. We must replenish our Ojas on a consistent daily basis, otherwise at some point our immune system "funds" go bankrupt. A depleted immune system can show up as allergies, being susceptible to cold and flu viruses, chronic fatigue syndrome, yeast infections, numerous digestive disorders, being overweight, low back pain, stiffness, even to the extent of severe imbalances such as cancer, heart disease or AIDS.

IMMUNITY

Immunity is based on the simple fact that the body is able to fight off disease on its own. It's all in how we look at germs, bacteria, or viruses. Bad bacteria and good bacteria are flourishing simultaneously inside and all around us. The Western model is, "kill them no matter what!" This is what happens in taking antibiotics. It indiscriminately kills the good and bad. This weakens the inherent strength of your immune system. There may be a time and a place for taking antibiotics, such as life-threatening situations, but for the most part in the West, people are popping these drugs like candy. Western medical doctors are dispensing them like it's Halloween, "the real trick or treat." Overuse of "antibiotics" (anti-Life agents) is unnecessary. What we need to do is support our own natural immunity from within by building its pro-biotic (pro-life) agents.

118

There is a crazy factoid: we have more bacteria living inside us than we do cells! This means the ratio of good to bad bacteria must be in balance. The following things will increase bad bacteria: cigarettes, alcohol, drugs; pollutants in the air, water and soil; too much sugar or refined food products; canned, irradiated or processed foods; and negative emotions such as excessive anger, fear, greed. All of these will weaken your immunity. When the "good" bacteria is flourishing it keeps the bad in check, thus we will have a healthy immune response to whatever comes in from the outside. Keeping the count of good bacteria up vs. bad is one of our main objectives to maintaining vibrant health. Taking probiotics such as Acidophilus or Bifidus is one way to maintain the equilibrium in the GI tract. Keep in mind you want to maintain balance of bacteria throughout the whole body, i.e. skin, mouth, and blood, through an Ayurvedic lifestyle. Some of the ways to maintain that delicate balance would be: cooking your own food that is appropriate for your Prakruti, practicing asana regularly and in a manner consistent to your Prakruti, as well as getting plenty of rest, ample activity, etc.

Look at animals and how they live in harmony with nature. You don't see animals running to the doctor or spraying this and that to kill the germs around them. The key to a good immune system is from the inside out, not from over cleaning or under cleaning.

For example, let's compare two opposite extremes: America and India. America is obsessed with cleanliness to the point of sterility. On the other hand, India is lackadaisical, it is normal to see "waste" of all kinds, out on the street. In America our immune systems are weak and dependent on chemicals/drugs. In India their systems are hyperactive and over functioning due an abundance of microorganisms everywhere. That's why I tell people to prepare their immune systems well before going to India, because you are going from a sterile environment to a thriving petri dish. One is neither better than the other, as both extremes weaken the body and are unhealthy.

Spiritual practices build the energies of Ojas, Tejas and Prana. Stick with your practice long enough and you will go beyond Vata, Pitta, Kapha, the grossest forms of energy available to us. Until we wake up, we will remain living a mundane animal life, from the cradle to the grave. The alchemical ability to transform the gross physical energy of your animalistic nature, to that of a Buddha, an "Awakened One," is available if you want it.

10

CLEANSING AND REJUVENATION

Ayurveda can identify the dis-ease process in the early stages before it manifests into a chronic problem. There are signs and symptoms early on that are signals to pay attention to. It's as if there's a little guy on your shoulder reminding you to be aware of those constant nagging pains, and if ignored you'll be flat on your back wondering what hit you. If only you had listened, the long road back to recovery could have been avoided. There is an old saying, " an ounce of prevention is worth a pound of cure," or for you metric people, "a gram of prevention is worth a kilo of cure!"

An example of how Ayurveda uses diagnostic tools to help in catching something before it becomes chronic is looking at the quality of the nails on your fingers and toes. If they are "healthy" they will have a rich pink color, are strong, and grow straight with no lines or spots in them. If they are broken, pale or have serrated lines and white spots, then there is a deficiency of minerals or other elements in the diet. The fingers represent acute problems and the toes express long-term chronic problems. There are other methods as well. Reflexology of the hands, feet and ears can tell you what is happening energetically in every organ and tissue.

By simply pushing a point on your foot, you can tell if an organ is congested or not. Two other mirrors are your tongue (coated or not) and the iris of your eyes, which may have shaded or discolored areas, indicating the condition of all the internal organs. Many signposts are being provided all the time, if you are open and aware to read them.

If you need to cleanse because there are signs of ama then Ayurveda recommends Pancha Karma, which is a cleansing, detoxification program with rejuvenation at the end to build healthy tissue. This process helps to eliminate ama early on before it manifests into a full blown disease. There will be an accumulation of Kapha after winter, Pitta after summer, and Vata after fall.

That's when the doshas have accumulated during their respective seasons. Many people are unaware of how to fast and cleanse properly. Ayurveda states, it's best to perform Pancha Karma at the juncture of the seasons. If this is not possible, at least do a once a year "spring cleaning." After this, you must nourish the tissues and organs you've cleared by introducing food and herbs that build. If you try to feed a weak, clogged organ it will not absorb the nutrients. It's not just cleansing that your body needs. It's cleansing and rejuvenation.

Another misunderstood concept is fasting too long, or cleansing too much. If you do, your body will feed off healthy tissues and organs, thus debilitating you. A general rule is a kapha person can fast the longest, 5-7 days. A Pitta person can fast 3-5 and Vata maybe 1-2 days. Each individual needs to take into account many factors before considering a fast or before doing Pancha Karma. Consult a qualified practitioner for personally prescribed programs. Once, I fasted for 21 days before I knew anything about Ayurveda, pretty crazy for a Vata person like me! But oh well I learned my lesson the hard way.

Pancha Karma can be described as "five cleansing methods" that purge the system of Vata, Pitta and Kapha when needed.

There is a "Purva Karma" pre-cleansing therapy or the "ripening" process that occurs before the actual Pancha Karma is administered. Most people mistake Ayurvedic massage to be Pancha Karma when in fact it is only the beginning step.

The Purva Karma goes as follows: You are given a deep oil massage using an abundant amount of medicated oils to prepare the dosha for evacuation. This is done in a succession of 7-10 days in a row. After the thorough massage you are put in a sweatbox, which you lie down in with your head sticking out. Then herbs are steamed up through the slats on the bottom of the box. This begins the "ripening" of Vata, Pitta and Kapha over the next 7-10 days. You're also eating a diet of simple food called "kitchari," which is a rice and mung dal preparation with Ghee (clarified butter). Each individual's response to this treatment is different as to when the dosha is fully ripened and ready for removal via one of the five cleansing actions or Pancha Karmas. The Ayurvedic doctor or qualified practitioner will know when you're doshas are ripe by your "pulse reading" which is an art form in itself. Various signs and symptoms will indicate when it is time to perform one or more of the five "Pancha Karma" techniques.

The specific Pancha Karmas are: Basti, therapeutic enema, for removal of Vata from the colon; Virechana, herbal purgative for removal of Pitta from the small intestine; and Vamana, therapeutic vomiting for Kapha via the stomach. (Remember me telling you the main sites or "homes" of VPK are the colon/ Vata, small intestine/Pitta and stomach/Kapha). The ripening of VPK happens by the combination of the diet, massage and sweat box over the 7-10 consecutive days. Slowly VPK gets pulled from the deeper tissues into the GI tract where they are then released through one of the three main methods above.

The remaining two are called Nasya and Rakta Moksha. Nasya is nasal administration of medicated herbs and powders for the brain and nervous system. Good for better concentration and elimination of toxins in the brain. Rakta Moksha is for cleansing of the blood by using leaches. They are used at selective sites

123

on the body where stagnant blood has accumulated, creating ulcers on the skin.

Mulla, did your father leave much money when he died? "No," said Mulla Nasrudin, "Not a cent. It was like this. He lost his health getting wealthy and then lost his wealth trying to get healthy."

RASAYANA

Rasayana is the rejuvenation therapy that aims at promoting strength and vitality, thus increasing immunity and longevity. Rasayanas enhance Ojas. Rasayana is the next step of the whole process of Pancha Karma. It is an essential ingredient that is overlooked in most methods of cleansing. The rejuvenation or Rasayana phase is even more important than the cleansing part. For this is when the body is fed nourishing ingredients for various cells, organs, and tissues. Many highly evolved herbal combinations that take weeks to make are given at this stage. There are some available in the west but most are banned from entering Western countries via India. You can however use some simple yet powerful foods and herbs as a replacement.

Some of these "super foods" and herbs are : Blue Green Algae from Klamath Lake in Oregon, USA, a rich natural wild source of vital minerals, proteins, essential fatty acids, anti-oxides etc. It is considered the most nutrient dense food on the planet. I mentioned earlier how it nourishes the blood, as it's qualities are similar to getting a blood transfusion. It's Tridoshic, which means it serves all three doshas. Some more Rasayanas on my list are: Triphala which is "three dried fruits," (Amalaki, Haritaki, Bibhitaki) made into powders with amazing nutrient density. You take this to cleanse and rejuvenate the body. This can be used as a regular addition to anyone's regime in keeping everything in the body working smoothly. Especially digestive disorders like: constipation, bloating, gas, and removal of undesirable fat. A few more are various ginsengs, shatavari (for ladies), ashwaghanda (for men), saffron, bee pollen, aloe vera, noni, almond milk, cows milk, ghee, dates, figs...

Another favorite in the Ayurvedic "tool box" is Chyawana Prash. It is an Ayurvedic jelly, containing 25-80 herbs plus the amla fruit (Indian gooseberry, Emblican officinalis). The Amalaki is the main ingredient. Amalaki contains 3000 mg of vitamin C, plus bioflavanoids, antioxidants, B complex, and carotenoids. It boosts digestion; increases muscle mass, lowers blood pressure and blood cholesterol, and enhances healing of tissue. It's available at most Indian grocery stores, online or in your favorite health food store.

Other key factors for creating a Rasayana effect are: plenty of sunshine, rest, along with everything else I've mentioned throughout this section on being nourished and balanced for who you are: music, colors, scents, gem therapy (vedic astrology), chanting, singing, whatever you love that is uplifting. Daily self massage called "Abhyanga," helps to pacify high Vata. You can use sesame oil for Vata, coconut for Pitta, and corn or sesame for Kapha. Also remember to take into considerations: age, season, geography, the work you do, and so on.

CONCLUSION

Ayurveda as you have seen is the language of Nature, the language of life and living. It's principles guide us to live in harmony with the greater Universe, thus providing the answer for not only healing the individual but the entire planet. There are many examples of each type of mind quality, but there are no "set rules" to live by. There are "tendencies" we need to be aware of to create balance. Be natural and playful with the integration of this truly wholistic science into your everyday living. The degree to which your awareness grows will in turn match the flow that you have with nature. Since Yoga is the sister science to Ayurveda , our next step is to explore that mysterious world. You now have the golden key. This is your invitation to unlock the door to this magical, mystical adventure within.

PREM'S RULES

As you have probably already guessed, I have no "rules" that I live by, in regards to sex, ganja, coffee, alcohol, food, sleep, or other lifestyle choices. I live by the "guidelines" laid out by these systems of Yoga, Ayurveda and Tantra, as a reference, yet I have my own "internal barometer" to gauge whether something works or not. My main criteria is if something takes me "In" or "Out." That is, if I'm feeling clear, at ease, present, joyful, playful, I know I'm on the right track. If I feel tight inside, heavy, confused, spaced out, serious, depressed during or afterwards.........I know I'm off. I am no longer afraid of anything in life for it's not the outside thing to be aware of, it's the internal reaction to it. For everything on this planet to me is considered Divine.

So I advise you to do the same. Don't take all this "spiritual" stuff so seriously and box yourself in with a lot of unnecessary rules and regulations. Yes of course be sincere in your pursuit of the "truth" and check out what others recommend, but live free in Conscious self-referral, otherwise you miss out on all the magnificence along the way.

Trust your "higher self," the voice of your heart. Sometimes it doesn't look or feel so pleasant. That's alright. It's all relative. Nothing is right or wrong in the eyes of Consciousness. Existence is, what it is. What YOU make out of it, is what's most important.

PART III

ASHTANGA YOGA

The Royal Super High-Way

All day I think about it, then at night I say it.
Where did I come from, and what am I supposed to be doing?
I have no idea.
My soul is from elsewhere, I'm sure of that,
and I intend to end up there.
This drunkenness began in some other tavern.
When I get back around to that place,
I'll be completely sober. Meanwhile,
I'm like a bird from another continent, sitting in this aviary.
The day is coming when I fly off,
but who is it now in my ear who hears my voice?
Who says words with my mouth?
Who looks out with my eyes? What is the soul?
I cannot stop asking.
If I could taste one sip of an answer,
I could break out of this prison for drunks.
I didn't come here of my own accord, and I can't leave that way.
Whoever brought me here will have to take me home.
This poetry. I never know what I'm going to say.
I don't plan it.
When I'm outside the saying of it,
I get very quiet and rarely speak at all.

— Rumi

11

WHAT IS YOGA?

Rumi so beautifully puts into words our human dilemma: living here on earth. Yoga takes this existential question of, "what is life all about?" and puts us on the path to discovering for ourselves what it is, not from our heads, but from our hearts. The first premise to begin with is that we will never be able to directly figure it out with our minds, so relax and trust that all will be revealed. Life is a Mystery to be lived. A mystic is one who must be courageous enough to venture within. Yoga is that passage into the unknowable. It takes us beyond the limited constructs of our mind and draws us into the vast world of Consciousness. There is this feeling of not being quite at "home" here on Earth. Yoga is our ticket back to that place of rest, our true "home" within.

The word Yoga means, "to unite or join together." It's a way to unite with the "One" who looks out from our eyes and hears with our ears. It is a method that guides us carefully along the beaten path of those who have gone before us. Ten thousand years ago these ancient Rishis, as in Ayurveda, put together a set of principles to guide us step-by-step through this maze we call Life. Before we begin to look at this pathway, we first need to know what our starting point is. For if we don't know where we are, how can we possibly know where we are going?

Let's start by clarifying a few misconceptions about Yoga. I am asked over and over again the following questions: "What is Hatha Yoga?" and "What is the difference between Ashtanga (vinyasa) Yoga of Pattabhi Jois and Patanjali's Ashtanga Yoga?" Let's start with the first one. Hatha Yoga is a term generally used to define all the physical posture-oriented forms of Yoga that are currently out there, such as: Iyengar, Bikram, Sivananda, Kripalu, Kundalini, Power Yoga and Ashtanga Vinyasa Yoga .... The list is growing daily! Most of these styles are more recent forms of Yoga Practice (late 1800's), except Ashtanga Vinyasa Yoga, which is said to be the "oldest" living form. The classes called "Hatha Yoga" are typically gentle stretching and breathing, of which Sivananda and Kripalu are examples. There is a wide spectrum of styles to choose from, from dynamic/intense to gentle/calming. The most dynamic form is Ashtanga Vinyasa Yoga. There are styles that are off shoots of Ashtanga called, Power Yoga, Hatha Flow, Vinyasa Flow. Bikram and Kundalini are other examples of the dynamic styles. Iyengar is somewhere in between, with a particular focus on alignment.

There was a definitive text written in the 15th Century about Hatha Yoga called, the Hatha Yoga Pradipika, by a yogi named Swatmarama. Around the 17th Century there were two other texts called, the Gheranda Samhita and the Shiva Samhita. In the treatise of the Hatha Yoga Pradipika, Swatmarama says, Hatha Yoga is a stairway to the heights of "Raja Yoga" of Patanjali, hence a preparatory stage of physical purification that renders the body fit for the practice of higher meditation. Swatmarama lists only sixteen postures (asanas) and some breathing techniques (pranayamas). Along with this he goes on to describe Chakras, Nadis, Mudras, and Bandhas.

In the Gheranda Samhita, a yogi named Gheranda focuses mostly on a cleansing regime called Shat Karmas (six cleansing practices), which are similar to Pancha Karma in Ayurveda in their detoxifying effect on the body/mind. The Shiva Samhita (unknown author) talks about 84 different asanas, only four of which are described in detail. It also deals with abstract yogic philosophy, mudras, tantric practices, and meditation. These three texts are considered to be the basis to the many styles of Hatha Yoga Asana practices.

The word Hatha is divided into two parts. "Ha" which means sun and represents the male principle of outgoing energy: firey, dynamic, yang. "Tha" means moon and represents the feminine principle of ingoing energy: cooling (water/earth), passive, yin. Hatha Yoga, thus means the method for uniting and balancing the inherent male and female energies within each one of us. As in Ayurveda, these ancient practices were developed by the Rishis in remote jungle hermitages or high mountain caves.

The Ashtanga Vinyasa Yoga method is said to have its origin in the ancient text by Vamana Rishi called the Yoga Korunta, which Krishnamacharya received from his Guru, Rama Mohan Brahmachari, at Mount Kailash in Tibet. Krishnamacharya later passed on this Hatha Yoga system to Pattabhi Jois, who is my guru or teacher. This method is said to be the original Hatha Yoga text on Asanas dating all the way back to Patanjali. I have no idea how accurate this information is since I've never seen evidence of any of these very old manuscripts, which were supposedly written on Palm or Banana leaves. I've heard of numerous texts that were written this way and still exist in Indian archives, but the Yoga Korunta was apparently eaten by ants, so there is no proof to back these stories. I can only repeat what I've heard over the years.

Krishnamacharya taught many of the major Yoga teachers of the 20th century, along with his son T.K.V. Desikachar (Viniyoga) and B.K.S. Iyengar. His teachings make up the three most popular Yoga asana styles on the planet and have had a huge influence on modern Yoga today. Pattabhi Jois or "Guruji," as I call him, says that the Yoga Korunta is based on the Yoga Sutras of Patanjali. Patanjali wrote his commentary on Yoga some 2500 years ago.

Patanjali's Yoga is also called, Raja Yoga, or the "Royal Way." I imagine Vamana Rishi, who wrote the Yoga Korunta, was commenting on the Yoga Sutras, as does the Hatha Yoga Pradipika. To top it all off, Guruji has written a book called "Yoga Mala," his commentary on the Yoga Korunta and his own experience of practicing for many years.

India is shrouded in a lot of myth and mystery, as are most Mystic traditions, so I have no idea what's accurate and what's not. My judge and jury has always been, see if what's being said resonates or not.

"Believe nothing, no matter where you read it, or who said it, no matter if I have said it, unless it agrees with your own reason and your own common sense."

— Buddha

So before you pass judgment on something, test it out with your own experience. Don't just act on "blind" faith; until you are perceptive enough to understand for yourself. Trust without some sort of verification borders on the ridiculous. It's important for you to know that spiritual texts are filled with conjecture and hearsay. As you can see, within just this lineage there are many translations and commentaries of the ancient Vedas. Keep in mind that anything written or spoken was relevant for that person at that particular time.

You know the game of "telephone," where you get in a circle of 50 people, and then one person tells the one next to them a "secret?" That person then passes the message on to the next, until it goes all the way around to the original person who started it. The message is always completely different than how it began, and the more people there are, the more convoluted the message becomes. Can you imagine how many times information gets twisted around in 10,000 years?!!! Any book—the Bible, Koran, Yoga Sutras—all have hundreds of translations and commentar-

136

ies passed on through the ages. So we must be realistic in our acceptance of these texts as the "gospel truth."

Only from personal experience can we walk away with an authentic expression of this or any tradition and be able to pass it on. All I know for sure is what my own experience of the practice of Ashtanga Vinyasa Yoga has been and from here on that is what I will write about. After all, Guruji has called his institute in Mysore, 'AYRI', which stands for 'Ashtanga Yoga "Research" Institute'. The word research stands out for me since this word means ongoing. It's not just the dead past being conveyed to us. We are all participating as research scientists of this ongoing living Yoga tradition.

Now as long as we have minds that filter and interpret, ideas are going to get distorted, and we must be careful what we say. It's amazing to me that anything gets communicated with the way the mind works with just simple things, let alone more complex ideas like Yoga. Any discussion of Yoga must come from your own experience; otherwise you are just repeating something someone else said and it might not be accurate. This is why the Rishis had the authority to speak on these topics, since they had access to all of life through their Divine Insight. The problem lies in us being mere mortals, and reading the texts with our spin on them. The Rishis were aware of our dilemma, hence most of them kept quiet since anything they said would have been misinterpreted anyway. The ones who chose to speak made their message always, "check it out for yourself, go within and see if what I am speaking is true." They knew if they simply gave us the answer it would not be clear unless we verified it for ourselves.

Somebody asked Mulla Nasrudin why he lived on the top floor, in his dusty old rooms, and suggested that he move. "No", said Mulla "No, I shall always live on the top floor. It is the only place where God alone is above me." Then after a pause, "He's busy, but he's quiet."

12

ASHTANGA YOGA "SUTRAS" OF

PATANJALI

The Yoga Sutras of Patanjali are 196 simple, yet profound, statements on the yogi's journey within. The root source of our suffering is the incessant mind. This mechanism of mind is based on the dead past, and has been put in place very early on in our life. Patanjali describes very accurately, step by step, how to be free of this attachment to the mind. He alerts us that the mind is but a tool to observe. He lays out a direction of how to be more Conscious. He doesn't say anything about "controlling" the mind, since that would be the mind coming in through the back door to control itself! He says, observe it.

Patanjali guides us through the inner world the same way a master scientist would describe the phenomena of the outer world. Out of Patanjali's ancient text, the basis for Ashtanga Yoga was born. As I mentioned in the Ayurveda section, Vedic knowledge was passed on from teacher to student through sacred phrases, known as sutras. As there were no pens and paper, learning was through this oral transmission via poetic Sanskrit slokas, that the student chanted over and over again until they were committed to memory so the student had access to them when needed. This was an exercise to remind the student of their own divine nature originating from the words of their ancestral roots with the Rishis. In each sutra was encoded a deep message that supported the process of going within. This is how students learned in those days, which is sometimes true even today in India. In this first written definitive text on Yoga, let us explore the process in the context of modern day life.

What's important to note here is that if you only learn the sutras to be able to repeat them back like a parrot, they lose their essence. They were intended as a guideline for one's life, not just to be memorized chanted verse. The first of Patanjali's Yoga sutras is quite profound: Om atha yoga nushasanam, which translates as, "Now the discipline of Yoga begins." Not yesterday or tomorrow but NOW. He says be open, Be Here Now. Be disciplined to have the capacity to discover something new about oneself. Notice the connection between discipline and disciple. A disciple is one who is open and receptive to explore themselves.

This sutra begins with the sound Om. Every book or prayer you read from the Vedas always starts with Om, and ends with Om. It's a way of creating "space" for whatever follows. When you chant Om, you move into space, as it is said that Om represents the sound or vibration of the Universe. After all, "there's no place like OM." There's no exact meaning to it, since it is meant to be a nonsensical word. It symbolizes various aspects of Consciousness, but mostly it's a sound that reverberates in space and creates a mood of silence, the absence of sound. If it represents anything, it represents time and space, which don't really exist anyway. The true beauty of it, is it takes you above and beyond the mind. This was the ancient Rishis' intention.

The second sutra sums up the entire journey of what Yoga is all about. Yogas chitta vritti nirodha, which translated means, "Yoga has the ability to quiet the mind." Note that it says, "has the ability to," not that the day you start doing Yoga the mind game is over. Yoga creates the possibility, the situation, to still the mind. The layers of Karma (actions) you have accumulated in past lives, or this life, will determine how many "veils" are covering the treasures revealed within a quieted mind.

If you go deeper into the workings of the mind, you realize that future happenings are repetitions of the past. We are simply repeating the past over and over again. A scary thought, but true. These Karmas, or actions, good or bad, have to be cleared. The answer lies in meditation, observing the workings of the mind in a relaxed way without judgment. Living from this place lets you clear the past programs, because you are stepping outside the realm of mind. Anything that leads you to yourself is considered meditation. You can create this in walking, eating, breathing, etc. Meditation is the "art of witnessing" everything. When you withdraw your awareness from everywhere and just let it rest within yourself, then you have arrived "home."

The action is not what counts. What does is the quality you bring to your action. There are a million and one illnesses of the body/mind, and yet one simple solution: MEDITATION. The "golden key" you hold in your hand and have always had with you is PRESENCE, which meditation bestows upon you. In the disappearance of Mind, the appearance of Being occurs. "Absence" or "Presence," it's your choice. One or the other is happening; both cannot exist at the same time. You are either HERE NOW or THERE THEN.

"Be focused on action and not on the fruits of your action. Do not become confused in attachment to the fruit of your actions and do not become confused in the desire for inaction" (2:47)-Bhagavad-Gita.

The third sutra, Tada drashtuh svarupe vasthanam, means, "then the seer is established in oneself." Here, Patanjali states, the "Witnessing Presence" is experienced through Yoga and available only when the mind is quiet and still. It is from this place one can live with grace and ease. Patanjali then goes on to describe in great detail the mind and how it operates. At this point I am going to select various passages that emphasize what I feel to be the essence of Ashtanga Yoga.

141

Patanjali talks about Avidya (false knowledge or ignorance), which creates Maya (illusion). The scriptures of Yoga, Ayurveda and Tantra speak about this world being an illusion. Not that it physically doesn't exist, but that your mind creates an imaginary world around what the senses perceive. It's like the famous blockbuster movie, "Matrix," which portrays a world within a world beyond what we can "normally" see. This is created from living out your "samskaras," or your past accumulated knowledge, and then projecting it into the future. Most of the time we're not living in the reality of what is because we're not present.

That's Aviyda, the root cause of suffering in the world. This was Buddha's basic premise in his life's teaching: Life is "Dukha" or suffering based on this illusory dream made up by our mind.

13

ASHTANGA YOGA:

A GLIMPSE OF THE EIGHT LIMBS

YAMAS

Ashtanga means eight limbs or steps. The first is called Yama, which is defined as "self restraints" or containing / managing your energy. Yamas describe opportunities for you to look introspectively and notice where energy is leaking. By observing the Yamas you build a reserve of energy that allows you to respond, rather than react, to life. This is needed to grow and ascend.

There are five Yamas: Ahimsa, or nonviolence; Ashteya, or non-stealing; Satya, or truthfulness; Aparigraha, or non-possessiveness; and most importantly, Brahmacharya, going in the direction of God. Each Yama helps create an upward spiral of energy. If we are to move in the direction of God, then a "sin" is anything that takes us away from this journey upward and distracts us from going within. Each yama is a way of instructing the yogi on managing his or her energy.

The first is Ahimsa, which means not to harm any living being, especially oneself. There is no need to torture yourself or anyone else in the name of spirituality, because violence in any form leaves you feeling exhausted. The second, Ashteya, which means, when you take something which is not rightfully yours, it will weigh heavily on your mind and pull you down. Satya, or truthfulness, is a virtue that frees your mind. Lying is one of the most energy-consuming of all human acts. Telling one lie leads you to telling many more to cover up the original. Aparigraha, the fourth yama, can be explained as 'not grasping' anything- person, place, or thing. Being possessive will also pull you down, because holding on to anything creates suffering. Brahmacharya sums up all the Yamas by saying, if we are to move in the direction of God, you must be attentive to your energy. Most of the time this word is interpreted as "celibacy." A natural celibacy is considered true Brahmacharya, but a forced one is destructive. Having said that, it's important to remember, that if you are living in a yogic way with awareness, there is no need for rules like yamas, because harmony with the natural order of the Universe will be effortless.

People are constantly looking for a guru outside themselves, to tell them what to do. The word guru means, 'someone who shines light where there is darkness. The ultimate guru and light is inside oneself, your "inner guru." Moving to the center of your being will then give you direction. This only happens by taking full responsibility and walking through the doorway of meditation. Meditation doesn't help you to be a Buddha, it only helps you to be aware of your Buddhahood. Living masters are examples to show us what is possible, but ultimately we need to find our own way. A guru can tell you about Ashtanga Yoga or meditation, but ultimately we must travel the path alone, or as I like to say, ALL-ONE, which is very different from the feeling of loneliness.

NIYAMAS

Niyama means, "fixed observances," or adhering to disciplines with regularity. When you hear "discipline," what do you usually think of? It may evoke a feeling of rigidity inside. It may connote enforcement or obligation. Everything we do with this concept of "discipline" feels like a job, but in truth it isn't. The literal translation of discipline is, "to have the capacity to discover something new about oneself." I think that's a better way to interpret discipline. The hardest part of any practice is to show up. When you stand on your Yoga mat, you're in a space of openness to discover something new. Niyama means the ability to come back to your practice again and again, without force or rigidity. Approaching life this way will invoke a totally different energy than the usual mechanical approach.

I have been practicing Ashtanga Yoga for 30 years, and every day I start my practice fresh. There is always something new for me to uncover. It becomes an adventure, an inner exploration. If I did it mechanically, then it would be boring. Einstein makes an excellent point by saying, "If A equals success, then the formula is: A=X+Y+Z. X is work. Y is play. Z is keep your mouth shut!" You can relate this to your practice: practice is some work, some play, and if you can keep your mouth shut and just do it, you're guaranteed success!

There are five aspects to Niyama; Saucha, Santosha, Tapas, Swadhaya and Ishvara Pranidhana. Saucha, or cleanliness inside and out, are ways of keeping the body/mind clear and clean through: daily baths, asana (posture) practice, brushing your teeth, eating pure whole foods, and keeping your thoughts and deeds pure. Santosha, or contentment, is to be at rest within oneself. Contentment never comes by accumulating more things. It's an inner fulfillment that you have all you need. The feeling is one of deep satisfaction, of being whole and complete. Tapas, or purification, is the "fire" generated from the intensity of your spiritual practices. Swadhaya entails study of the Scriptures and observing

145

oneself, whether through the yogic disciplines of conscious breathing, watching your thoughts and feelings, experiencing your body, or using mantras, etc. It's embracing the words of wisdom from those who have gone before us, giving us verification we are on the right track. You are then left rooted in the experience of, "the 'One' who looks out from your eyes." The source of all that is. Ultimately here is where you want to live.

Finally, Ishvara Pranidhana, or surrender to God. This last Niyama is the most important one. It is surrendering to: God, the Universe, Existence, Creator, the Source, the Great White Spirit, Allah, Jehovah, Lord of the Rings, sorry I got lost there...... Whatever name you come up with to symbolize the energy which is greater than self. When you're able to relinquish the need to identify with what you are doing, this will free you up to enjoy the show. You understand that whatever we do, the final outcome is not in our hands. Making an effort without letting go leaves you only creating more ties to oneself. The notion that there is something to do is a false idea created by our egos. We are all merely an instrument of the Divine.

Yama and Niyama are similar to the ten commandments of living. When you adhere to these observations you develop strong roots. They create a foundation for the ascension process and if they are not understood properly there will be no way of getting off the ground. The cosmic joke is, we seem to need some kind of method to get back to where we already are! Ashtanga Yoga is a process of waking up from the illusion of needing to go anywhere outside oneself, ever. Patanjali compassionately guides us one step at a time to look within, so it's not a shock coming out of our deep sleep.

Much internal energy is consumed when we misinterpret words. We know intuitively it doesn't feel right to think or act a certain way, yet we buy into what others say about it. We have created many dual patterns within, which keep us fighting with ourselves constantly. When this happens everything starts to feel unclear. You begin to doubt your intuition and your own experience of life. Therefore, it's good to step back and gather your energies and see what fits. Most of what we've learned is from others in society, making us "believe" their way is the only way. We must recognize that the people we have revered the most—priests, rabbis, brahmins and gurus—are the ones doing all the interpretations for us. They have set themselves up as the mediator between God and the rest of us. They've created the confusion and they seem to have the solution, very clever!!!

Yamas and Niyamas are the foundation for living in alignment from your heart. Niyama is the next logical step to create regularity in your disciplined life. It may appear controlling when you hear words like regularity, discipline, restraint, but this is only a device to positively redirect your energy. If you're taking it all too seriously, you've missed the point. The best way to know you're on the right track or not is if your having more fun, celebrating, laughing a lot and enjoying life to the fullest, All-Ways.

ASANA

The third limb is the one we're all familiar with when we hear the word Yoga. Typically this brings to mind the image of someone wrapping their leg around their head or sitting in some sort of pretzel pose. The funny thing about this is that out of the 196 Yoga Sutras, Patanjali refers to only three or four on asanas, mainly the crossed legged, seated positions which create a firm, yet relaxed posture for going deeper into one's Self through meditation. This is the main purpose of asana, is to secure a platform for meditation. We have come to use the word asana as the definitive word representing Yoga. The way Patanjali speaks about asana, is where we end up after many years of Hatha Yoga physical practice. So according to Pantanjali, asana is a small step but a pivotal one, since a strong foundation is needed for ascension.

The main sutra on asana is ,"Sthira sukham asanam," which means, "when balanced in asana, a simultaneous feeling of opposite qualities is created." One quality is Sthira, the other is Sukha.

Sthira is a feeling of strength, stability and firmness. Sukha means happiness, lightness and space. In asana, you want an experience of being rooted, grounded and firm, yet with a feeling of exhilaration and lightness. This is the ideal of course, and in the beginning it may not always be possible to have both.

Only with restraint (Yama) and regularity (Niyama) can asana happen. Otherwise, sitting silently becomes an impossible task as the body is so restless, it revolts. One way or another your body or mind will attempt to lure you out. Have you ever tried to sit for a long period of time in "pure" silence? Sounds pretty simple, but not that easy. The body/mind is always pulling you away from going within. Like a young child that doesn't want to listen or sit still, it resists by creating some kind of discomfort or distraction. The body is not ready to be disciplined: it is spoiled, lazy and restless. The mind does the same trick by constantly chasing thoughts and feelings to divert you away from sitting in meditation or going within.

The concept of asana can be a great boon, or if not put into proper perspective, an obstacle. Frequently, people get involved with Yoga by doing asanas as an exercise, and their egos expand from the practice because they feel or look good from doing it. They also get quite accomplished at mastering advanced postures which again may boost their ego. My initial attraction was watching all these "beautiful" people practicing and I wanted to look like them. They radiated something I wanted, but if I had stopped there, I would have missed the whole point of asana. It is to keep the bodily temple healthy, free and clear of accumulated toxins, but most importantly, it serves as a platform for Divine observation, prayer and devotion.

Imagine entering a temple that is filthy dirty inside with cobwebs hanging everywhere. How would that feel? Probably not real conducive for worship or meditation. The same thing is true for our living temples. Keep your "temple" fit and strong in order to be able to sit and penetrate into the depths of your Being. It takes a tremendous energy to pierce the veil of illusion. The mind

148

has such a strong hold on reality. If asana is not approached in this manner, it will remain just an interesting exercise that creates strength and flexibility. Moreover, it can create more attachment to the physical form. The secret behind asana, if used correctly, is that it shows us how to go beyond the physical. We can transcend it only when we go thoroughly into it. For those who are stuck doing asana purely as an exercise, I'm sorry to say are making an "ASS-ana" out of themselves.

Continual "Presence" is our "best tool in the box," since we are only on our Yoga mats for a few hours each day. What do we do with the other 14-16 hours of our everyday living? One of the greatest Consciousness exercises that I utilize is bringing my full awareness to whatever I'm doing. When I'm eating, I'm fully there tasting my food, savoring the smells, feeling the textures in my mouth. When I'm walking, I'm feeling my body walk, my feet in connection with the earth, the wind across my skin as I move, the sounds and sights that are there to behold. I am constantly engaged, using all my senses in ways to bring me out of my head and into the "living" moment. This is my "true" Yoga practice. This is easier said than done as the mind is always looking for something new to chew on. The importance of being present carries over into the seven or eight hours we sleep every night (that's one third of our life, or 26 years if we live to be 80!) Since we spend much of our life "asleep," we need to learn to access more of our Consciousness during these hours as well. If you are Conscious throughout the day, this stream of Consciousness permeates into the sleep state. This is why sleep is such an important part of our life.

Another way to look at this is, the same Consciousness that was there when you were a child is the same Being living in you now as an adult. Your body has changed shape and experience has accumulated, but the "Witnessing Presence" who was there from birth is still there observing until you die. I keep a picture of myself as a child around the house to remind me of the innocence that is still there hidden inside, my "inner child." I acknowledge

149

this Being in myself and others because I know this innocence still lives. It's only the accumulation of memories which cloud our current reality. We can live with innocence once again once the cloud is lifted.

My asana practice sets the tone for the entire day. It creates in me a state of Presence that lasts throughout the day. When I step off my mat I am still observant in all that I am up to as I move about. It also works in reverse. When you are vigilant and watching where you allow your energy to wander off into, you're not all over the place when you do your practice of asana. If you have been spacing out all day, when you come to your mat it is harder to gather your awareness back. That's why asana is not the end of your Yoga practice. It is only the beginning. In practicing the "Art of Presence," you build and secure an energy that contributes to how Conscious you are during your asana practice, and life. That's why Patanjali in the Yoga Sutras invites us "to practice consistently over a long period of time with intensity." It gives a cumulative benefit of storing the energy and using it for moving vertically, not spreading horizontally.

Ashtanga Vinyasa Yoga, unlike other styles, is a dynamic moving form of Yoga asana. It takes what Patanjali has said about asana one step further, by adding the therapeutic qualities. It cleans and clears all the Nadis (pathways). It purifies all the organs by making the body squeeze and move in different positions, and pushing toxins out through the skin, bowels, lungs and the bladder. In this Tapas (purification, one of the Niyamas), there is a calming of your body and mind that allows you to sit still in the seated asana of which Patanjali speaks. This is one of the main reasons for practicing asana from the spiritual aspect. Once the body is cleansed and purified, then it is prepared for sitting. The three best-known "asana" in the Yoga Sutras are Padmasana, the traditional lotus posture, Siddhasana, another seated posture that requires less flexibility, and Sukhasana.

Osho has a form of emotional cleansing called Dynamic Mediation, where through super-active exercises, you throw out all bottled up emotional garbage, so you are then able to sit in meditation. He developed this because he saw it was not possible for people of this day and age to sit motionless for long periods of time. Until the body is clear of the restlessness that comes from physical and mental toxins, it will be hard to sit still long enough to go deeply in and connect to your original source. Ashtanga Vinyasa Yoga method is a "Moving Meditation," which is what life is after all, isn't it? It prepares us to move and breathe and be Conscious of whatever shows up in our everyday living. Asana is only for one to two hours of our day. To carry it over into everything we do is the true meaning of practicing Yoga, not just being able to wrap your leg around your head.

The root source of Ashtanga Yoga is in the eight steps or limbs. Asana is but one aspect. I tell my students, "whatever I see you do on your mat is most likely how you live your life off the mat."

PRANAYAMA

When the body can rest in asana and there is a sense of peace from living a life of Yama and Niyama, then you can regulate your breath, which is the next limb. The fourth limb of Ashtanga Yoga is called Pranayama, which means breath awareness. The classical image of Pranayama is being in a seated posture regulating the breath. An example is: inhale to the count of 5, hold breath in for a count of 5; exhale 10 counts, hold 5, inhale; and repeat several times. That is one way to define Pranayama. I will go over what I feel to be the deeper meaning of this science of breath.

Practicing Pranayama allows you to have power over your mind. In changing the rhythm of your breath, notice if you breathe a certain way when you enter a certain state of mind. When you're angry the breath becomes fast and irregular. When you're sexually aroused, what is the breath doing? When you become frightened by something or someone, how does your breath move? Or, when you are looking at a beautiful sunset, or the precious face of a baby, what does your breath do then? And of course there is the methodical way I mentioned, inhaling and exhaling a particular rhythm. Notice your breathing in all these circumstances. You will experience a pattern. The mind moves with the breath, the breath with the mind.

Another way of breath awareness that can be observed throughout the day, is noticing which nostril is predominant. Every couple of hours in a 24 hour day, the breath moves through this cycle, one side stronger than another. If the left nostril predominates, you feel calmer inside, cooler and more passive. When the right nostril predominates, you're more stimulated, warmer and active. Pay attention to how the breath changes and how it affects your experience. Moving with your breath—let's call it a "Living Vinyasa"—is matching what you do to what's happening with your breath. If you are breathing from the left you are more likely to be meditative. If from the right, you are typically more active. Being sensitive to this rhythm you are swimming with the stream, not against it.

Part of the science of Pranayama is consciously affecting your "state" by altering your breathing pattern. If for instance, your right nostril is predominant, doing a pranayama that changes it to the left predominant will create a feeling of calmness. If you are breathing left and you need to be active, an active pranayama will opens the right nostril. I have observed in myself that when practicing Ashtanga Vinyasa Yoga both of my nostrils are fully opened, meaning that I have integrated my energies and created balance.

Dualities such as male/female, active/passive, and solar/lunar characterize both the larger world and our body/mind. When you do alternate nostril breathing, it balances the left and right hemispheres of your brain, which balances the right and left sides of your body, which in turn are reflected as the male and female energies in each of us, whether we live in a male or female body. The word Hatha Yoga means, "Union of Sun and Moon

Energy," or harmony of the male and female aspects of who we are.

It's important to understand the underlying reason breath in Pranayama is so important. What matters is how it operates, not the mechanical control that most Yoga practices prescribe: hold your breath for five, exhale ten, etc. Observe the subtle nuances and the quality of your breath and mind, and how they affect Consciousness. That's what Pranayama's all about. The seated observation of the breath in a systematic way is a mirror in which we can look at ourselves as we do in asanas.

When you're in a stressful situation it's possible to regulate your breath so that you can relax. I was asked recently if I get nervous when I speak in front of people. In the past I was petrified, because I was overly self-conscious and extremely insecure. I gauged my self-image by other people's perceptions so I had a lot invested in what people thought about me. My breathing was shallow and held tightly in my chest. I would calm myself down by doing a set of pranayama before speaking to groups, which helped at the time. Now, as you can see with this book, I'm not worried anymore to say what I feel.

So regulating my breath gave me some space. It was a temporary relief, but my mind could recreate the tension again at any moment. Now, my breathing is relaxed and calm naturally, which allows me to access unlimited resources within, effortlessly. True pranayama has become part of my life. The tool of sitting watching the breath and counting is no longer necessary. Of course I still do formal sittings to aid in particular situations or health reasons. Sometimes I like to do a set at 4:20 am and 4:20 pm just to shift my reality. When I am free from my mind, I become a conduit, a vehicle, an instrument of the Divine watching the cosmic comedy of my life.

*   *   *   *   *   *

By the way have you heard of the eighth chakra? I call it the "Clown Chakra." You know the image of this funny-looking character with a big red nose, wild and crazy multicolored hair, and baggy clothes with big floppy shoes? When this Chakra opens, the other seven open as well. You become ecstatically happy and it happens quite spontaneously. This is when you realize how silly you've been your whole life. You begin to laugh uncontrollably, a deep Buddha belly laugh, at how you've been chasing a dream, when all along you had everything you could have ever dreamed of, right Now. This is the nature of the fool. He acts like a fool on the outside, but down deep inside he is full of Wisdom. He has a joy from the realization that life is one big cosmic joke. God has played the ultimate trick on all of us by hiding Within. The very place we consistently refuse to look. We go on wandering for years, if not lifetimes, looking everywhere outside, when we only had to look Inside. That's fucking funny! What a sense of humor! If you were going to hide something, how clever is that? Right underneath your very nose!

SOME INTERESTING YOGA RESEARCH ABOUT BREATHING

There is an institute in India called Kaivaladhama which discovered some very interesting facts about breathing. You know the place I described earlier, where I learned all the crazy cleansing practices? They did research on how different postures and breathing exercises affected the nervous system, using modern scientific instruments and protocols to measure their effects. There's a system inside each of us that regulates all automatic bodily functions, like your heart beating, digestion and breathing, called the autonomic nervous system (involuntary). This system is wired to function automatically.

One part of the autonomic nervous system is breathing. We don't have to tell ourselves to breathe. Yet, we have the ability to control our breath, so as much as it is an involuntary operation, it is also voluntary as well. At the Institute, they observed how yogis, through their breath, tapped into this nervous system. By learning how to control their breathing, the yogis were able slow the heartbeat down to the point where it was barely pumping. They could put a spike through their arm, remove it and there would be no bleeding. These individuals were buried alive for three days, and were very much alive at the end of that time.

They were able to directly affect their autonomic nervous system through controlling the breath. When you connect to your nervous system through the breath, you have mastery over your body and mind. That's why Pranayama is important, but it has to come naturally, not forcing it. There is sometimes benefit to controlling the breath, but if you're not ready it can hurt you. That's why many Yoga books caution the reader not to do Pranayama or breath control without a teacher, especially when holding the breath for a long periods of time. Pressure builds up in the body, similar to a pressure cooker, and can blow out a weak organ or tissue. It's like playing with fire. If your body is not prepared properly and the channels are not clear, you can damage it, especially any organ that is weak. Again, that's why you have to be healthy, and it's important to not do strong Pranayama until the body is ready. However, simple breathing exercises to bring overall better health and affect the quality of the mind are okay.

PRATYAHARA

"If you don't go within, you go without" — Prem

The next step or fifth limb in Ashtanga Yoga is called Pratyahara. This is a very interesting word that is often misunderstood. Pratyahara means "turning back to the source." It usually gets translated as "withdrawal of the senses." A turning back to the source is a beautiful way to put it. In recognizing that our energy is constantly leaking out, we can understand how Pratyahara is a valuable step in redirecting it in. Since it is necessary to redirect

the force of energy inward and upward, it's easy to see why Pra
tyahara gets translated as turning away from the world. Yogic
texts that emphasize you must withdraw your senses from the
world," are basically saying, "don't enjoy sense pleasures because
that is not Yogic." Utter nonsense! The secret is, the world doesn't
use you up, your mind does. Everyone is operating from the
mind, so there you have it. If you want to identify the "devil,"
that's it. It's not this mythical figure with horns on his head, it's
our mind that has conjured up a demon within. This has created a
living hell on earth as opposed to Christ's, "Heaven on Earth."
Therefore, we can't point an accusing finger to say the world is
screwed up. Existence is what it is. It is simply just there in its
rawness. It's how we create it to be in our mind that matters, and
how we participate in it matters most. This will determine
whether we screw up the world. We have a choice, but it is not
possible to remedy the situation if the direction you are taking is
opposite to the direction you need to go. There are many problems, but only one necessary solution. Herein lies the solution to
all of our woes. Head in the direction of Source, go within.

Since we were young, we've been fed contradictory information leaving us never sure what is true and what is not. We go on
believing superstitious lies, trusting the adults that have perpetu-
ated them out of fear and denial, but mostly out of ignorance.
Look around the globe- do I have to spell out the madness that is
printed in every newspaper and magazine around the world? Utter confusion based on no substance. All rooted in what the ancients have called Maya, the illusion, the myth that life is the way
it is, based on what we know from our minds, which is crazy!

Our mind interprets the sensory information and turns it into
a belief system that we grow up with as a Christian, Buddhist,
European, American, Asian. We have five senses that are fundamentally openings for experiencing the world. Your eyes are
windows, your ears are openings for sound to enter, all of your
skin is meant to feel sensations. Your taste is for perceiving what
nourishes you and what doesn't. Your nose is for allowing fra-

grance of whatever scent to enter and penetrate your Being.

Pratyahara is a turning of your senses inward. Simply to experience is to become like a child once again. No meaning behind it. Quite difficult to do. Try it sometime. Look at a flower or sunset and notice what happens. It is one thought after another. But there's a "home" inside waiting no matter where you go. The source is always Present. (Presence=Present=gift)

I wrote this poem a few years ago for a lover:

PRESENCE

The greatest gift, I can ever give you, is the gift of my
Presence............
Feel the Love spring forth from the deep knowing
I am with you Now, fully awake, alive.
Rest with me here.
Feel the space to be who you truly are.
For together we can change the world
by simply Being.

DHARANA

The sixth limb of Ashtanga Yoga is Dharana, which is translated as concentration. Pranayama is the bridge you've crossed over between mind and body. Pratyahara brings you to the gate, the door where you're ready to enter the vast worlds within, then it's possible for concentration to take place. Before this preparation it's not possible. You may have glimpses, but then quickly fall back to "sleep." Dharana brings your awareness to one point like a laser beam, now you have direction to your Consciousness. Your energy is not dispersed in many directions. It's focused and concentrated. It takes you to the goal, and what's your goal? In Yoga, it's to go in and up.

It's possible to abuse the power you gain through these practices. Hitler read Vedic texts. He explored many esoteric practices, along with becoming a vegetarian. He performed rituals and produced symbols like reversing the Swastika, which in India is the symbol of power. It made him extremely charismatic and convincing in the eyes of the German people. The culture at the time felt weak and powerless from the effects of World War I, so any sense of relief was welcome. Even the horrid one offered by Hitler. It's the dark force verses the light force.

Patanjali warns us about the alluring power gained by harnessing this energy from Yoga in an entire chapter called the Vibhuti Pada. He states there are incredible powers available, but to be careful not to get sidetracked as you progress along the path of Yoga. Scientists talk about harnessing energy. Einstein understood how to generate energy, which resulted in the development of the atomic bomb. He later expressed regret in playing a part in developing the means to unleash the atom's awesome power after the bomb was used to kill so many people in Japan. What we're doing in this Ashtanga Yoga practice is not to explode, but to implode, which brings the energy higher within and up.

DHYANA

The seventh limb in Ashtanga Yoga is Dhyana, which means meditation. This again can be misinterpreted. Meditation is not something you can force upon yourself. It has to happen naturally. If you're not ready for meditation, you will sit there thinking about sex, money, pain in your body, or a thousand and one other things. You're not prepared! Dhyana means it happens spontaneously, it's in the flow and effortless. You have done the necessary steps: Yama, Niyama, Asana, Pranayama, Pratyahara, Dharana. You have concentrated all your energy in one direction so the possibility for Dhyana has arrived. Now you're "ripe." All your energies are gathered and focused. You're at the door aware, fully awake, and ready to soar. It is this continuous flow of Consciousness in the direction of God, the "Original Self," the Witnessing Presence, that is Dhyana.

So Dhyana is beyond form, beyond time and space. When you sit in meditation you disappear into the void. I have had the experience of wondering, "where am I?" as I return back to my body from sitting in meditation. I'll look up at the clock and three hours had flown by. I've had this happen many times as well in the writing of this book, disappearing into a portal, only to come back many hours later. I've also sat for a few minutes that felt like an eternity! The majority of my meditations have involved a lot of struggling. The momentum of thoughts was very strong and the tension in my body left me feeling exhausted. I was not fully prepared to let go and drop in.

You can only create the situation for meditation to happen. There's a deep wakefulness, as the final step is dissolving. You are waiting for that final melting and merging. The object has dropped and the subject has not fallen asleep, as the Witness is Present. You never know when it will come and what will remain is your ever Present Being. Like a gold miner picking away searching for gold, he keeps going no matter what, because he never knows when he will strike it rich.

SAMADHI

The last limb of Ashtanga Yoga is Samadhi, which means, fully dissolved. "Life is not a question, it's not a problem to be solved, but a mystery into which one dissolves oneself." Once again I bring out this beautiful phrase to demonstrate what we are here for. This is Samadhi. The drop, your Consciousness, merges with the infinite sea of Consciousness. If you could follow an actual raindrop falling into the ocean you would see it touch the water and dissolve instantly, becoming part of the ocean. At that point you cannot distinguish that single drop from any other.

This is called Maha Samadhi. Dhyana is the process of dissolving oneself; the mystery concludes as one dissolves completely and disappears into the ocean. There are many types of Samadhi which give us glimpses of this fully dissolved state. I imagine it is God's way of teasing us to carry on to the end.

Here is an inspiring account of Swami Paramahansa Yogananda's "glimpse" of Samadhi, from his book called "Autobiography of a Yogi." He lived the final days of his life in Encinitas, California where I first began my journey with Ashtanga Yoga. I spent many a day in his ashram along the magnificent coast of the Pacific Ocean sitting in deep contemplation, feeling the peace surrounding me and the Presence of this saint who walked along this same path.

"My body became immovably rooted; breath was drawn out of my lungs as if by some huge magnet. Soul and mind instantly lost their physical bondage, and streamed out like a fluid piercing light from my every pore. The flesh was as though dead, yet in my intense awareness I knew that never before had I been fully alive. My sense of identity was no longer narrowly confined to a body, but embraced the circumambient atoms. People on distant streets seemed to be moving gently over my own remote periphery. The roots of plants and trees appeared through a dim transparency of the soil; I discerned the inward flow of their sap.

The whole vicinity lay bare before me. My ordinary frontal vision was now changed to a vast spherical sight, simultaneously all perceptive. Through the back of my head I saw men strolling far down Rai Ghat Road, and noticed also a white cow who was leisurely approaching. When she reached the space in front of the open ashram gate, I observed her with my two physical eyes. As she passed by, behind the brick wall, I saw her clearly still.

All objects within my panoramic gaze trembled and vibrated like quick motion pictures. My body, Master's, the pillared courtyard, the furniture and floor, the trees and sunshine, occasionally became violently agitated, until all melted into a luminescent sea; even as sugar crystals, thrown into a glass of water, dissolve after being shaken. The unifying light alternated with materialization's of form, the metamorphoses revealing the law of cause and effect in creation.

An oceanic joy broke upon calm endless shores of my soul. The Spirit of God, I realized, is exhaustless Bliss; His body is countless tissues of light. A swelling glory within me began to envelop towns, continents, the earth, solar and stellar systems, tenuous nebulae, and floating universes. The entire cosmos, gently luminous, like a city seen afar at night, glimmered within the infinitude of my being. The sharply etched global outlines faded somewhat at the farthest edges; there I could see a mellow radiance, ever undiminished. It was indescribably subtle; the planetary pictures were formed of a grosser light.

The divine dispersion of rays poured from an Eternal Source, blazing into galaxies, transfigured with ineffable auras. Again and again I saw the creative beams condense into constellations, then resolve into sheets of transparent flame. By rhythmic reversion, sextillion worlds passed into diaphanous luster; fire became firmament.

I cognized the center of the empyrean as a point of intuitive perception in my heart. Irradiating splendor issued from my nucleus to every part of the universal structure. Blissful amrita, the nectar of immortality, pulsed through me with a quicksilver-like fluidity. The creative voice of God I heard resounding as Aum, the vibration of the Cosmic Motor.

Suddenly the breath returned to my lungs. With a disappointment almost unbearable, I realized that my infinite immensity was lost. Once more I was limited to the humiliating cage of a body, not easily accommodative to the Spirit. Like a prodigal child, I had run away from my macrocosmic home and imprisoned myself in a narrow microcosm."

Each enlightened being, whether it be- Patanjali, Buddha, Christ, Krishna or Osho, had their own way of expressing the Divine. They lived in the state of pure Ecstasy. The word Ecstasy comes from the root ex-stasis, meaning, "to stand outside oneself, "which is what happens when we have an experience that is too powerful for the body to contain. These Beings were perfect examples of Consciousness expressing itself through the full potential of the human form. Out of compassion for others these Beings gave back by sharing their light in a global way, pointing us in the direction of our true nature. In my eyes, this is how the Yoga Sutras came to be.

I know there are many other enlightened ones living right Here and Now on this planet, spreading their Love in simple ways with pure intentions. Quite unassuming, unrecognizable as a Buddha or a Christ, they may be your next door neighbor, or even the homeless guy on the street. How can we truly tell until we are there ourselves?

It is our birthright as human beings to merge with this source and recognize our Divinity. Each of us one way or another is on our own personal journey of the dissolution of the individual ego.

After all, what else are we here for? Ashtanga Yoga is one particular way the ancient yogis lived and shared the light that was always there, to which we have been temporarily blinded. It's like the old gospel song Amazing Grace: 'Amazing grace how sweet the sound, that saved a wretch like me! I once was lost, but now I'm found, was blind but now I see.'

IN SILENCE

A guide has entered this life in silence.
His Message is only heard in silence.
Take a sip of his precious wine and lose yourself.
Don't insult the greatness of his Love,
for he helps those who suffer, in silence.
Polish the mirror between the breaths.
Go with him, beyond words.
He knows your every deed.
He is the one who moves the wheel of heaven, in silence.
Every thought is buried in your heart;
He will reveal them one by one, in silence.
Turn each of your thoughts into a bird
And let them fly to the other world.
One is an owl, one is a falcon, one is a crow.
Each one is different from the others
But they are all the same in silence.
To see the Moon that cannot be seen
Turn your eyes inward and look at yourself
IN SILENCE....

— Rumi

BIBLE REFERENCE

I mention the Bible repeatedly throughout this book, because I grew up with it as a Catholic and I know most people in the West were influenced by it one way or another. More so than, say, the Bhagavad Gita, Maha Bharata, Ramayana... And even though the Bible and Christ are saying the same thing as these Eastern teachers and texts, we are probably more attracted to the latter, since Christian dogma was jammed down our throats as kids. Another reason I mention the Bible is to bring out the fact that Christ was a Yogi and it has been an alternate theory that he went to India and Tibet during his supposedly "lost 18 years" when he was 12 to 30 years old (the time span the church conveniently lost when talking about Christ and his Life Teachings).   There are some very interesting hypotheses on his actual life and death. One is made in a very controversial 1951 book by Nikos Kazantzakis called "The Last Temptation of Christ," and a 1988 movie with the same title. The film was banned in many countries of the Christian world as blasphemous by depicting Christ engaging in sexual activities and showing him with many "human" emotions such as doubt, fear, depression, reluctance, and lust. There are several books out on Christ and his journeys to India and Tibet: "The Aquarian Gospel of Christ" by Levy, and "The Lost Years of Jesus" by Richard Bock. They are about those missing years of Christ exploring Yoga, Consciousness and Meditation, in Asia. Now we have the most recent controversial book and movie that stirred the world of course called, "The Da Vinci Code," which brought to light that Christ had "another life" hidden by the church to propagate their lie. There are documents substantiating the belief that Christ never died on the cross and lived a full life in Kashmir, where there is a grave site in his name.

14

REVELATION OF "THE PYRAMID CODE"

Catchy title, yeah? It's the Yogic version of the Da Vinci Code. I knew it would pique your curiosity. Now that I've got your full attention, here I go: It all began with a vision becoming a reality. A friend of mine, Rupali, was arranging a month-long intensive (workshop) about Ashtanga Yoga and Ayurveda for teachers and students.

She was setting up the entire program for me to come in and teach on the Island of Oahu, Hawaii. The class had 25 participants, with a waiting list of people to get in. I was traveling at the time, so she emailed me a few months before we were going to start, asking for the "manual" we were going to use for the students. I hadn't even started to put it together. I promised to get it to her as soon as possible, but as the time drew closer I still didn't have it done.

She kept after me every few weeks asking if I had it yet, and even though I assured her this would get done and I was working on it, I kept putting it off. The truth was that at the time, I was not ready to put it down in words yet. I intuitively knew it was in me somewhere, but it wasn't coming out. A few weeks before the intensive was to begin, I was back in Kauai and she called me on the phone and asked me once again about the manual. I said,

"Sorry, I don't have it completed yet." Since I hadn't come up with anything on paper, she decided to come to my place to help me put it together. She flew in for the weekend from Oahu to the neighboring island of Kauai, which is my home three months of the year. I felt relieved, because I didn't know how I was going to do this on my own. The material we came up with together didn't feel like it captured the essence of what I really wanted to say, so I asked her to give me one more day and then we could print it. She got back on a plane and I was faced with the pressure of coming up with something fast.

I was caught up in my head about how to present this information in a manual to be used as the template for teaching. I wanted to be clear on how it came across, but my mind could not wrap around the mystery of the practice in words. Was it even possible to put into words the essence of Ashtanga Yoga and Ayurveda and thirty years of empirical study? I continued to struggle to create something I felt good about that would convey the foundational principles in a concise and authentic way, but nothing came. I sat for hours writing and crumbling pieces of paper up and throwing them in the garbage. I was now feeling desperate, and out of frustration I began to cry. I thought I would telephone her, letting her know "I can't do this," cancel the workshop and ask her to give everyone back their money, but I didn't. I went to bed that evening feeling distraught, vulnerable, and confused about what to do. I eventually drifted off to sleep, but just before I did, I felt a quiet prayer of help enter my heart and a state of complete surrender take over me.

In the middle of the night I suddenly awoke full of energy and ideas for the manual. I began to write, and literally could not keep up with my hands as the pen moved across the pages at lightening speed. I saw an image of a Pyramid with clearly marked principles relating to Ashtanga Yoga. That night my understanding of what I had been studying and teaching for many years became crystal clear. The essence of all I experienced became systematically defined as principles of a living system, and a core central to all truths was revealed to me.

These principles were channeled from the Causal Level of Consciousness, the space of "Cosmic Intelligence." This space of Collective Unconscious was somewhere beyond my limited mind and intellect but is available to all who dare to dive deep into the expanse of Oneself. It was information that I now see was congruent with many of the ancient texts. It was in my words and images but as you read on, there is this thread or vein of truth ringing through all of what I present. Again, not me personally, but transmissions from beyond. For several years now I have presented this material to students all over the world. What follows is what came to me that night.

The Sri Yantra, The Mandala of Creation, Projected into 3-Dimensions

Sculpture © '96 S.Tenen / MERU Fdtn

Fig. 1A

167

"THE PYRAMID CODE"

It started with a vision of a Tetrahedron, which is four triangles of equal measure put together making a three-sided Pyramid. Eight Tetrahedrons then merged together to form a Double Pyramid, which is one four-sided pyramid on top of another. One is going up into the sky, the other, into the earth. Each of these four Tetrahedrons above the earth symbolized four principles with it's own clearly defined set of energies inside of them. I later found out through a Quantum Physics friends of mine, that they do not perfectly fit together. Yet somehow I saw them magnetically drawn together creating this double Pyramid shape.

The core is a multifaceted Crystallized Center taking the shape of some sort of Polyhedral (many Tetrahedrals formed together creating what looked like a ball with many spikes). It looked as if the Polyhedral was a bright Sun glowing inside the center, radiating out light in all directions. The Earth also has a crystallized magnetic core. This fuels the dynamic movement of this spinning vortex form as this whole mass was spiraling through space. I now know why I envisioned it this way, because if you meditate on the picture (fig. 1A) which is called a Sri Yantra, in 3D, it symbolizes the web like matrix of the Universe. The Sri Yantra in 3D is an image of a pyramid also. (There are many other Sri Yantras painted on canvas in the Tantric Tibetan tradition that are quite beautiful, check them out.) It demonstrated to me that everything I'm experiencing in Yoga, Ayurveda and Tantra are "alive principles" not merely dead words or belief systems. It also captured in a 3D image the web-like matrix form of the Universe, in which nothing is separate or distinct on its own.

I also got that energy exists in an infinite field of pure potential, as one gigantic quantum energy soup. In the Chaos Theory of Physics, a scientist came up with a term called the "butterfly effect," which is when a butterfly flapping its wings in Tokyo, could cause tornadoes in California. All that happens in the Universe is not random at all. There is a Cosmic Law in place. Here is an amazing quote by Albert Einstein, a modern day "Mystic":

"A human being is part of the whole called by us universe, a part limited in time and space. We experience ourselves, our thoughts and feelings as something separate from the rest. A kind of "optical delusion" of consciousness. This delusion is a kind of prison for us, restricting us to our personal desires and to affection for a few persons nearest to us. Our task must be to free ourselves from the prison by widening our circle of compassion to embrace all living creatures and the whole of nature in its beauty. The true value of a human being is determined by the measure and the sense in which they have obtained liberation from the self. We shall require a substantially new manner of thinking if humanity is to survive."

— Albert Einstein, 1954

Everything in life is interconnected one way or another. After all what is above? and what is below? It's all relative to where you are. Is some one standing on the south pole upside down? There are positive and negative poles, for instance: if you flush a toilet in Australia, the southern hemisphere, the water goes clockwise down the drain and in America, the northern hemisphere, it goes counterclockwise. I did it here in Hawaii and it's true! I watched it swirl counterclockwise! But in reality there is no up or down, right or wrong, black or white. We as Humanity, are making all this stuff up in our heads. It is our mind again, trying to make sense out of a Uni(One)-Verse(whole) that is whole and complete in itself. Dualistic thinking is mind and matter, the logical linear way of Science. I am speaking and writing metaphysics. I recognize that what I am saying here cannot be proven scientifically, but I am alright with this. The question is, are you? Can you be at rest with the Mystery of Life without having to label everything within it? To give up your imaginary world about how it all works? I am asking you to "step outside yourself" for a moment (an ecstatic state) and experience a World of Wonder and Awe.

The Four Pyramids above the surface are the ones I will write about. The first pyramid contains the principle, "From the Inside Out." The next, "From the Ground Up." The third principle, "From Gross to Subtle Energy." And fourth, "Everything moves in a Vortex." All this appeared to me in a lucid dream form, in images and symbols, as I wrote page after page of what I am about to share with you. It was quite "trippy," experiencing this shape within, and believe me, I am not good at math, geometry or physics.

The four pyramids below represent latent energies. They are hidden from the everyday reality of our five senses but they are just as important as the pyramids above. The Mysterious energy that animates all of life is perceptible with our inner senses only. For instance, a seed that holds the tree within it. There are worlds upon worlds that are beyond all sense of reason and logic. Looking up in space and wondering what's up there is another unexplainable happening. I want to remind you what Ayurveda has said, that we are a micro-cosmos existing within the macrocosm. Some of us call this Mysterious energy God, I choose to call it, Existence. We are part of the "Cosmic Dance" or "God's Cosmic Play" called Leela, in Sanskrit.

PERSONAL EXPERIENCES WITH "PYRAMID ENERGY"

Before going into the actual principles I want to share with you some profound experiences that I've had with Pyramids over the years. I already knew about the energy of a pyramid, as I had various insights into their awesome power of harnessing energy. I remember as a young boy, my friend's father, who was a science teacher in high school, built a small copper tube four-sided pyramid as an experiment for his class. It's dimensions were twenty centimeters by twenty centimeters on all sides. He put his razor blade after every use inside the center point of the pyramid on the ground and it remained sharp for a year! He put pieces of fruit inside as well and could keep them there for weeks without rotting. I remember seeing this and thinking that was incredible!

Another one along the same lines was with a company called Cell Tech, now known as Simplexity Health. I've worked with this company for 20 years now. It is an edible "Micro Algae" harvesting company . Back about 18 years ago the company built a double pyramid green house in which they grew trays of sunflower, buckwheat and alfalfa sprouts. They harvested hundreds of kilos of raw sprouts. These were then frozen and freeze dried at a later time for distribution/shipping purposes. This product was amazing for its energetic physical boost and its delicious taste. Myself and many people that I knew were having incredible results: more physical and mental energy, immune system enhancement, improved digestion etc. I witnessed the greenhouse firsthand. It was quite an impressive structure, say 30 feet or about 9 meters on all sides. One pyramid went up from ground level and one dug down into the earth. I got inside the center of it, where the vortex of this double pyramid's energy lies. There were staircases stacked with trays of sprouts in and all around this "power spot." The vibrant energy of these green plants was unbelievable!!! It's hard to describe how alive and radiant they were. They were beaming with life force juice, and the attendants who watered and harvested them were as well. All the growers were very busy most of the day keeping up with the prolific growth of these "super sprouts." I could see for myself in the short time I was there why these workers were so energized, and the sprouts as well. Being that it was so labor intensive compared with the cost, Cell Tech decided to stop growing the sprouts and distributing it as a product, but while it lasted it was a hit, everyone in the company loved them.

A few years ago, I went to Paris for the first time to teach a workshop. Some of the students brought me to the Eiffel Tower. As I came closer to this massive structure, I began to feel a strong pull drawing me to the middle. I walked right to its center. As I looked down I noticed a small metal plate about 10 x 10 centimeters that marked the exact center of the four legs of the tower. When I stood on the plate and looked straight up through the center of the tower, a rush of energy suddenly came through my body. I stood there in Samasthiti (feet together, standing at attention) buzzing like I was high on some kind of drug. I then did a handstand and then a headstand on the plate. After that I sat down in Lotus, "Padmasana," and meditated on the same spot, which attracted a crowd of curious tourists. (I probably could have made some money if I put out a hat!) I told my friends they had to experience this exhilarating energy rush. That day I experienced the vortex of pyramid energy coming from the sky and channeling through the configuration of the tower, through me into the earth. The four corners of the Eiffel Tower are similar to the four corners of a pyramid, which is the same kind of energy, but in a different form. Check it out if you get a chance to go to Paris, but don't call me or use my name if you get thrown in jail for causing a commotion.

To bring this to even a more personal physical experience is that when we take the seated asana position of Padmasana (Lotus) or any other crossed legged seated meditation pose, we take the shape of a Tetrahedron. The sacrum (sacred), the base of the spine, is also a triangle shape, and forms one corner of the pyramid. The right and left knee make up the other two corners. If you lean slightly forward and imagine lines connecting down from the head to your two knees, you will see you are a human pyramid. Patanjali's use of the word asana, seated pose, captures that energetic quality of the pyramid. This is the most powerful position we can put ourselves in, to create the vortex energy of a pyramid. What follows is an energetic look at why this is what we want in our practice of Ashtanga Vinyasa Yoga.

—§—

15

THE WIZARD YOGI

INSIDE/OUT

*T*he first Tetrahedron of the double Pyramid is called Inside/Out. This is the most essential of all the pyramids for Ashtanga Yoga. The vision that first came to me was only this, a single Tetrahedron. It then took shape with seven others to form the completed double Pyramid form. Along with this vision, what came to me in words were the guiding principles of Inside/Out. These are the magnetic forces that bring you back to your core when you drift off into the past or future. It is your anchor to Presence and connection with your physical and energetic bodies. When you consciously connect with this principle it pulls you magically back In. Symbolizing the three corners of the base of one Tetrahedron, the main tools in the bag of a "Wizard Yogi" are, the Bandhas (Mula/Uddiyana), Ujjayi Breathing, and Drishti. (It is also known as Tristhana, "three places." Some people spell it Tristana, which literally means "three breasts." Got to watch this Sanskrit stuff..... This could be the correct meaning in that a breast provides nourishment, but for some reason I don't think that was their intention).

THE BANDHAS

Let's start with the roots. So we begin with Mula Bandha. Mula means root and Bandha means engaged. On the physical level it is a muscular contraction of the perineum, the pelvic floor. This origination point is different for a man and a woman.
{ DISCLAIMER: This will be one of the only things throughout this whole book that I have not had a direct physical experience of since I am not in a woman's body. Like most men I haven't got a clue, but I will give it my best shot being the inquisitive one that I am. I have talked to many women about their experience and I have explored by whatever means possible to delve deeply into the mysterious abyss called Woman.}

Here's a little comic relief to support my case:

A man walking along a California beach was deep in prayer. All of a sudden, he said out loud, "Lord grant me one wish." Suddenly the sky clouded above his head and in a booming voice… The Lord said, "Because you have TRIED to be faithful to me in all ways, I will grant you one wish." The man said, "Build a bridge to Hawaii, so I can drive over anytime I want." The Lord said, "Your request is very materialistic. Think of the enormous challenges for that kind of undertaking. The supports required to reach the bottom of the Pacific! The concrete and steel it would take! I can do it, but it is hard for me to justify your desire for worldly things. Take a little more time and think of another wish, a wish you think would honor and glorify me."

The man thought about it for a long time. Finally he said "Lord, I wish that I could understand women. I want to know how they feel inside, what they are thinking when they give me the silent treatment, why they cry, what they mean when they say 'nothing', and how I can

174

make a woman truly happy." The Lord replied, "You want two lanes or four on that bridge?"

MULA BANDHA

I will start with what I know for sure. For a man Mula Bandha is the pelvic floor, the space between the anus and genitals. Sometimes I've heard it described as squeezing the anus, that is not a completely accurate description. In Hatha Yoga the exercise which focuses on anus control is called, Ashvini Mudra. Mula Bandha's focal point is the mid-point area of the perineum, a layering of connective and muscle tissue around the pelvic floor, which has one of the highest concentration of nerve endings in the human body.

For a woman Mula Bandha begins on the pelvic floor, but it also goes deep inside the vagina to the head of the cervix, "womb with a view."

A woman's genitals are internal, men's are external. A man's feelings are more superficial, on the surface. It is our nature. Women feel everything deeper in all aspects of life since this is their inherent nature. There is the possibility for a man to develop his "feminine side" but it is not normally available for most men. This goes for women as well with developing more masculine energy. How you balance this is the art of Hatha Yoga.

Our inherent energies as men and women are being challenged in this day and age more so than ever before. This is why we must evaluate how this system of Yoga can best serve us in the twenty-first century. Biologically we are the same as thousands of years ago, yet we have lost touch with our native ancestry of living in harmony with nature.

Psychologically we are faced with many incongruent life circumstances since life is accelerated in this technological age. The best reference point to begin with is our body's core energy. This being the physical manifestation of this energetic point is called Mula Bandha.

Practicing Mula Bandha keeps you from "leaking" your energy down and out. The "truth of life" is not for those who dissipate their energy and become frail and weak. It is as if you have dropped a bucket in a well and in pulling it out of the well you hear water leaking. By the time you pull the bucket up all the water is gone. You look and there were holes in the bucket. We are like this leaking vessel, dipping into the "well of life" and coming up empty again and again.

UDDIYANA BANDHA

Uddiyana Bandha is the next piece to the puzzle that often gets overlooked. Uddiyana means "flying upwards." My experience of this Bandha is that it is an extension of Mula Bandha. To speak about it we must create distinctions, but in actuality there are none. When we contract Mula Bandha by engaging the pelvic floor, Uddiyana Bandha then lifts the energy higher inside and up. Physically the lower part of the belly is slightly drawn in and up.   This gives you a feeling of lightness yet rooted in the pelvic cavity. (This is no to be confused with Uddiyana Kriya, a Yogic cleansing practice which is hollowing out the entire abdominal cavity).

Apana Vayu is the energy that moves things down and out, i.e.: urine, feces, menstruation, or birthing of a fetus. So when you lift the energy up by accessing Mula and Uddiyana Bandha, this first seals the energy in.

By holding mula bandha, you are redirecting the flow from going down and out. Apana Vayu then merges with Prana Vayu, which is in the heart region, which has a naturally occurring upward movement. Uddiyana Bandha transforms this energy of Apana into Prana to go even higher.

For your information there are three other Vayu's that move energy around. One is Samana vayu, responsible for digestion, next is Udana vayu centered mostly in throat and responsible for speech and communication and finally there's Vyana vayu, responsible for circulation.

Holding Mula and Uddiyana Bandha creates a centered, grounded experience in the base of your body. It establishes a firm foundation in the pelvis which allows space in the vertebras to extend out from there, creating length in the lower back. It also protects the back by stabilizing these core muscles in and around the pelvis. This creates a healthy lower back that will then move properly when needed in asanas or life situations that demand strength and flexibility in that area. Without this established in a practitioner, there is the possibility of injury to the lower back in many of the "back bend" asanas. Most importantly, it supports your everyday activity of living in your body with the freedom to do what you want, like you were as a child. It also creates a vortex of spiraling energy in this area known in the Chinese systems as the Dantian, or the "hara." You know the term from the Japanese warrior of committing, "Hari Kari," which a ritual suicide when one is attempting to save his Honor by killing himself? The knife or sword was put to the Hara area and plunged into the abdomen. The hara is recognized as the source of power that is unleashed in all martial art forms, namely Kung fu, Karate, Aikido, etc.

Joseph Pilates, who created Pilates movement therapy, was a dancer who understood the principle of good back health from learning Yoga. Obviously, he understood Mula/Uddiyana Bandha, as it is emphasized in the training he developed called "core strength," although the actual term Mula or Uddiyana bandha is not mentioned. I would like to point out here that many people who have studied Yoga, Ayurveda or Tantra, like Joseph Pilates, have put their names to a process that is rooted in the principles of one of these ancient systems. Yet there is often no acknowledgment to the original source. I am bringing it to your attention so that you are aware that many therapies, diets, etc. are based on these inherent natural principles. One of the reasons for this book is to give credit where credit is due. Also, that the revival of these systems are popular because "truth" never dies. What is true today will go on forever. Plus it is always good to go to the source of something to understand it.

The bandhas also generate an intense heat. A fire is ignited and fueled by awareness which radiates upward. For wherever you place your awareness, energy will flow there in the form of heat, buzzing vibration, tingling. This heat creates a purification like no other kind of heat. Toxins are released from deep tissues. The mind is purified as well by the stillness within. For stillness leads to a purging of all the old samskaras, or old patterns revealed so that you may consciously let them go.

Energetically Uddiyana pulls kundalini (latent, potential energy) upwards towards the Sahasrara Chakra or the thousand-petaled Lotus at the top of the Head. The Lotus is a spiritual symbol used in all the ancient texts to signify the majesty of one of the most spectacular flowers on the planet. Its spiritual significance is that it is growing in a muddy swamp, yet it emerges so magnificently beautiful!!! From the base Chakra, Mula Dhara Chakra, where Mula Bandha resides, we move in and up to the highest plane of human spiritual existence. When fully in bloom, the Lotus flower at the top of the head elicits the most heavenly fragrance for all to enjoy. An absolutely poetic image that the Rishi's envisioned to inspire us to go Within, to discover for ourselves.

Start with your body: this keeps you grounded and centered in your physical being. Most of the time the mind pulls you away from your physical experience, what is real now. Focusing on Mula / Uddiyana Bandha is a device to help pull you back into Presence and be fully in your body. Even if only for a glimpse at first. There are momentary gaps of Presence and then back to the incessant mind. Continually coming back to the Bandhas in your practice of asana reminds you to be rooted and centered in your Being Here Now. When you drift off into thoughts or feelings, remembering the Bandhas will immediately bring you back into the moment. As you practice consistently day after day, week after week, year after year, then you begin to live more in Presence.

Then when you step off your mat, you still experience Mula Bandha because you're centered and rooted there.

Managing your energy keeps you alive and vibrant. Notice where you give your energy. Is it to your job? Making money? Your family? Are you constantly obsessed with thinking about sex? Are you pulled in many directions trying to make a name for yourself? There are a thousand and one ways, "good or bad," to distract us from our primary focus of "waking up" spiritually. Observe where your bucket is leaking and shift it so you can go higher. You need all the juice you can to climb this mountain within. If you manage your energy then there will be no need for outside stimulants to keep you going all day. Notice how people are hooked on coffee, tea, cigarettes, chocolate, or sugar to keep them functioning throughout the day. Our culture is bankrupt not only financially but energetically as well. We are living off of borrowed energy that is not really there. Taking stimulants when there is no reserve (Ojas) is like whipping a tired horse.

Mula Bandha is a reference point to orient yourself. If you look at Mula Bandha on a purely physical level, it's not possible to keep it contracted for long periods of time. Try holding your bicep muscle or any muscle for that matter for longer than a couple of minutes. From a healthy functioning muscle stand point, you contract it when you need to and then it falls back to a state of rest, otherwise it will fatigue. So activate it physically when you need to for demanding poses or things in life, then relax it but keep an energetic feeling always centered around there. It takes awareness at first, then it becomes second nature. It's such a relief to know that you don't have to be holding it physically all the time! I can't tell you how many people have thanked me for sharing that with them. So relax your anus, since it's impossible to keep it tight all the time physically!

There is also the likelihood of it being overly stimulated to the point of chronic contraction, thus energizing the area but not moving the energy in and up. There is a subtle distinction I am referring to here. The physical is there, but if you get stuck in only the physical it can disrupt the flow as well and become congested. Then there is the likelihood of becoming a "tight-ass" or an "asshole." Isn't it funny how the best jokes are the ones that have a bit of truth to them?

ENERGETICS OF MULA BANDHA

I point out once more that it's not just the physical we are concerned with here, otherwise we would be circus performers. Being able to pick yourself up and jump back or press up into a handstand is impressive but falls way short of what we are moving towards with Yoga. We are enamored by all these feats of strength and flexibility, thinking this is the goal. If you cannot accomplish them in Ashtanga then you become frustrated and feel as if you are doing something wrong. You may never be able to jump back, so what? This practice is about tapping into something beyond your self.   Ecstasy again means "to stand outside oneself." The feeling of being in the "zone" as some athletes call it, is a feeling of elation. There is energy that is moving through you. Grace is there, available all the time, yet we block it by going back into our heads. There is the element of Ashtanga being very gross and physical, and maybe those of us that are attracted to it are usually athletically inclined. But there is an undercurrent that is there if we open up to receive the grace. Get out of the way, then you flow through your practice or life. For after all our practice is a mirror.

Guruji says "Mula Bandha twenty-four hours a day!!!" How is that possible? It's not physically but energetically for sure. My interpretation of this Zen Koan like expression, is when you are Awake, you are Awake even when sleeping! The Witnessing Presence that lives within each of us is always available. It is a way of speaking about waking up inside and staying awake. We are constantly falling back to "sleep" when our minds occupy our awareness. Living fully awake and alive is our birthright. It is who we are. All the rest is made up in our heads from lifetimes of

180

nonsense and lies. The process of Mula Bandha is to continually hammer away at WAKE UP, WAKE UP, WAKE UP!!! When you become awake do you need your alarm clock going off constantly? What better method to awaken than to be fully there alive in the core of your body. The center of power and energy for your whole being.

All these methods that I am speaking of are devices, tools to wake us up. So when I talk about holding Mula Bandha, I'm speaking about it in an metaphorical way. I constantly chant out 'Mula Bandha' in class to remind everyone to come back from "wherever land." I see the whole room enliven with awareness for a moment then some of them slip back into being unconscious. There are a few people who give me this look like, "how did he know?" Well, nine times out of ten people forget it. Every once in a while someone will pass "wind" and that leads me into my comic relief comment by saying "mula bandha" or "no anal exhaling!"

When this area gets highly magnetized by constant stimulation it wakes up an energy that is lying asleep. I feel it as an electrical current moving, a tingling vibration up my spine, which spreads throughout my whole body and beyond similar to an orgasm. That will get you up in the morning for practice! This is the magical energy called Kundalini. It is latent, potential energy waiting to be tapped into. Our sex energy is rooted there as well and is synonymous with kundalini. This is our most primal energy source. Yoga and Tantra recognize this power and know how to harness this for higher purposes. Most people only get a glimpse of its power through sex and ejaculation. The magnitude of its force is unimaginable. It is atomic power compared to a matchstick flame.

When I observe a beginner who is doing Yoga for the first time, I may notice they are right there experiencing themselves with total Presence but have their knees bent and cannot touch their toes. Next to the beginner is a so called "advanced Yoga practitioner" who can do all the intricate postures. They look picture perfect. However, I can see their mind is drifting, constantly wandering, spacing out, going through the motions mechanically. Their approach to the practice becomes like a job, not a joy, because they are lacking in Presence. They are merely going through the motions like a "good" Yogi.

Who is more advanced of the two? It doesn't take time to come to Presence. A beginner can be more advanced in the true sense of what the practice of Yoga is all about, if they are able to tap into the Presence within. This is not a common occurrence, and therefore the disciplined, regular practice of an art form like Yoga is necessary to bring one to that place. There is, however, the danger of advanced practitioners being so convinced of what they know, they close themselves off to new, valuable information or insights. There's an expression in Zen, "Beginner's Mind," to be like a child, open and innocent, to explore. This is why I appreciate someone coming to me new, as opposed to a 10, 15, or 20-year practitioner with many bad habits to break. There is the rare, humble, long-time student who surrenders to what is Now. This again is the true sign of a disciple or advanced student, to be open to discover something new. After all, there are layers upon layers of levels to delve into.

Over time, your awareness, through intention, is more energetically stimulated than purely a physical effort. It is also a reference to speak about something which supports your life on many levels. Whatever you're involved in, doing Mula Bandha can be accessed. That's why I refer to it as a metaphor, because it's subtle, not so much physical, but its effect on your life is profound. The Bandhas are phenomenal in all aspects of life. It helps with everything you partake in, whether it is playing a traditional sport, dancing, hiking, surfing, or enjoying sex. Whatever it is, you will be better at it because you are rooted in your core and are fully there experiencing whatever it is you need in the moment. All martial arts teach you to be rooted in the core of your body. How do think Master Martial artists break bricks or boards? It's virtually impossible to do it with only your arm without breaking your hand first. When they hit a solid object and snap it in two, they tap into the energy coming from their power center. This energy, when harnessed with intention, can kill. In Yoga we're not using that energy for destructive purposes or defending ourselves, rather we're using this to enliven our bodies.

The Martial Arts have techniques in which you learn to defend yourself, but also to learn how to access that power within. Most Martial artists never have to use this energy to defend themselves. However, the source of the power you generate comes from the grounding that exists from the practice. A true martial arts master is a peaceful warrior who is soft, relaxed and gentle but pulsing with confidence and strength. A very valuable lesson which Ashtanga Yoga also teaches. Watch a cat jump, you see a relaxed animal spring into action. They are not tight and tense in their body. They have no mind to get in their way, which is our greatest inhibitor most of the time. There are many powers inside we are not accessing. It's best to start from the root and go up. Thus, we begin with Mula and Uddiyana Bandha.

In the practice of Ashtanga Vinyasa Yoga, we are constantly challenged to move from an energetic place as opposed to physically muscling our way through the practice. Tapping into this energy can help us to float gracefully through what appears to be quite difficult postures or circumstances. You can use this in all aspects of your living. Herein lies the test if you are gaining anything from your practice. Do you move with equanimity on and off the mat?

UJJAYI BREATHING

The next thing to observe is Ujjayi breathing. Often, in other forms of Yoga, either the emphasis is on abdominal breathing, or there is no emphasis on breath at all. In abdominal breathing, you relax the belly completely, while breathing naturally in and out, similar to the way a baby breathes. In Ashtanga Yoga, we breathe just the opposite. You breathe with the entire upper thoracic cavity, fully expanding in all directions as you inhale. The action of the ribcage is to expand the lungs equally: front, back and the sides, as if you were blowing up a balloon. While this is happening, keep the lower abdomen held firmly in place. On exhale, the ribs fan back in towards the navel, completely emptying the lungs. First there must be a rooted, grounded, feeling engaging Mula and Uddiyana Bandhas. Mula bandha stabilizes the pelvic floor, while Uddiyana Bandha keeps the lower abdomen firm and slightly lifted, on both the inhale and exhale. This is what allows the expansion of the rib cage; otherwise the breath will be blocked from expanding fully. Try it. It may be hard to grasp without a teacher to guide you, but I wanted to point out the distinction. It's all in how you manage the Bandhas, to secure a powerful Ujjayi breath.

Ujjayi breathing is not necessarily better than abdominal breathing, it just has a different effect and benefits. When you breathe from your abdomen it creates a calm feeling inside, appropriate for certain gentle, calming kinds of Yoga. In Ashtanga Yoga, which is very dynamic and powerful, you want to generate lots of heat and sweat profusely. Breathing this way stimulates your energy, but you can still remain calm and quiet inside.

Ujjayi Breathing is Sanskrit for "victorious." It is a throat-sounding breath. You breathe through your nose, but create a deep resonant sound in the back of the throat by slightly contracting the glottis. It's important to keep your sense of hearing engaged on this sound. It sounds like Darth Vader from Star Wars. Keep it slow and deep. I continuously remind students in class, this practice is done one breath at a time. Don't get ahead of yourself. The inhale and the exhale should be the same length. If your breath is broken, fast, interrupted, or if you are holding it, then you're most likely forcing the pose and need to back off. This constant monitoring helps to regulate the flow. This will enable you to synchronize the breath and movement, which is vinyasa. This keeps you right where you need to be in any given moment, observing whatever shows up.

*   *   *   *

One of my favorite sayings from Guruji is, "mouth is for eating, nose is for breathing." I love his sense of humor! He wanted us to know when breathing in Ashtanga Yoga, you use only the nose, because there are vital channels activated by the air passing in through the nostrils, as opposed to the mouth. The nose is made for breathing. We have hundreds of tiny hairs inside the nasal passages to filter debris and warm the air as it comes in.

In mouth breathing, the air passes quickly, straight in and down into the lungs. It goes in and up towards the third eye center, which activates the "master," mysterious, endocrine gland, called the Pineal Gland. As I said earlier, not much is known scientifically about this gland, but it is talked about in yogic texts as being a source of psychic, paranormal powers. In addition, mouth breathing can have either a dulling effect or an over stimulating one. Let's say you have a cold and your nose is plugged up: you open your mouth and you're breathing like a "caveman" or "cavewomen," which has a heavy, slow, dull, lifeless effect (Tamasic). If you breathe quickly through the mouth it creates a stimulating, exciting, dispersing effect (Rajasic). What we want is a calm, clear, inspiring, alive, balanced effect (Sattvic).

People tend to breathe through their mouth when exercising because there is a greater demand for more air. Breathing through the mouth can create a hyperventilation which stimulates the nervous system to be in a fight or flight response- even when it is unnecessary for the body to react in this way. This causes the loss of a lot of energy, and can bring on a feeling of fear. Drawing in air (prana) from the nasal passages, you can regulate the flow and amount much more easily. The problem with mouth breathing is that it floods in, and is less easy to control, while nose breathing creates a smooth and fluid stream. I tell people, the inhale and exhale should flow evenly like the pouring of oil. This calms the nervous system and brings a feeling of "relaxed strength."

I've had students ask me, "are you supposed to breathe ujjayi breathing throughout the day?" Or , "If you do Mula Bandha all the time, why not Ujjayi breathing as well?" I have to laugh and tell them if you breathe like this in public they'll lock you up in the looney bin! People will definitely think you are a bit strange.

My experience is this: Ujjayi breathing is beneficial for all types of physical exercise. Now if you want to experiment with it in other activities such as running, hiking, biking, by all means, go for it. It brings more aliveness and awareness to whatever you do, so why not. Plus it helps you to be more centered, especially with the conscious Presence of grounding your energy with Mula and Uddiyana Bandha.

Notice that when you're practicing the mind begins to wander and gets lost in thoughts. Mula Bandha brings you back, the breath brings you back. It's Presence you want in your practice. Through this it carries over into your everyday life. Integrating this into your life is what matters. Many awareness techniques are available from various teachings. This is the way we cultivate Presence in the Ashtanga method. No added bells and whistles, simply your full awareness rooted in the core of your body. Consciously breathing and moving, through a string of postures linked together nourishing every cell of your body. What more could you ask for?

DRISHTI

The third point, or corner, of the first pyramid, is Drishti. Scientists tell us 80% of our energy goes out through our eyes. The remaining 20% is left for the other four sense organs: ears, nose, tongue, skin. Drishti means "to gaze." It is not meant to be an intense stare, that I often see students doing. It's simply means witnessing through relaxed eyes, the windows of the soul. When practicing Ashtanga Yoga, there are nine drishti points, as taught by Pattabhi Jois. They are: thumb, navel, toes, nose, third eye, to the right, to the left, up, and at the hand. All dependent on which asana you are in. It helps the "wandering eye" syndrome. Drishti trains the mind to observe by creating a double-arrowed passive awareness. Rooted within, looking out: internally focused, yet watching what happens outside as well. It is a form of Pratyahara, the fifth limb. Directing your energy back "Home," yet another device to keep you Present. Keeping your energy from leaking in many directions. This is also why in deep meditation we close our eyes. It brings the 80% of our energy that normally goes out, In.

As you have seen, the tools of Inside Out—Mula and Uddiyana Bandha, Ujjayi breathing and Drishti—bring more aliveness to your practice, because they create Presence. When you step out of Presence, you're absent. You lose touch with your core essence and expose yourself to many of the destructive behaviors you might have avoided, if you were awake and aware.

ONLY ONE RULE

The sky is suspended blue ocean.
The stars are the fish that swim.
The planets are the white whales I sometimes hitch a ride on.
The sun and all light have forever fused themselves into my heart
and upon my skin.
There is only one rule on this Wild Playground
Every sign Hafiz has ever seen reads the same.
They all say,
"Have fun, my dear; my dear, have fun,
In the Beloved's Divine Game,
O, in the Beloved's Wonderful Game."

— Hafiz

GROUND UP

The second Tetrahedron is called, "From the ground up." This is another valuable tool for the "Wizard Yogi." It's making contact with the surface of the earth's energy with whatever part of the body is touching: feet, hands, arms, abdomen, back, pelvis. You're creating structural integrity by employing basic laws of mechanics. Ashtanga Yoga begins with a standing pose called Samasthiti. This is the first asana (pose) in Surya Namaskar. (Sun salutations are the opening breath and movement section of the Ashtanga method). There are numerous vinyasa sequences throughout all six "series." The first asana, Samasthiti, brings our awareness to the core and root of our feet which is where we need to begin this practice.

The word Samasthiti literally means, "balanced standing." How can we have balance in our stance without firm roots? Bring awareness to feeling your feet together. How do they feel standing there on the earth? Is your weight equally distributed between your left and right foot? Feel the trunk of your body sitting atop your legs and feet. From the ground up, build the pose upward with integrity and strength. From the ground up, is energetically similar to mula bandha. It is as if you have bandhas in your feet.

It's the best place to start for anyone. For example in Samasthiti, I always connect in with my feet first then move to feeling my legs; make sure mula bandha is engaged; then move up my spine creating length and space throughout all the vertebras; and lastly hold my arms active at my side with the neck and head continuing to lengthen upward.

Gravity pulls us towards the earth and we are constantly moving and flowing with this force, whether we are conscious of it or not. A sense of groundedness brings you more in alignment with this very powerful karmic law, gravity. If you don't obey its rules you feel the heaviness of it. Levity, the energy we are cultivating in Yoga, is the opposite of gravity. You find a weightlessness in the pose. That's why we sit in a crossed-legged pose for meditation. It is the best way for you to sit and have your spine vertical for a long period of time. It creates the feeling of being rooted, yet elongated. Samasthiti, as the first pose, sets the tone for everything that follows. It is the birth of your practice that day, as Savasana or "corpse pose," is the "death" of your practice, the last pose where you lie down and completely let go. Just as each breath is another form of birth and death; inspire-birth, expire-death, Savasana reminds us of how precious each moment is.

In Samasthiti, you experience the least amount of surface tension from gravity pushing down on your body. Similar to a "plumb line," which in construction they use in measuring something to be perfectly vertical. In the body the plumb is the centerline which goes right through the core of your body. You can also experience this sense of weightlessness when you do a handstand correctly. Connect with the energy of the earth as you place your hands upon it. Feel the abundance of energy, coming up from the earth, into your hands and through your arms and continuing to move upward out through your feet. Handstand is the same experience in Samasthiti but in reverse; now your hands, have bandhas in them.

I like to set up the intention from the very start with accessing this connection between my body and the earth. I begin by feeling my energy radiating out in six directions, all emerging from my center, Mula Bandha. First, from Mula Bandha down to the core of the earth, then from mula up into the infinite sky, third from just below my navel forward and out into the horizon, fourth, out my back from navel center into the horizon, and finally five and six, from navel right and left into the horizon. If you open yourself up to it, you can access a force that is always abundantly there.

*   *   *

As they say in Star Wars, *"May the Force be with You." George Lucas is a mystic. He explored many disciplines that inspired him to bring this concept to the movie screen. He hung out with notables like Joseph Campbell, who gave him many insightful stories that he used to create his story line. He studied many Eastern religions, namely Buddhism and Hinduism. I loved the futuristic Yogic like characters, namely Yoda and Obi-wan Kenobi, the Jedi masters. Cool stuff.............Love that trilogy of movies !!!*

Moving from the ground up creates a firm, solid foundation. In this principle it's important to recognize each person is working with a different bodily proportion. Some have long legs and arms, some short or long torso with short legs or long torso etc. There are many variations on the theme. In recognizing this, you need to vary your stance accordingly, shortening or lengthening to give you a sense of groundedness. Feel if there is more weight going into one foot than the other, or when the hands are touching the ground in "down dog," is there more weight in one hand than he other? This affects the central core, your spine, tremendously. The source of most internal rotations and imbalances stem from not being in your "roots."   If you begin from the ground up, you can correct it, otherwise the imbalance is always going to return since you are not addressing the root cause.

Another often misunderstood dilemma is with being able to jump back from a seated position, Dandasana, into Chaturanga (push up position). If when sitting on the floor with legs stretched out straight (Dandasana), and your arms are fully extended but cannot touch the floor, then it will be very challenging to jump back because there is less clearance for the body to swing through. It's possible over time to do this, by getting your core energy strong to lift you high enough off the ground to clear the legs coming through. For a person with this anatomical structure, it will be very frustrating for them to do.   Especially when they see people with longer arms than torso, easily lift themselves up and jump back. Just based on simple physics, you can see how anatomical structure makes all the difference in the world. I also want to mention here that Dandasana, the first sitting pose in the

Primary Series of the Ashtanga Yoga, is, "a seated Samasthiti." Let's call it "balanced sitting." Beginning here creates a foundational base and structure before moving into the next pose.

Every practitioner can move and change their position, and the teacher plays a significant role, by observing and supporting each student, according to their individual needs. Even though everyone may be doing the same pose, they're not really. Like roots in a tree, the deeper the roots, the taller the tree can grow. If your feet are incorrectly placed the whole pose is incorrect. It's your foundation, and if you build a weak foundation, that which you place above it cannot stand very long before it collapses. Any tall, natural, or man-made structure is built upon deep foundations or roots.

After the feet, I look at the legs, so I'm building from the ground up, and have them adjust their pose from there. If you're not observing the foundation, it puts a lot of stress on your ankles, knees, wrists, and elbows, and injury can follow. I have seen a tremendous number of injuries caused by forcing vulnerable joints into uncompromising positions because people are unaware of their relationship to gravity and joint mobility. Pain is a signal in the body to stop!

A WORD ON INJURIES

The first series of Ashtanga Yoga is one of the most amazing healing practices for correcting and healing a troubled body and mind, but if done incorrectly can damage just as much or worse than any other mode of sport or movement. The Primary Series of Ashtanga Yoga is called "Yoga Chikitsa," which means "Yoga Therapy." I call it "Yoga Surgery," since it goes in and heals any disorder "without the knife." I have seen it over and over again heal and repair severe problems and injuries, that in the West if you went to a Medical Doctor they would tell you, you needed surgery. (There are times when the medical world is the only option, especially emergency medicine: for instance, if I break my arm I'm not going to go to an Ayurvedic doctor!) I have seen in myself and others heal traumas from cars, motorcycles, sports, medical procedures or surgeries through this practice. In fact, I rehabilitated a torn ACL in my knee from carelessly playing competitive street basketball through patiently using primarily the First Series as my medicine along with ayurvedic herbs, and other healing techniques. Do it with wisdom and intelligence and reap the rewards. Do it with ignorance or overzealousness, and reap the damage done.

It's not the fault of the system or method, but often overzealous teachers cranking people into positions or postures they have no business doing. I've heard again and again in the Ashtanga community, that a teacher has told someone their supposed injury was not an injury at all, but an "opening." I say for the most part that is nonsense, or shall I say ....Bullshit !!! That kind of pain, in my experience, is a signal to back off and is one of your best internal teachers, because it tells you you're doing something incorrect. If you don't stop doing it you're on the road for disaster. On rare occasions, there is a "setting" that happens, a realigning of a bone that sounds horrific, but this is an exception to the rule. Let's add a preface to Guruji's, "Practice and all is coming" quote by saying, " with patience and practice, all is coming." It's so individual how long it's going to take for "challenging" postures, it may never be possible for some, but most of all go slowly and be sensitive to the needs of your body. Explore each day in your practice and over time you will be guaranteed to progress.

Your practice will reflect the way you live. If you rush through your practice this will be reflected in your life, or if you are overly serious or guilt tripping yourself about not being able to do a pose or comparing yourself to others, mostly likely you do this in your life. Are you joyful having fun, light, vibrant? Again, this reflects your Life! We must watch how we mechanically race through the series just to say, "I practiced today." Savor each breath and notice how your life will have the same quality.

THE "OLD" DAYS OF ASHTANGA YOGA

Now once upon a time back in the "Old School" days (70's-80's) there was a total of four sequences called Primary, Intermediate, Advanced A, and Advanced B. Intermediate is now known as Second Series. In Sanskrit, it is called Nadi Shodana, which means purification of the gross and subtle pathways. It is known for its effect on the nervous system, as there are many poses that awaken the spine from back bending, along with deeper hip and shoulder openings. The poses also demand more strength.

"Advanced A," is a combination of what is now called Third and Fourth Series, rearranged slightly different. This series in Sanskrit is called Sthira Bhaga, which literally means, "Steady Divine Power" or "strength building," as Guruji calls it. This sequence of poses demands even more strength and awareness. It builds core power like no other series of poses can. This was as far as I have gone. I now practice 1st, 2nd and 3rd, when I'm in a stable living situation. When I'm traveling or on the road, I practice first series only, as it keeps all the "pipes" clean and helps me stay strong. It also helps me establish balance immediately when I land somewhere new. It has been such a blessing for me to have this tool as I travel. (I don't know what I would have done without it.)

"Advanced B," Fifth and Sixth Series, are poses I've never attempted to do. I've seen a few people practicing this when I was just getting started back in '78, unbelievable! Cirque de Soleil moves, I can't imagine ever being able to do them. Even some of the Advanced A was too much for me. It has been the most challenging physical and mental discipline I've ever experienced.

THE ASHTANGA METHOD AS IT IS NOW TAUGHT
BY PATTABHI JOIS

It's important here to mention, if you are going to take on Ashtanga Vinyasa Yoga as a method, let's be consistent with Guruji, Pattabhi Jois, and his current way of going about it. Otherwise we create a lot of confusion in the Global Brotherhood of this system. If you are an authorized or certified teacher, you are in alignment with AYRI of Mysore. This keeps a coherent flow wherever you choose to go, whether that's in Los Angeles, New York, Paris, Sydney or some small town in the middle of nowhere. You can walk in and know the same method is being taught. The personality of the instructor can still shine through, but the sequencing and principles are not lost. I can't tell you how many times I've had people come to a class of mine and say, "Yeah I know the series," and then proceed to do........ I don't know what! I am attempting to say here that to uphold this system let's be consistent with the lineage. Of course we can add our insights and experiences to the teaching but let's not alter the foundation of the practice and still call it Ashtanga Yoga. Plus we need to be open to change with what he sees fit. After all Pattabhi Jois, or Guruji, is the living "Grandfather" of it all and out of respect let's go with him. If not, go off on your own and call it whatever you want, just don't call it Ashtanga. This doesn't mean we have to be walking, talking, clones of Guruji. We can as I said, be unique expressions of this living system without diluting its principles.

The beauty of this method is after practicing you begin to see the poses are only mirrors reflecting back to you what you need to look at inside yourself. I also saw after years of practicing and mastering some of the advanced asanas, it didn't make me any more spiritual than someone else. It only means, I can do something with my body that any dancer, gymnast, martial artist can do, perhaps many times better than me!!! What's so special about wrapping your leg around your head? It took me a while to get this, but hey, better late than never! It's also been a very humbling act to practice these series and see where I am at not only physically, but more important, mentally.

I feel like I've barely scratched the surface and more is being revealed everyday. This is exciting to me! That gets me up in the morning knowing there is always something new to uncover and explore. I heard my dear friend and brother David Williams (one of the first Westerners to practice Ashtanga back in the early 70's) say, "Before you've practiced, the theory is useless, after you've practiced the theory is obvious."

GROSS TO SUBTLE

The third Tetrahedron or tool, of the Mystic Yogi, is to move from "Gross To Subtle" and back again at will. It is based in the things I've already mentioned. First you begin with your body. You get in touch with the physical side of who you are. This includes noticing and feeling the position of your feet, legs, bandhas, your breath and what's happening inside yourself. How is the spine feeling? What's the breath doing? Am I fully Here, Now? Stick with the physical sensations happening in the moment. I always tell students to "get out of your head and into your body." I want them to feel a sensory experience, of warmth, tingling, buzzing, some kind of physical sensation, not just spin ideas and images around in their heads. It's an internal exploration in awareness having little to do with your thoughts and feelings. If thoughts or feelings come, which they will, without struggle, return to the experience of what is happening. Just watch it, don't give it any energy, then come back to being Present in your body using the Inside/Out principle to ground you in what's real NOW.

The subtle energy circuits, existing beyond the five physical sense organs in Yoga, are called the Seven Chakras and 72,000 Nadis. Another name for this vast network of ethereal channels is Meridians in Chinese medicine. The Rishis of Ancient India have stated in numerous texts, there are 72,000 Nadis (channels or tubes) in the entire body. I have no idea how they came up with this number, but I imagine it's to make a point, there's a lot! The digestive channel is one of the many tubes that exists in our body. The Lymphatic and Circulatory system is another intricate set of tubes. The Nervous system is yet one more extensive set of nadis. The body has literally miles of this "wiring" branching throughout its entirety, from the tips of the toes to the top of the head. There are the physical nadis you can see and count if you cut open a cadaver, and then we have all the subtle channels; together they number 72,000. We are basically a bunch of tubes running in every possible direction, distributing energy in one form or another. We are literally a tube within a tube within a tube!

When you have mastered the physical, the more subtle things begin to emerge. Until this time, you are most likely making it up in your head. Once you've connected with your physical energy through the grounding tools of Inside Out and Ground Up, the ethereal realms reveal themselves naturally. It's like this; if you go beyond the confines of your limited mind, the Conscious Presence of all that is, makes itself available. Until you are rooted in Presence, you will not have access to extra-sensory vision. You will be mechanically going through the poses, getting some physical benefits, but the "key" to enter the vast worlds within will be just beyond your reach.

Making only a ten degree shift in your awareness will grant you access. You are now able to feel all the subtle movements becoming real life experiences you're fully there, alive and awake. Until this time you were "asleep" and were relying on someone else's experience; now you are having your own! It's perfectly alright to get guidance or direction, but when someone else colors your world, it will forever remain in your imagination. You will never fully grasp it. It would be similar to someone describing to you the wonderful taste of chocolate, without ever tasting it for yourself. Better yet, what a spectacular sunset or rainbow looks like, without ever seeing one. Not possible!!! But we continue to do this all the time with the spirit world.

JIVA BANDHA

Another bandha rarely talked about is Jiva Bandha, a subtle energy activator. It is done by placing your tongue behind your two front teeth, on the upper palate. You can perform this while doing Ujjayi breathing in your asana or pranayama practice, meditating, or even throughout the day as you see fit. You can feel the subtle activation when you are quiet enough inside. It creates a circuit from the base of your spine to the top of your head and back down again through the tongue, to the base of the spine. It is an energetic loop or vortex. Circulating this energy through this channel is one of the best exercises you can do in preparation for more intense techniques that require years of practice.

In this practice of circulating the energy you may get a glimpse, a lightening flash, of what's to come. In order to activate this energy to its full potential, you need to pierce through the various layers or Chakras. The groundwork must first be established. Here is where the preliminary work of Primary, Intermediate and Advanced Series prepare the circuits to handle the voltage you are about to access. The voltage is known as "Kundalini Shakti," which runs through the main channel or nadi called, Sushumna. It is difficult to connect with Sushumna Nadi unless you have done this necessary preparation. Jiva Bandha helps to magnetize the energy along with concentration at the third eye center.

Jiva Bandha also helps in keeping the face relaxed and the throat open for Ujjayi Breathing. It's an internal detector letting you monitor any tension that may be created in the jaw, face, and eyes from struggling and fighting inside oneself. As a teacher I see an assortment of contortions on students' faces: clenching their jaws, eyes bugging out, their foreheads wrinkled. It's "facial Yoga" right before my eyes! It's actually quite entertaining. I know right away they're working way too hard in the pose, so I remind them, saying "relax your face," "Jiva Bandha." Just like when I chant out "Mula Bandha" in class. I see myself when I teach, as this "little guy" on people's shoulders prompting them to be aware of things that they forget about themselves. Eventually they hear their "own voice" which is, after all, what I want to happen.

EVERYTHING MOVES IN A VORTEX

This is the last Tetrahedron of the Ashtanga Yoga Double Pyramid. The Wizard Yogi lives with the realization of this energetic law of "Everything moves in a Vortex." A vortex is a whirling or spiraling mass of energy with a center point that is pure stillness and silence, filled with potential energy. A perfect example of this in nature is a Tornado or Hurricane. In the "Eye" of a hurricane is a stillness and deafening silence.

I have friends on Kauai who survived the hurricane "Iniki" that hit on, strangely enough "9/11"-1992, and devastated the whole island. They told me it was a very strange feeling to have winds up to 180 miles an hour (290 kilometers) ripping everything in its path and hurling it in the air. Then as the "eye" passed over them there was a stillness that was eerie beyond belief, as the back end of it came again several minutes later , spiraling in the opposite direction, continuing its rampage.

All things in nature are represented in spirals: the DNA that is the genetic blueprint of our body/mind, the Earth spinning around the sun, our galaxy spiraling at thousands of miles an hour through space, the way all plant life grows, and the energy within a Pyramid. In close examination everything that exists has a circular flow about it. Nothing moves linearly except mind and man.

"Manas" is the Sanskrit word which means mind. Drop the "as" (or "ass") on Manas, and what do you get? Man! Mind=Man. Hu, means God. So a Hu-Man is a God-Man or God realized, God-Conscious-Man. Mantra literally means "to lift you beyond

198

your Mind" or take you out of your Mind. That's why it is such a powerful tool, especially AUM or "OM". This is our birthright to be a 'Human Being', but we must In-volute (spiral inward), as opposed to E-volute. Let us In-volve ourselves in Life, instead of E-volve. Darwin got it all backwards. It's not about evolution, it's about involution; otherwise we remain as our brother animals. Once more a secret revealed right under our noses!

There is a very interesting discovery that a group of archeologists made while excavating around the Pyramids of Giza, Egypt. They found there is a Pyramid going upside down into the earth. This adds a whole new dimension to the Pyramid structure energetically. I mentioned earlier, double pyramids were used for sprout cultivation, because they have twice the vortex of energy; one coming up from the earth and one down from the sky. Its main emphasis is to harness the Prana, life force energy, into the central vortex of the Pyramids. Prana is inside and all around us, and we are a mini Pyramid as well, so in connecting with the six directions, we are accessing the power of the Pyramid in our living form.

How to access it depends on how open you are to receive. Pyramids seem to be funnels for this energy to move through and get magnified. We have a tangible laboratory to play in; our energetic bodies. Knowing that this is available and that it exists, gives us permission to explore for ourselves. Anything that I ever read that seemed a bit far out or strange in Yogic texts began to become my reality as I went deeper into these Mysteries. I then could go back and read them and finally say, I honestly "know" what they are talking about. Before that point it was simply more information to fill my head with and repeat back to people, to impress them. This made me feel like a hypocrite, because I wasn't truly feeling it or living it, and it took energy out of my sails, since I was incongruent with what I was walking and talking. This is of vital importance: be authentic and real with what you know and your life will be one of a flow. What I'm describing here is to relax your mind through all these methods, then when the time is right for you to Know, you will. Stay open and patient, TRUST that "All is Coming."

There is a vortex of energy lying dormant at the base of your spine called Kundalini. It is rooted in the base chakra, where mula bandha gives you access to Muladhara chakra. Most books on Yoga depict an image of a cobra coiled up at the base of the spine. The image of a cobra was chosen because in ancient times people were more in touch with nature. So they chose things in nature to represent energies of the subtle realms. They observed how the cobra could miraculously rise up from the ground and stand straight up without legs. That was mysterious to them. Which is how they experienced the current of energy up their spines. In modern times with the familiarity of technology, we could describe that energy as electric. It's an electrical current that we can access, a switch, if you will, at the base of the spine called 'Mula Bandha'. It is the magical button for the "Wizard Yogi." We are in fact, bio-electrical organisms. As Guruji has said, "control your anus (Mula Bandha) and the world will take care of itself."

What we're doing in Yoga is waking up or switching on the Kundalini energy, the latent spiritual force which goes up the central access of the spine called Sushumna nadi. On either side of this central nadi are two additional pathways called, Ida and Pingala. These are related to the Ha and Tha of Hatha Yoga. They weave back and forth at each chakra from the base, Muladhara chakra, to the third eye, or Ajna chakra, and ending at each nostril. Right nostril being Pingala, or "Ha," and left nostril, Ida or "Tha." There's a symbol from Western medicine called the caduceus. The insignia consists of a staff and two serpents spiraling around it with wings spread open wide at the top. The staff represents the spine where Kundalini moves. The two snakes wrapping around the staff are Ida and Pingala. Hippocrates, the father of Western Medicine 400 BC, brought forth this symbol from the earlier Greek physician, Asclepius from 1200 BC, which I imagine he got from Yoga, since Yoga (8000 BC) predates Asclepius. Just a wild guess...........

200

The chakras are the infamous pathway of the serpentine Kundalini energy which starts in the root chakra, and culminates in the brain at the pineal gland represented as the third eye. The Pineal Gland in the brain is magnetically charged, igniting the "Light Body" of man and blossoming like a new flower, the seventh chakra, Sahasrara the thousand petaled lotus, at the top of the head. The physically cocooned caterpillar is now a spiritual butterfly. A Resurrection occurs and our spiritual eye, the third eye, opens. We then have, metaphorically speaking, grown wings of spiritual flight!

Its funny because the caduceus symbol that Medical Doctors use as the single emblem to represent their profession (which I'm sure most doctors have no idea what it really means), happens to symbolically represent this same process of resurrection and traveling up the spine from the root chakra. The magnetically crystalline pineal gland is charged, causing a chain reaction from within. Resurrecting the Kundalini, energizes the pineal gland and causing a morphic resonance that allows you to unfold spiritually the cells in your body. The cells begin to vibrate at an accelerated speed. They move so fast that disease is no longer possible in your physical body. Thereafter you will probably never need a Doctor again!

Each Chakra has a latent spiritual force that is awakened as Kundalini rises. The first Chakra, Muladhara, is about Security and its color is red; the second is Svadisthana, it represents Creativity and is denoted by the color orange; the third, Manipura, is Power, color yellow; the fourth is Anahata, Love, color green; the fifth is Vissudha, Divine Communication/Communion, represented by blue; the sixth;, Ajna, is Clairvoyance, and its color is indigo; and the seventh is Sahasrara, Infinite Wisdom and Liberation, represented by violet. Notice all seven colors of the chakras make the colors of the rainbow.

The root chakra corresponds to the planet Saturn and the zodiac sign Capricorn which in turn corresponds to the metal Lead. Leo is chakra seven and corresponds to the Sun and Gold. As you

201

go up the spine in correspondence to the metals of each planet we see that Lead turns into Gold. This is the reason behind the great work of Alchemy, which is said to cause Lead to turn into Gold. It's symbolic of the serpentine Kundalini energy rising up the Sushumna channel at the top of the head, causing the "Sleeping One to Awaken," to be "Born Again." As Jesus once said, "Truly, truly, I say to you, unless one is "born again" he cannot 'See' the kingdom of God."

This principle of "Everything moves in a Vortex" gives an added mysterious touch to the whole mix of "the Pyramid Code." This Universal Matrix of Life moves in this way, then you can tap into it with your own energetic body, since you are a part of the greater whole. Based on everything else I've gone over up this point, you can see a theme. There is an inherent energy born out of your "Being-Ness." Yet another vehicle to ride while traveling Inward and Upward.

SUMMARY OF "THE PYRAMID CODE"

These four Pyramids essentially "switch on" the magnetic attraction inside by bringing your awareness to them. This then allows you to see clearly beyond the restriction of your limited mind. The more you remove the weight of thoughts and feelings through your connection to Presence, the less effect they have on your Conscious Awareness. Remove the obstacles and instantly you are back Home. As you space out and drift off into the past or future, these magnetic attractions draw you back into your central core of Being.

In experiencing the "Inside Out Principle" through Bandhas, Breath and Drishti, you then come back to Presence. "Ground Up," the second corner of the pyramid, helps you to be Present by grounding your physical energy first, anchoring you to the Earth within and around you. Thus establishing the principle of structure and integrity. The third corner of the pyramid is "Gross to Subtle." You begin with the physical body and over time move to the more ethereal energies all around. You're watching, feeling and experiencing the physical body first to then be able to connect with the subtle energetic currents in the Nadis and Chakras. Lastly, all energy is in the form of spiraling vortexes. Understanding how to use them can help you to pierce through the veil of darkness which inhibits our going higher. The combination of all of these tools are what guides you to the Light within Yourself.

16

"MYSORE STYLE"

ASHTANGA VINYASA YOGA

THE MOST ANCIENT FORM?

he subject of whether Ashtanga Vinyasa Yoga is the oldest known form of Asana has been an issue of debate amongst the Yoga community for decades. Most of the other forms of Hatha Yoga are very recent, by recent I mean within the last hundred years. Yoga first came to America in 1893 with Swami Vivekananda, but it wasn't until the early 1960's during the massive hippie movement, when the Beatles were doing meditation with Maharishi Mahesh Yogi, that its fire ignited. In the early 70's, Rajneesh, later known as Osho, created a strong interest in Consciousness and its practices. Later on in the same decade, there was yet another wave of Yogic enthusiasm, stirred by various styles of Asana practice such as Iyengar, Kundalini and Bikram, which gained in popularity throughout the 80's and 90's. It was also during this time, that "offshoots" or altered versions of Ashtanga Yoga, like Power Yoga, Hatha Flow and Vinyasa flow, came to popularity. In 1975 when the onset of Ashtanga began in the west, Guruji came over to teach his first tour (I was part of his second tour in 1978).

The source of Guruji's teaching comes from the ancient text the Yoga Korunta. I honestly feel Ashtanga Yoga is the most complete and precise method reflecting the essence of Yoga asana. I will attempt to give you my reasons why. Asana is a particular method used to explore Consciousness. It becomes a mirror for the body/mind. It is unique to each individual how one approaches the practice. One of the best ways to do this, is to create an environment where you allow your own personal journey to unfold in each moment. This is the beauty of the Ashtanga Mysore method. Most other styles of Yoga Asana are constantly pulling students out of their experience by instructing the whole class to all do the same thing, like the childhood game of "Simon Says" or "Follow the Leader." Everyone is at a different place in their growth and development, so the experience must match the individual. I don't know of any other group style which addresses this issue except the traditional "Mysore Style" practice of Ashtanga Yoga.

In the Mysore style an individual is given the freedom to practice alone yet within a group setting. The qualified teacher then has the ability to assist each person as they see fit. It allows them to give personal, specific instruction to that individual, whether it be physical or verbal, without disrupting the rest of the group. This experience is very similar to one on one, private instruction. A qualified teacher will never give a student more than they can handle. They can determine this by observing the quality of someone's breath, focus and awareness, as well as their body type.

At one point in the history of Ashtanga Yoga (I believe it was the mid to late 80's) the Iyengar method began to spill over into the Ashtanga method. This was extremely helpful at the time since we needed the additional information to assist us in the "cleaning up" of some poses. We were hurting ourselves and others by pushing too hard in the practice and using "Nike-like" enthusiasm ("Just do it!"). Getting on our mats and going for it! Then Iyengar practitioners and teachers were curious and began

206

to check out Ashtanga classes. Out of that, they started offering comments and suggestions to better stabilize or establish safe body standards, for example, vulnerable joints. Now it was helpful to a certain extent, but when it got to be too "heady," meaning too much talking in class or the use of props, this took away from the flow of the Ashtanga sequence. The value of the Iyengar method or any other method, is that it supports the mechanics of the body in asana. This type of teaching is great in a workshop setting.

A workshop is a way to give a more detailed look at how things are done and daily practice is to discover for yourself what works and what doesn't with individual differences considered (Mysore class). They serve two completely different purposes. The "stop and go" Iyengar style is not appropriate for a flowing practice like Ashtanga. It breaks up the continuity created in a Mysore atmosphere. Guruji always quotes Vamana Rishi in the Yoga Korunta as saying, "O Yogi, do not do asana without vinyasa." In other words, "don't practice asana without movement and breath (meditation) associated with them." With the combination of both you do not lose your heat and it allows for deeper levels of Consciousness to awaken. If not, (like a friend of mine once said) "we're only jump'in around like a bunch of wet monkeys." The main point of Asana after all, is vibrant health. Saying one style is better or more spiritual than another, is ludicrous! No matter what form of Yoga asana you choose to practice, make sure that it takes you In, otherwise it is just another glorified version of stretching.

When I first learned Ashtanga, we were taught to take 8 breaths in each pose. In Guruji's book written by Lino Miele, he specifically says, 8 breaths. Now, the standard is to take 5 breaths in the "led" ashtanga classes. Let me take a minute to speak about the "Led Ashtanga" classes that are being taught around the globe. They are subject to the same predicament as any other led class from any other tradition. People definitely compete with each other and their attention is distracted. My understanding of how the led classes began, was about 10 years ago or so, Guruji started leading people through the Ashtanga Primary series, while counting the "vinyasas" outloud. This was started as a method to teach the proper vinyasa of the sequence, since over the years he saw many people practicing "incorrectly" all over the world. So he wanted to create a consistent, coherent method guiding us back to its original form. Out of this the "led class" was born. Now Guruji teaches led classes on Friday and Sunday. Before this time it never existed in India.

In a mysore class, it is appropriate to take longer than 5 breaths per pose. Perhaps even more breaths on one side or modifying the pose, whatever is suiting the individual's body needs. I personally encourage this method of practice. I recently read in an interview with Manju Jois, Guruji's son, where he says, "of course you can modify a pose to serve the student, my father did this with me in the beginning of my practice."

I think Guruji is often misunderstood since he doesn't speak fluent English and when he does, his words sometimes get twisted around. I know from being with him for years, his intention is pure. He comes from the school of thought, "1% theory, 99% practice." He doesn't spell things out, it's not the Indian way. He gives us much room for our own interpretation. Unfortunately students who have not put sufficient time into their practice, end up spreading misinformation.

THE SUN AND "SURYA NAMASKARA" WORSHIPING THE SUN OR "SON"

Another reason why I say that Ashtanga is the most ancient form is the fact that the whole practice is based on "Surya Namaskara," the worshiping of Surya (Sun). The emphasis is on the transformation of the Sun living within us and the acknowledgement of its power to sustain life on our planet. The Sun god is depicted as far back as 10,000 BC. in the oldest known source of recorded symbols, hieroglyphics. The ancient Yogis worshipped the Sun by performing this rite facing east towards the rising sun and chanting mantras going with each movement. We do this practice in Ashtanga Yoga (except now we do it without chanting the mantras, although this is how Guruji learned it from Krishnamacharya). We do Surya Namaskara throughout the whole practice keeping the fire of the sun (agni) stoked within us for divine purification (tapas) inside and out. Some forms of Hatha Yoga teach Surya Namaskara, but the Ashtanga method has it as a consistent thread woven throughout the entire practice.

THE SUN AND THE "SON"

Here's where it gets very interesting!!! Some say that Christ the "Son" of God, is actually only a representation of the "Sun." There were enlightened Beings like Buddha, Krishna, Muhammad that walked the earth, but Christianity took it to a whole new level to elevate Christ to be the only begotten Son of God. Here is what Thomas Paine (1737-1809) a radical, revolutionary during the American colonies' struggle for independence from England, said about Christ and Christianity: "the Christian religion is a parody on the worship of the Sun, in which they put a man called Christ in the place of the Sun, and pay homage to him the adoration originally paid to the Sun."

The Bible seems to be more about Astrology than anything else. Christ had 12 disciples which represent the 12 signs of the Zodiac. The sign of the cross is the symbol used for dividing the Zodiac into the four major groups: Earth, Water, Air, and Fire signs (notice the similarity of 5 elements of Ayurveda). December 25th, the proposed birthday of Christ, is merely a pagan day of worship of the star Sirius being the brightest star in the sky at that time. Easter, the day Christ was said to "rise from the dead," represents the time when the transition of the darkest time of the year moves into the start of lightest time. (There are many more "coincidences" if you want to do your own research, by all means do. Watch the documentary "Zietgeist: The Spirit of the Age.")

The story of Christ (meaning "Anointed One" like Siddhartha being called Buddha, "Awakened One") in the Bible was developed politically by the Roman Emperor Constantine in 325 AD. The Bible is the first "Christian" document made by the Vatican, which has ruled the World for the past 1700 years!!! It has been enforced by whatever means necessary through physical persecution during the time of the Dark Ages, the Crusades, and Inquisition, or in the form of mass guilt which works quite insidiously by eating at ones heart. Giving the people in power their best tool ever of control! Knowing this puts into perspective the hidden messages of the Bible. But it doesn't take away from the fact, the Sun is the most powerful force on our planet to sustain life along with the symbol it represents to purify our body and soul. There are gems scattered throughout the Bible, yet we must know what to look for to understand their deeper meaning. Along with this we must explore other sources which add to the missing parts deleted from Christ's message or any other mystics words. It comes down to this: Jesus was a Divine messenger, but his message of love got twisted to serve the organization built around him 300 years after his death.

17

ASHTANGA YOGA AND AYURVEDA

The "Mysore Style" practice of Ashtanga Vinyasa Yoga is based in Ayurveda. Each individual needs to find his or her own way of using the principles in their Yoga practice. Guruji specifically mentions in his book "Yoga Mala" on pg. 41, "As the bodily constitution (prakruti) of each human being is different, it is important to practice the asanas accordingly." To me, this is a firm statement addressing the Ayurvedic approach of Ashtanga Vinyasa Yoga. If your Prakruti or Vikruti is either Vata, Pitta or Kapha, how would you practice Ashtanga Yoga? Since Vata tends to be unsettled and ungrounded, the first step is to get yourself grounded to the energy of the earth through Mula Bandha, which is very important to start the practice. It gives you a center, a rootedness to get you into your body, and to control the tendency of Vata to go up and out, dispersing your energy. Mula Bandha helps to keep the energy built up inside from leaking out, while at the same time it stabilizes the pelvis. Another grounding force is bringing awareness to your feet and legs in the standing poses, establishing the "ground up" principle. This helps you to connect to the Earth and "grow roots." You can stabilize and strengthen the rooting force of gravity through your feet and legs with the help of Mula Bandha.

Next, you want to increase the heat in the body because Vata tends to be cold. The Ashtanga practice heats you up. Typically, those with alot of Vata don't sweat very much, but since the practice increases Pitta, it induces sweating. Most Vata people barely sweat but Ashtanga seems to open the flood gates. It helps them to detoxify the body, and increases circulation too. This practice is very good for digestion, and Vata people frequently have irregular and sometimes poor digestion, absorption, assimilation and elimination. Also, you want to slow down your breath and movements, to slow down your mind and thoughts. All the movements in Ashtanga Yoga should be flowing with the breath. Vata people tend to hold their breath or breathe very shallowly. Hearing the sound is beneficial since the sense of hearing is associated to Vata. People with increased Vata tend to move the eyes alot, their energy is dispersed via the eyes. Remember, 80% of our energy that is allotted for our senses goes out with the eyes, so Dristhi in the pose can be another way to direct the energy in. The last thing for Vata to do at the end of the practice is to relax completely, in Savasana. Relaxing your energy is important for Vata especially because they are always on the go. Vata=Movement.

Ashtanga Yoga is a also great practice for a Kapha person. Think about the attributes of Kapha, and create the attributes of Vata in the practice because they're opposite. Since a Kapha person tends to be slow and heavy, you want to speed up the breath and movement, and create more lightness. Kapha people have a tendency to be lazy and don't bring a lot of energy into whatever they're doing. They have to be stirred up, and bring more intensity into their practice. Heat is very good for Kapha because of their tendency is to be cool. An intense fire will also help to liquify the Kapha to start losing weight. They'll get more energy and enthusiasm, which the Ashtanga practice can give to them.

The main thing for Pitta people is to back off on the intensity of the practice because they're very fiery and intense about everything. Because Ashtanga Yoga is naturally a fiery, intense practice, it's important for Pitta types to slow their practice down. They need to make their breath slow, calm and more relaxed. Pitta people need more space because they are usually so driven to accomplish and to go to the next level of practice. They love to be challenged, which stirs them physically and mentally. This can end up being a form of torture, since their tendency is not to back off but to want more.

This is the beauty of understanding Ayurveda. Each Dosha has different qualities and when they're recognized it becomes easier to address the needs of the individual. This is especially important for teachers who can make a tremendous difference in how they communicate to students, which enables them to not only understand themselves better, but to practice whatever lessons they need to learn. You know the expression, "you teach what you need to learn the most."

Listen to your body. If it needs to rest, let it. Watch that your mind doesn't take over in your practice. Be honest about your energy. Ayurveda states "to work at half your capacity." This means if you can run ten miles and you're exhausted, then run five. Many people tend to expend all there energy every time they do an activity. Then there is no reserve left (Ojas). Each time they do this they weaken their immune system along with all the other vital organs: heart, lungs, kidneys, etc. This is important to remember, and Yoga and Ayurveda reminds you to be aware of this. Also Vata and Pitta students need to watch their Ojas since the wind and fire can dry it up. So Vata and Pitta need plenty of Ojas increasing things in their diet and lifestyle.

REST DAYS

I'd like to mention the importance of rest days, appropriate for all three doshas. Some students want to practice straight through, seven days a week; others ask, "should I practice everyday or is it alright if I just do a couple days a week?" I tell them that I practice regularly, only taking one day off on Saturdays and moon days, full and new.   Rest days are crucial in order to maintain a healthy balanced body and practice. It is very easy to disturb your Prakruti (constitution) by "under practicing," as for a Kapha person, or "over practicing" as for a Vata or Pitta person.

Women take what is called "Ladies Holiday" when they are menstruating. These days are for "rest," to give the body a break. It's important for women to honor this time of rest. The body is working in a downward/apana way, to cleanse itself. In practice, through bandhas, we are primarily moving energy upward, following prana. Therefore, to practice while the blood is flowing down, is counterproductive to what the body needs at this time. It can also create discomfort in the uterus as engaging the bandhas puts pressure on this area. The energy that would normally go into your practice should be spent rebuilding the blood in the system. Women also tend to have sensitivities in the low back and lower belly which make the practice of strenuous asanas very uncomfortable. (If there is discomfort you can practice passive gentle asanas to relieve the pain and stagnation there.)

The explanation for why we rest on full moon day, is because the energy is so high on full moon. (you know the term "lunatic?") On full moon days, it is statistically proven that more accidents happen and more people are admitted to mental hospitals on full moon than any other time of the month. New moon is a day of rest because typically the energy is low, so why not just go with it and rest.

One last thing in relation to practicing, I tell people that even if you only do a little everyday, (for instance: Surya Namaskara/ some standing/ finish.......) is better than sporadic practice once or twice a week.

I practice regularly because for me, it is like brushing my teeth or taking a shower. Do you only do this once or twice a week? Sounds ridiculous, but of course you brush and bathe regularly. It is part of your healthy lifestyle. Also if you practice regularly there is no need for Pancha Karma or radical cleansing regimes.

214

You are consistently wringing out your body of any toxins (Ama) that may have accumulated over time. This is the whole point of doing Fasts or Pancha Karma or taking herbs to cleanse. Practicing regularly the Ashtanga Yoga method keeps all the organs and tissues vibrant. So you are less likely to need a formal cleanse or fast unless absolutely necessary.

CONCLUSION

I want to sum this up and remind you that the most important thing regarding Yoga is that it's necessary to first establish a firm foundation with Asana, the first rung of the Yoga ladder. Look at the postures as doors to enter into the deeper worlds of Patanjali's Yoga sutras. The best way to enter it is by going deeper into your own physical body first. Use this as your laboratory to explore before entering the more refined subtle energies.

The more sensitive you become in your physical body, the more naturally you will gravitate toward things that bring you balance in your everyday living including healthy relationships, foods, environments, colors, scents, books, movies. The best news about this is that you don't have to look for someone else to tell you what's good for you. Through your connection of the source of all that is, everything becomes revealed to you spontaneously.

It's important to listen to the needs of your body, not the desires of your mind, then all of this is available right now. Until you integrate it into your everyday life and living it, it only remains another Philosophy. More knowledge spinning around in your head, taking up space. Live in the Mystery and see what shows up. The more awareness you bring to everything you experience, only then can there be true freedom. For how can you have "free will" or freedom if you are not free from the reactive mind? Again Patanjali sums it up beautifully in the second sutra, "Yogas chitta vritti nirodha." Yoga has the ability to quiet the mind. Silence and stillness are its fruits. Your freedoms await you by going within.

In building and harnessing all this potent, juicy energy, now what to do with it? Well Tantra has a solution. This energy is like precious gold. Spend it wisely, invest it in your further "involution"- In and Up. Let's explore this very controversial subject in the next section.

PART IV

TANTRA

The Path to Divine Ecstasy

18

INTRODUCTION

There were these two monks transcribing a copy of an ancient manuscript. One of the monks suggested that they get the actual text to make sure what they were transcribing was accurate. He thought he would go down into the basement of the monastery where the originals were stored and retrieve it. After some time, the other monk began to wonder what happened since he was waiting for his brother to return. He went down to find out, and what he heard and saw shocked him. The other monk was standing against the wall, wailing uncontrollably and banging his head against it. "Why are you banging your head?" the monk said excitedly. The other monk turned and pointed to the original text which lay nearby. "Look," he cried, "it says here, celebrate, not celibate!!!"

This seems to be a joke, but I bet most monks would be banging their heads against the wall if, say, the Dalai Lama discovered this text and exposed its folly. Celebration or celibacy, which one sounds more spiritual to you? I have a feeling that most people would say celibacy. This is because people have the image of what's spiritual tied up in the smokescreen of religion. We tend to glorify the ascetic practices for their amazing feats of "self control" and condemn those that are sincerely ecstatic, enjoying life to the max (I'm not talking about the hedonistic person that is merely in it to get off on whatever rush presents itself).

One way or another we have all been duped. For most of us, even as we enjoy ourselves there is always a hint of guilt around it. But it's okay to celebrate or have fun without a reason behind it. We have been lied to about our most precious energy, Sex. Sex is emphasized in Tantra, since the ancient Tantric Yogis realized that this is our vital energy. This is the source of how we celebrate our lives or repress them. When you understand it for what it is, rather than deny its Presence, only then can you go beyond it. If not you repress the very essence of who you are, your very life force.

I am well aware that Tantra is a vast topic and I am only opening one arena of it. It is however our most potent energy for a reason. It not only creates Life, but gives Life.

I'd like to show in a simple chart the synergy of Ayurveda, Ashtanga Yoga, and Tantra and how they build upon each other to create a Divine Union of Sex, Love and Prayer. Sex is the base, Love transforms the base energy, and Prayer is the culmination. A pyramid is then formed with the essential energies of all three.

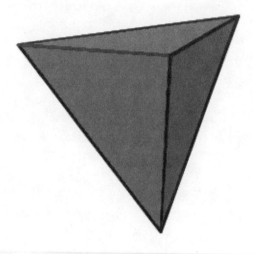

PYRAMID (tetrahedron)

AYURVEDA	**ASHTANGA YOGA**	**TANTRA**
OJAS	PRANA	TEJAS
KAPHA	VATA	PITTA
FOUNDATION	VEHICLE	ENERGY
FUELS	MOVES	TRANSFORMS
EARTH/WATER	AIR/ETHER	FIRE/WATER

SYNERGY: All three systems together are more powerful than each individually.

19

PAST AND PRESENT VIEWS OF
SEXUALITY

PAST VIEWS

As a society we have gotten lost in the maze of Sexuality. Look at how almost everything sold today is through sexual innuendo by all the advertising venues around the world. Sexual material generates the highest revenues of everything sold on the internet. On the other hand Tantra, when approached reverently, guides you on how to transform your Sexuality into a Divine pathway. Therefore in order to fully embrace the science of Tantra, its important to look at what has shaped our view of sexuality in society, up until now.

The Tantrikas of the past, the yogis of Tantra, knew that playing with this energy was like playing with fire. Tantra explores what some religions call the "dangerous" energies. Yoga also says to be cautious, as sex will supposedly bring you down. It's important to note that Yoga tends to be exclusive in its approach; Tantra inclusive, yet in reality the end outcome is the same: Liberation. If you don't understand sex, it will "pull you down," but on the other hand if you know how to use it, it can "lift" you up. Fire can burn or it can transform.

The misinterpretation of Tantra has come from moralists of all religious sects. Even the Brahmin priests of Yoga warned us of the nature of sex, in a negative way, hence the practice of "brahm"- acharya. The word brahmacharya, as I stated before, can be trans- lated as celibacy, yet its actual meaning is "to go in the direction of Brahma, or God." The definition of Tantra is: to accept exis- tence as it is, not negative or positive, no duality, but go beyond it all. Everything can be used as a force which allows you to ascend, if you know how to apply it.

If all was created by God, how can anything be evil? The origi- nal religious meaning for "sin" was "that which takes you away from going within." Simply put, anything on the outside that lures you from your center of Being is a sin, and that which guides you in is virtuous. If sex takes you out, because you don't understand it, then it is evil. Using this interpretation for sin makes it a pretty easy barometer to determine what to do and what to avoid in your life and living. Then as I said in "Prem's Rules" (pg.127), there is no need for the guidelines of Yama and Niyama (moral and ethical codes of Yoga) or the Ayurvedic die- tary rules and lifestyles. You live it from your whole Being, know- ing what resonates or not for YOU. If people lived in society with this kind of clarity there would be no need for laws, or the police to uphold them. There is no need to listen to what someone else says about something, when you are connected within yourself. We have gotten so far from our center, our inner wisdom has be- come clouded. So we are in need of some direction. The only problem with that is, who to trust? People in power want that kind of control. If you are feeling unsure you will look to others for answers. Go within and you will find out for yourself who is wise or who is not. That's the only way to confirm anything.

All the formal religions and cultures are responsible for keep- ing a lid on our most precious essence, Sex. Guilt and shame are their knives that cut at our roots, making us feel insecure and dependent on the outside. Over and over again we cannot get past this guilt without feeling "wrong" because the programming is so strong. This is why the emphasis is on Sex in Tantra. It is the medicine for the modern age; transforming this energy from sex, the base, into love at the heart, and then finally to prayer, residing at the top of the head. This is our divine pathway and expression as human beings. Deny this essential truth and we deny life itself.

We are in the same boat as our friends the monks. Deep down is this feeling that sex is somehow the root of all evil, or shall we save that one for money? (Money as we know, has also been proposed to be unspiritual). What it comes down to is the fear of handling our own inherent primal energy. This is the underlying fear of all fears, to be truly alive and vibrant. There are a thousand and one ways we sabotage our aliveness. We have to open ourselves to our most essential life force.

Marianne Williamson's quote made famous by Nelson Mandela's Inauguration speech of 1994. In which he says:

"Our deepest fear is not that we are inadequate. Our deepest fear is that we are powerful beyond measure. It is our light, not our darkness, that most frightens us. We ask ourselves, who am I to be brilliant, gorgeous, talented, and fabulous? Actually, who are you not to be? You are a child of God. Your playing small doesn't serve the world. There's nothing enlightened about shrinking so that other people won't feel insecure around you. We are all meant to shine, as children do. We are born to make manifest the glory of God that is within us. It's not just in some of us, it's in everyone. And as we let our own light shine, we unconsciously give other people permission to do the same. As we are liberated from our own fear, our presence automatically liberates others."

MODERN DAY VIEWS

There is a feeling of brotherhood amongst men, an authentic experience of love which exists without sex. I remember back in the early 90's a wave of men's groups emerged that I participated in. It was a valuable experience to see how we as men have lost touch with our true manhood. This bond is an important one in the development of a healthy man. In this day and age we have lost contact with this initiation into manhood and our feeling together as men.

Now it is predominantly a competition that breeds violence in all the "gladiator"-like sports, American Football, Rugby, Ice Hockey, Boxing and most of all the Business world. Look to what extent it's gotten out of control with the many wars taking place all over the planet, along with rampid pollution of all our air, water and soil. We are faced today with global suicide. This confusion has been built into our society as hatred and superiority based on fear. Now it is magnified into a worldwide paranoia of terrorism. Sex again is at the root.   There is no way we would act like this unless we were brainwashed to be at odds with other men from an aggression built up over sexual repression. Remember John Lennon and the hippies of the 60's saying, "Make Love not War?"

There is a convoluted energy that makes us feel uneasy. This in turn allows the people of power, who know we are frustrated, divert our energy and channel it into fear, then hate. In repressing our energy, then they channel it into a cause that serves them. Granted, if we didn't have outlets like our aggressive sports, the earth would have already been completely destroyed. If we continue abusing ourselves, mass destruction is likely because the tension is getting so high. If we had a feeling of love in our hearts how could there ever be War?

Here's what Einstein had to say about violence and war:

"Any intelligent fool can make things bigger, more complex, and more violent. It takes a touch of genius and a lot of courage to move in the opposite direction. I know not with what weapons World War III will be fought, but World War IV will be fought with sticks and stones."

226

If women, on the other hand, had the power to run the world, there would be peace and love throughout the planet. In one of the only serious talks I've ever had with my two daughters, Shanti and Mira, I attempted to describe to them how I saw the situation here on Earth at this time, regarding men and women. I told them to first embrace who they are as women and not to pretend to be men and get caught in the competitive world of men. Yes, participate, but keep your sense of femininity as you move through the world doing whatever you choose to do. I kind of apologized to them for being a man, and for how men have basically polluted most of our resources on the planet, and how we've killed in the name of God or country, millions of people. Basically men have put the planet in the state it's in today. I told them that they had to live in this World run by men, yet they can add their own beauty and light as women.

Men need to learn to listen to women for they have "the instructions and the manual," as my friend Ed Kaiwi, one of the original nine royal families of the Hawaiian people and an active Kahuna (shaman) on Kauai, has shared with me. Ed explained that the Hawaiian people came from Lemuria, the land of Mu, and passed this belief on through a verbal tradition for thousands of years. It became their "living code." The women in their society were revered and respected. Men, as Ed went on to say, "are instruments in the implementation of the instructions of women and they, the women, hold the key to understanding what needs to be done to bring balance back to the planet, otherwise men will fuck it up beyond repair, as you can already see." In other words, we need to listen to our women and follow their lead until we can be "whole" again inside ourselves as men, and we develop our feminine energy through practices such as Tantra and Yoga. Tantra has the answer for the ailing mind of man in the art of sacred sexuality.

There needs to be forgiveness for "man," for if you recognize the root cause of his violence, you'll see he is frustrated and doesn't know how to channel or manage his sexual energy. It comes out distorted through the "warrior" within each man. The distinction between a man and a woman is how it manifests. Man naturally has an external energy and his expression sexually is outward in the form of penetration. His sword is his lingam (penis). In his desire to penetrate he uses an exterior sword, or now bullet, to penetrate the flesh of another out of extreme sexual frustration. This may seem far-fetched but look at the energetic similarities that are there and tell me if it doesn't fit.

Woman are able to support and encourage men by giving them the needed instructions, but we as men must listen. Woman are naturals at this Art of Tantra. They live in their hearts very easily. Men need guidance since most of the time we live in our heads and confuse love with sex. We immediately go into sex without recognizing it is Love we truly want. Being able to move our sex energy out of the genitals and into the heart is one of the greatest gifts Tantra and Yoga have to offer men.

Women, however, have had so much guilt put on them from the beginning of time. Look at the story of Adam and Eve. The story portrays how Eve entices Adam to eat the apple, causing the Human race's "expulsion from Eden." Pointing the finger at women is much easier than accepting our responsibility. When women truly embrace their femininity they are powerful beyond belief for they are one step above men. Yet men look at softness and passivity as a weakness when in fact it can be our greatest strength. Look at how water shapes rock along a river or ocean shore, over time it even molds them.

From an Ayurvedic perspective men have more cosmic fire or Pitta and women more water or Kapha. This makes men typically more fiery and aggressive. Women are softer, and nurturing in nature similar to Kapha.

ENERGY RELEASE FOR MEN

Exploring the state of mind you are in when you enter into sex, is of the utmost importance. The more tension-ridden the mind is, the more momentary the sexual intercourse. The greater the tension the quicker the ejaculation, because a tension-filled mind is looking not for extended pleasure, but for release. You feel dissipated as well. It is a constant cycle of building and re-leasing like a sneeze. You are left with just a feeling of relief! A momentary glimpse into Samadhi like bliss, then you slip back into feeling wasted and disillusioned. This creates a dependency to chase it again and again, like an addict. You must understand your vital energy, for life is your vital essence or sex energy. To relax is one thing, but to feel dissipated is quite another. Relaxa-tion means the energy is within and you are resting. To feel dissi-pated means you throw your energy out and lie exhausted. You are weakened with the loss of energy, yet thinking you are re-laxed. This often happens to Vata and Pitta people, when they exercise to the point of exhaustion.

We touch this energy for a moment in "ordinary ejaculation" then we feel cheated afterwards. We have one of the most potent tools in orgasm without ejaculating, yet we don't know how to use it. It is like giving the secret behind atomic energy to a child. He has no idea how to apply it. We have in our hands the most valuable and powerful source of our energy, yet we never get off the ground.

CULTIVATING POTENT ENERGY

This energy we cultivate through our spiritual practices is similar to a rocket launching. It's the same kind of energy we need to create a change of Consciousness in the body/mind. Have you ever watched on TV or in a movie a rocket ship taking off? Initially it consumes a lot fuel or power to get the rocket off the ground and into space. Once it's off of the Earth's gravita-tional field, it becomes lighter. Less fuel is needed once it is free from the pull. Similarly, our journey in and up requires every-thing we have to penetrate and lift us free of the pull our mind has to the world, especially in Sex.

Tantra is about accumulating energy to ascend, by building it through your sexual energy and lifting it higher. From the very beginning there can be a sacred experience of sex, which raises the energy up. In celebration and playfulness, energy is lifted upward. In condemnation or repression it is spun downwards.

In all the texts of Yoga, Ayurveda and Tantra, they say it takes a tremendous amount of energy to ascend, so that's why if you squander it on petty things there's no juice for getting off the ground! So this is the importance of not only Mula Bandha sealing it in, but to lift that energy in and up by Uddiyana, which literally means "flying upward."

"Too much coming, all is going" — Prem

THROWING AWAY YOUR WEALTH:

"Early one morning before sunrise, a fisherman arrived at a river. On the bank he stumbled across something on the ground and noticed it to be a small sack of stones. He picked up the bag and putting his net aside, sat down on the bank to await the sunrise. He was waiting for dawn to break in order to start his day's work. Lazily, he picked one stone at a time out of the bag, and threw it into the quiet river. Then he cast another stone and then another. He enjoyed the splashing sound, in the silence of the early morning, so he kept tossing the stones into the water, one by one. Slowly, the sun rose and it grew light. By that time he had thrown all the stones away except one; the last stone lay in his palm. When he saw in the daylight what he held in his hand, his heart almost stopped, he was breathless. It was a diamond! He had thrown a whole sack of them away. This was the last piece in his hand. He shouted and he cried. He had accidentally stumbled upon so much wealth, that his life would have been enriched many times over. But in the darkness, unknowingly, he had thrown it all away. In a way, this fisherman was fortunate, still one diamond was left. The light had dawned before he had thrown the last diamond. Some people are not even that fortunate. Their whole life passes and the sun never rises, the morning never comes in

230

their lives. This is what we do with our life if we don't catch ourselves. We throw our energy away in so many different ways and directions. This is why our sexual energy is so precious. It is the diamonds we throw into the river of life. Even before knowing what life is, we have discarded it. Life is dissipated without ever experiencing what was hidden in it; what secret, what paradise, what bliss, what liberation."

— Osho

Sex is our most vital energy — our only energy. We were created out of it. Your father's sperm and your mother's egg merged and then multiplied until you became a fetus continuing to grow from the original sex seeds. We must not fight it. Go with it totally then it is possible to go beyond it.

The whole method in your love making is to be there with all your awareness. The pleasure available is above and beyond any other experience if we go with it. Relax your breathing, whatsoever is happening in your body, in your mind, and feel the new circuit you create with your partner, your bodies together in a feeling of electricity. Now slowly bring your awareness to Mula Bandha, the source, stimulating the energy there to rise up to the third eye, as I discussed in the section on Ashtanga Yoga.

The more awareness you have on the third eye the deeper the lovemaking. Go with it and stay with this energy with your full awareness. There will be a moment where you disappear, and for the first time you will realize the attraction is not for intercourse but for Superconsciousness. If you can have even a glimpse, a lightening flash will illumine the darkness, then you can easily proceed on the path. When this has happened you have transcended the sexual experience. It doesn't mean that you will never have sex again but you see it for what it truly is. You have used the intensity of the experience to go beyond. Once your energy is transformed, nature and God meet in you. A meeting of body and soul, a union of heaven and earth.

Whatever you do out of this kind of awareness will be a creative act, for you are then naturally artistic in all of your living.

Only when you have mastered the inner intercourse of merging your own male and female energies, are you then able to go beyond the physical connection outside. This can be cultivated in yourself through your Ashtanga practice: Inside/Out, Ground Up........ Then this sacred beautiful dance of merging with your beloved can be heavenly. It is only through the recognition of this vital energy, our Ojas,Tejas and Prana, and using it to go higher will there be any chance for ascension.

20

PINEAL GLAND MAGNETISM

M any people have no idea what the Pineal Gland is all about. In Tantra and Yoga it is said that this gland has a "magnetic" quality to it. When you close your eyes and bring your awareness to your third eye, the pineal gland is activated. It makes it easy to go inwards and upwards in meditation, because it creates such a high charge.

It is also said that the head is considered north and the feet south, the back of your body the west, and the east the front. I am going to take a big jump here: north, being the most magnetically charged direction on earth, is similar to the Pineal gland in the head, the most magnetically charged area of the body. Being the Yoga researcher that I am, my hypothesis is that when you place your attention on the third eye your energy immediately goes to this gland. It works like a compass when you move it around: the needle always points north.

Or here's another one: when you use two magnets there is a positive and a negative pole to them. They are attracted to each other. So when you get one in close proximity to the other they collide together from the magnet attraction or charge. I can take one more giant leap and say Male and Female attraction is because of this magnetism. The Lingam is magnetically drawn to be inside the yoni from this pull. This is after all the deepest physical connection we can have with each other so of course it has a tremendous power and appeal.

When you sit down to meditate for the first time, depending on how "civilized" you are, it may be quite a challenge to sit and be with yourself. All your energy has most likely gone out into the world, so it might drive you crazy to sit and watch your mind. Since the body isn't moving any more, all your energy goes to what is happening in the mind. This is why in modern society people can't sit still. Their energy is constantly drawn out, so to sit still is torturous. Try an experiment for five minutes, sit with a pen and a piece of paper, and write all the thoughts that come to mind. You might want to quickly throw it away before someone finds it as you may be committed to an insane asylum!

We're all a bit crazy, some more than others. We are barely maintaining, and thank goodness for Pharmaceutical Medication, Alcohol, and Recreational Drugs such as Marijuana. Otherwise, the mental health institutes and jails would be even more flooded with wild, insane people.

Insanity, by the way, means, "doing the same thing over and over again and expecting a different result." Freud spoke of how his mode of psychotherapy could never cure people since it was impossible to cure them. He could however make them function as a "normal" member of society, but with his understanding of the human mind it was not possible to do anything else. Jung however took Freud's work to the next level by exploring Consciousness beyond the mind.

There is so much pent up energy wanting to release yet our only outlet is to divert it. Instead the solution lies in transforming it, otherwise it returns again and again. Please hear me now, I am not condoning the use of drugs. I am saying with the state of mental health of most people in the civilized world these are modern day distractions and buffers at best not solutions. **MEDI-TATION is your best MEDI-CATION.**

"Take hold of your own life. See that the whole existence is celebrating. These trees are not serious, these birds are not serious. The rivers and the oceans are wild, and everywhere there is fun, everywhere there is joy and delight. Watch existence, listen to the existence and become part of it. Then you become a lover — because love can exist only with a deep respect for fun, with a deep respect for delight. Love cannot exist with a serious mind. With a serious mind, logic is in tune. Be non-serious. I'm not saying not to be sincere. Be sincere, but be non-serious. Sincerity is something else; seriousness is totally different. Be sincere with existence, then you will be true; you will become part of this cosmic LEELA, this cosmic play."

— Osho

PINEAL GLAND AND THE THIRD EYE

In Yoga, Ayurveda and Tantra, they speak of a connection to the Pineal Gland the "third eye," but not much is known about it in Western science. I went to this amazing exhibit in New York City, "Bodies.....The Exhibition." It was one of the most amazing displays of the human body ever exhibited on the planet. I walked through this gallery of bodies laid out in athletic positions doing various things. They were naked men and women, embalmed in unimaginable ways. They were quartered, split down the center, opened, and dissected. It took me four hours to see and experience all the many bodies in numerous rooms. There were rooms on the circulatory system, the nervous system, digestive system, etc.

I mention all this because when I left, I was in complete and utter awe with the miracle of the Human form. Nothing could have even come close to this experience by looking in a book or going to a lecture, a movie about it or even in a medical school lab of cadavers. I was in the presence of the most Divine creation. All I can say is, WOW !!!!!!!!

There was nothing in the exhibit about the Pineal gland. I thought that was strange and asked one of the curators what it does and what's going on with it. He said, "it's the master endocrine gland" — but what does that mean? It's a tiny little gland about the size of a pea, and it sits right in the center of the brain in a tiny cave, behind and above the pituitary gland, which lies a little behind the root of the nose. (One of the reasons that we breathe through the nose instead of the mouth in Yoga is to stimulate this gland.) It lies directly behind the eyes, attached to the third ventricle which is connected to the spinal cord and the cerebrospinal fluid. It's a mysterious gland in that science can't figure out what it does other than it has some relationship with light and darkness and the secretion of the hormone melatonin which regulates sleep and wakefulness.

I'll mention a few other facts about the Pineal that are interesting for Yoga enthusiasts. Here we go: From the time of your birth to roughly the age of 13, your brain produces large quantities of DMT (Dimethyltryptamine), a psycho-tropic chemical that also comes from a plant called Ayahuasca or Syrian Rue. This is used in ceremonies originally in South American shamanic rituals. In other words, children under the age of 13 are basically "tripping." Some psychologists have linked this to what we term "childish behavior," playing, laughing, even having visions and other less scientific phenomena. After the age of 13, the Pineal gland begins to calcify and the production of DMT comes nearly to a halt, although the gland still produces other indole alkaloid compounds.

The human brain produces many other indole alkaloids that you may have heard which include but are certainly not limited to: LSD, Psilocybin, Mescaline, etc. All of these chemicals are found in nature, and all of these sources have at least one culture cultivating them and using them for religious purposes. Every single culture in the world has some reference to these chemicals and attribute them to some "Divinity."

Why am I making such a big deal out of this? It's that the practices of Yoga and Tantra done "correctly" will bring on the naturally occurring feeling of using these drugs. Why use them if you can access this on your own for FREE, without any side effects??!! This is what needs to be on TV to get kids off drugs. Teach them how to get high whenever they want.

It's interesting to note that the Pineal gland when dissected has a crystalline center and as I said is highly magnetized. It's like a computer chip in your brain. I also imagine the Pineal Gland to be a miniature broadcasting and receiving station. It's your own satellite network to the Universal matrix of telecommunication. You use it by focusing your awareness at the third eye, projecting or receiving whatever message you want into the ethers.   The more present you are the higher your chance of sending and receiving a clear signal. It's how we plug into the inter-Galactic web called the "INNER-NET." I do it all the time with people I Love and am connected to. I start by feeling an image of the person in my heart, then I project whatever message I have out from my third eye center.

21

SHIVA SHAKTI STORY

$\mathcal{T}$he following is a story told down through the ages of how Shiva and Shakti communed which lead to the birth of Tantra to the world:

(Shiva and Shakti are depicted on the cover of this book, dancing the dance of creation, in front of Mount Kailash)

Thousands of years ago, there lived a great god in the jungles of India. He was an ascetic and a yogi who resided in distant hermitages, sitting in yogic postures for endless hours. His consciousness removed from the world, led him to have no interest in human affairs. For he had transcended all passions and worldliness and dwelled in unending meditation on the divine, while contemplating the reality of his true nature: That which is never born and never dies.

Sometimes as this renunciate sat in meditation, he would get an erection and feel the throbbing power of his penis (vajra or lingam); yet he was not concerned. As his consciousness expanded and traveled to merge with the vastness of the whole universe, he simply observed the workings of his human form. His precious lingam arose to meditate with him as the ultimate manifestation of virility.

Meanwhile, the great Goddess Devi, Mother of Creation, decided the time had come to bring the powers of this great godman back from the vast expanses of the universe to the earth to test his strength and to reveal to him advanced teachings he had never even imagined. It was time for Shiva to transcend his own detachment and bring his Spirit back into his body, to be immersed in the world through his physical form and senses, to draw his Spirit more deeply into the Here and Now.

One day, as he was wandering through a village, Shiva saw Sati, and his heart was touched beyond control. All his yogic powers were of no avail. In one sweeping moment his heart became the ruler of his soul.......not to mention the ruler of his lingam. Shiva's consciousness merged with his heart, and his body suddenly longed for human contact and presence. This was exactly what the great goddess Devi had intended.

Eventually, Sati and Shiva fell in love, and married. They lived in blissful union for many years in a hermitage on the sacred Mount Kailash. Countless adventures followed. At last, Sati died. Shiva was inconsolable. He wandered about the land, mad with sorrow, for he had loved Sati as he loved himself, as an inseparable aspect of his own divine nature. But he needed this very human sorrow, for through it he tasted the humble descent of the lover into the dark night of the soul. He knew that love and union could no longer be separate from meditation and contemplation.

The other gods seeing his misery, decided to help. Sati was reborn, reincarnated into the being of an even more exquisite young woman, Parvati, later known and honored throughout India as Shakti. As soon as they met, they were reunited as husband and wife.

Shakti was a great yogini, devoted to Shiva, yet matching his powers in her own feminine way. She was the embodiment of pure energy, the mother and matrix of all manifestation. The source of her great power resided in her vagina (yoni), her sacred garden. Shakti represents the power that weaves the universe and manifests in all forms. Until Shiva and Shakti met, their respective qualities had remained barren, devoid of dynamic creativity. Each was waiting for the missing energy that would awaken his or her enlightened completion and allow them both to realize their ultimate mission: to become the creators, the father and mother of the world.

As they perfected their yogic practices, Shakti accepted Shiva as her guru, her teacher, and he taught her the ways of transcendence to guide her to her ultimate liberation. Shiva accepted Shakti as his guru; and she initiated him into his ultimate liberation through the fusion of the transcendental, or pure consciousness and Spirit, with the manifestation in and through the body and the senses. They became spiritual partners, co-creators of their ecstasy. Shakti taught Shiva to temporarily relinquish asceticism, to integrate the art of love and sexual union into his spiritual practice. Thus, from the path of Yoga was born the path of Tantra, the Yoga of Love.

Shiva and Shakti, in their blissful practices, discovered new ways to channel their orgasmic powers through spinning vortexes of their energy centers, or chakras, and developed the great path of Tantra. This science encompassed the knowledge and skills of music, astrology, massage, painting, dance, poetry, visualization, ecstatic ritual, meditation, and teachings for the "householders."

DIVINE HIDE AND SEEK

We are all in a divine game of hide and seek.
Look around, do you see me? I see you!
Dive deep into each other's eyes.
Look behind the looking.
What a sense of humor to come up with such a game.
Play-full-ness abounds.
Catch each other coming out from their "secret" hiding place.
I see you! Do you see me?

— Prem

22

BREATHING TECHNIQUES FOR

TANTRIC PRACTICES

In the ancient text called the "Vigyan Bhairav Tantra," translated as, "Techniques for Going Beyond Consciousness," Shiva, the Indian God of Rebirth and Disillusion, describes the whole science of Tantra to Shakti, his consort.

In this text Shiva goes about describing 112 techniques to take you beyond the Mind. They are written in the language of love. Shakti is asking Shiva, while in a deep embrace, about particular aspects of life, and he answers indirectly. For instance she asks, "Who am I?" He will not say directly, he will give a technique. He says, "do this technique and you will know." For Tantra, doing is knowing. How can doubts be cleared by giving only verbal answers? Mind itself is the doubt. Unless the mind dissolves, doubts cannot be cleared. If you have a mind it will project and cloud your awareness of the world. An answer may satisfy your mind, but then it only remains a philosophy. You will not change. You have not been touched deeply. This is what I love about Tantra and Yoga as they are practices to transform, and not simply philosophies. They go fully into it with both feet.

The breath is intimately linked with the mind. It serves as a bridge between the mind and the body.   Breath is always here Now. So Tantra, as in Yoga, uses it as a tool to go beyond the mind. There is a distinction in watching the breath in Tantra and controlling the breath in Yoga. You control the breath in Yoga with Ujjayi breathing or sitting and regulating the breath in Pranayama. In Tantra, you're simply watching the breath, not controlling it. It's a powerful technique. You experience a kind of portal of Presence: the space you enter through your breath is via a doorway into the unknown or unknowable.

This reminds me of the animated Disney movie, "Alice in Wonderland." In the movie Alice was hanging out in Nature watching butterflies, feeling very connected to everything around her, being this beautiful, innocent young girl. Suddenly, she notices this rabbit running by, singing and frantically looking at his watch. He was saying in a loud voice "I'm late, I'm late, for a very important date." She follows this rabbit as he jumps into a hole. She jumps down the hole with him and begins to free fall through space. She floats to the bottom as her dress becomes a parachute. She sees a doorway. She peeks in the keyhole, but can't really see very well because it's nearly closed. She sees the rabbit already on the other side running in the distance. All of a sudden the keyhole starts talking to her and tells her of a solution. It tells her she can drink a nearby potion, which will make her small so she can get through it. After drinking the potion, she goes through the keyhole, a portal into "Wonderland." As she wanders through the land many magical, wonderful, mysterious things happen to her all along her journey.

It's a beautiful children's story, yet powerfully illustrating in its childlike, poetic way. Walt Disney was another modern mystic and I'm sure he must have played with exploring Consciousness one way or another when making some of his movies, either with psychedelics or meditation or both! Who knows for sure?

We are living in our own wonder filled land if we drop into any one of the 112 Tantric techniques. I will mention only a few

244

more. If you want to experiment with all of them, I recommend Osho's "Book of Secrets," which is by the way my favorite book by him.

So the breath as in Yoga is our vehicle for riding beyond the confines of the mind. It's the first technique in Tantra to explore. Hopefully, you've already connected in this way through your Yoga practice. That's the whole point. If you aren't in touch with yourself, how can you connect with another human being? How can you connect with the world around you? You have to connect with yourself first, so you can have an "inner-action" with the world and other people. Our goal, if there is one, is to be inner-dependent , not independent or dependent on anyone or anything. The alchemical transformation requires harmony of self first, otherwise the fire of passion can burn you, not transform. As in Yoga asana, preliminary steps must be taken to handle the voltage that is running through all your circuits. This is the importance of having a solid Asana practice.

THEN WINKS

Everything is clapping today,
Light, Sound, Motion, all movement
A rabbit I pass pulls a cymbal from a hidden pocket then winks.
This causes a few planets and I to go nuts
and start grabbing each other.
Someone sees this, calls a shrink,
tries to get me committed for Being too Happy.
Listen: this world is a lunatic's sphere,
they don't always agree it's real,
Even with my feet upon it and the postman knowing my door
My address is Somewhere else.

— Hafiz

ANAPANA-SATI TECHNIQUE

This breathing technique is watching the breath coming in and going out called, Anapana-sati. Of course there is much more to it than that, as the incessant mind is keeping you busy as you're following the breath. There is a stream of thoughts coming and going like the breath and the technique is simply watch it all. Relaxed with no judgments, just watching, witnessing. This is the main form of mind purification in asana practice as well. You will recall me saying that the Ashtanga asana practice is a "moving" meditation. The only distinction between this and Anapana-sati is, in Ashtanga you are regulating the breath and watching it; in Anapana-sati, you are only observing it naturally coming in and out, without interfering.

This technique is said to be the main method of Buddha, which eventually led him to enlightenment. It is the popular method of meditation called Vipassana. It's a formal training conducted all over the world. It is set up as a ten day sitting, continuously watching the breath throughout the day. You sit for an hour get up walk a bit then sit again for an hour. The day begins at 4 am. with a wakeup bell and continues until 9 pm. There are about ten hours of meditation throughout the day, interspersed with regular breaks and rest periods. Every evening at 7 pm there is a videotaped lecture by the Teacher S.N. Goenka, known as the founder and reviver of this method, which provides context for meditators to understand their experience. Since I've never done the full 10 days I can't comment on it. I can only repeat what I've heard and what I know about meditation. It appears to be a very powerful technique of complete immersion. If this is what you need then by all means do it. I feel the one element missing here is how to make this work in real life. Sometimes complete isolation can be valuable for deep introspection but I've heard most people say that the effect of the 10 days slowly wears off since you aren't doing this in real life. Most important is daily consistent practice at least one hour per day.

We must be careful of emulating various sages or saints and taking on practices which served them at a particular time in their life. Buddha tortured himself for many years, thinking this was the way to enlightenment. Notice I say "thinking this was the way," since he realized afterwards it was unnecessary to be so extreme. His greatest realization out of it all was in the surrendering and letting go in the end. That was at the age of 35 after sitting under a Bodhi tree for 49 days, and vowing to himself not to arise until he found the "truth."

The classic image you have of Buddha, just before enlightenment, is him sitting under this tree. He looks like a skeleton, severely emaciated from fasting, and about to die. He was day after day watching his breath, bringing his full awareness to this. Watching and waiting, not impatiently waiting, but fully there awake and aware. Over many years, he began to clear himself of all the past conditioning in his own genetic makeup of core beliefs. He finally came to a point of release. He was faced with the death of his body, or the death his ego. The death of his ego happened, followed instantaneously by his Awakening. The full Presence of his Being dissolved when the absence of his Ego happened. When the light is turned on inside, darkness automatically disappears. This kind of determination is needed sometimes to take you to the other side. Buddha was a radical.

The next breathing technique is slightly different than the previous one. It is observing the gap between two breaths. You're watching your breath coming in, then at the very top of it comes a space before it moves into the exhale. You continue doing the same with the exhale, watching it go out completely and then at the very end there is space before it then moves to inhale. When you experience the gap, the space, between the inhale and exhale you become timeless and mindless. The gaps become longer as you clear the past impressions. All meditations lead you to this place of stillness, if only for a moment. This is what we crave in orgasm, timelessness and mindlessness, or space, which is a glimpse of Samadhi. This glimpse is similar to lightening on a new moon night. There is a flash of light in the darkness of the night that illuminates the sky.

"Love yourself," says Buddha. And this can transform the whole world. It can destroy the whole ugly past. It can herald a new age, it can be the beginning of a new humanity. Hence my insistence on Love – but Love begins with You, then it can go on spreading. It goes on spreading of its own accord; you need not do anything to spread it. "Love yourself," says Buddha. And then immediately he adds: "And Watch." That is Meditation, that is Buddha's name for Meditation. But the first requirement is to Love Yourself, and then Watch. If you don't Love Yourself and start watching, you may feel like committing suicide. Socrates says: "Know thyself," Buddha says: "Love thyself." And Buddha is far more true, because unless you Love Yourself you will never Know Yourself – knowing comes only later on, Love prepares the ground. Love is the possibility of Knowing Oneself, of Being Oneself."

— Osho

THIRD EYE TECHNIQUE

The third technique is called the Meditation on the Third Eye. It's also known as the Shiva Netri, or the "Eye of Shiva." This eye opens when you close your two eyes to the world and bring your attention to the "third eye." Again this is the eye Christ talked about when sharing about meditation. "The light of the body is the eye: if therefore thine eye be single, thy whole body shall be full of light." I experienced this "light" in the three hour meditation I used to do, as I described briefly to you in my life story, with Charan Singh. I brought my attention to the third eye using a Mantra given by him. When I brought my attention there, I saw a light and it grew to feel as if I was bathed in it. There was also a "celestial sound" called the "sound current," a conch shell, deep bells ringing or cymbals, a flute, the ocean, whistling of wind, the

248

sound of "OM." These sounds would intensify as the light grew brighter within me. Religions throughout the ages have used these objects to symbolize what they experienced in the inner world. These are some of the sounds and lights that are made by the priests of various religions: church bells, conch shells, cymbals, chanting, singing......lighting candles, ghee lamps, agni hotra "ritual fires." Now we perform these acts mechanically, yet we are out of touch with their true meaning.

The "sound current" as it is called, is related to the Ether element, which remember represents our most subtle sense, hearing. I traveled this way internally many times over the years. It is what Charan Singh called "Surat Shabd Yoga" or the "Yoga of Light and Sound." It was also known as "dying while living." It was an extremely euphoric feeling. I felt like I was traveling at "the speed of light." It didn't happen every time I sat, only when "I" disappeared. When I came back hours later I felt completely new, refreshed, and at peace within.

The sound comes from beyond this world, hence the name "celestial sound" or OM. It is what the Bible refers to as the "Word" ("In the beginning was the Word, and the Word was with God, and the Word was God" John 1:1) Shams-e-Tabrez, the guru of Rumi, the famous Sufi mystic poet from Persia, said, "We should see God with our own 'Inner Eye' and hear His voice with our 'Inner Ear'. We should penetrate the dark veil within and behold his glory."

You can do this technique by sitting in a comfortable seated position and begin to follow the breath as it comes in and goes out. Slowly, once your awareness begins to quiet, shift your energy to the third eye center. Keep your awareness there by continuing to follow the breath or use a mantra of your choice. You can use AUM if you want. Keep your full awareness centered at the third eye and stay with this for 15-20 minutes if you can. You can increase the time if you have done the preparation as I mentioned in the Ashtanga Yoga section, otherwise your body/mind will rebel. Plus it carries over into your lovemaking as I said earlier.

Watch as the mind wanders, gently bring your awareness back to the breath or mantra and be fully there awaiting at the third eye. Do not imagine that you are seeing something or hearing something. Cooperate with whatsoever shows up. Wait and let whatever happens take its course. If light comes, be with it. If the sound comes as well, listen with rapt attention, not moving at all. If you let your mind jump ahead you will only be in imagination. Do the technique and wait!

ST. FRANCIS OF ASSISI PRAYER:

Lord make me an instrument of your peace
Where there is hatred let me sow (show) Love
Where there is injury let sow pardon
Where there is doubt let me sow faith
It is in giving that we receive
It is in pardoning that we are pardoned
It is "dying" that we are born
That we are born to eternal life

NEAR DEATH EXPERIENCES..........

Some people have described this feeling of light and sound, when they've had a "near death experience" and returned to talk about it. They entered into a brilliant light. They're dying, they're leaving their body and dissolving into the light, then are suddenly jerked back into their body. When they spoke of this they said it was the most ecstatically beautiful experience. Something pulled them back whether it was a loved one, their family, bank account, or whatever. They were some how given another opportunity to live life with more aliveness and awareness than ever before. The individuals I've met, that have had this experience were extremely (sorry for the word play) "lit up." They were some of the most passionate people   I've ever met, full of enthusiasm for life. It gives a newfound respect for the phrase we throw around all the time, "Living life like there's no tomorrow." Try this out for yourself: imagine you were told that you only had one week to live. How would you use your time? It is a very powerful exercise. I use this all the time. The only thing that truly matters is how you live your life NOW.

23

TANTRA AND SACRED SEX

rue Tantra is a spiritual path and is practiced with an air of sacredness. As with all forms of spiritual worship, there is an acknowledging and honoring (worshipping) of a Divine Being. However, in Tantra, this deity is reflected and honored in your partner, rather than in an intellectual concept or vague image. Therefore, Tantra is not an abstract form of spiritual practice, but a practical one, wherein the experience with the Divine is brought down to the very realm of the senses. Of course, this is not to say that the tantrika (practitioner of Tantra) cannot choose to practice other forms of spirituality and worship. It's just that Tantra challenges lovers to see the Divine Presence of God in and through each other.

There is an image in Tantra of Shiva and Shakti sitting face to face in a crossed legged position, Shiva's lingam, or penis, is inside Shakti's yoni, or vagina. They are connected as one being, sharing on a deeply spiritual level, obviously not only through words. Words are after all only a small part of communication. The communication in this image of Shiva and Shakti is a communion, a merging of male and female energy. This is a beautiful metaphor and an actual experience that happens in Tantric sex.

This is why sex is such a powerful spiritual experience: when you can share at this level with your partner. In the sexual embrace you enhance each other's electromagnetic body, giving added life force to each other.

Tantra says go into the physical energy of sex fully to see what creative energy is all about. Explore it first in yourself, as you have been in your asana practice by exploring Mula Bandha and getting in contact with that part of your body by feeling the pelvic floor the seat of your sexual energy. Play with that energy by feeling it in your own body. You have to learn about energy in your own body before you can share it with another person. In the texts I've read and explored, there are different techniques of connecting with the energy by yourself first. This involves breathing exercises, playing with Mula Bandha and creating an energy circuit in your spine like the Jiva Bandha energy breathing technique . Then you're able to explore that energy with someone else.

SEXUAL TECHNIQUES OF TANTRA

I want to share with you some sexual meditative techniques of Tantra. The energy you've been cultivating through your practice of Ashtanga Yoga starts with Mula Bandha. Mula Bandha gets you in touch with your base energy, keeping sexual energy alive and moving upward.

Loving each other becomes a playful yet reverent experience of exploring in "childlike" ways. This is the essence of the sexual aspect of Tantra. All the preliminary playing and exploring you do in your Yoga practice brings you to the table of love. Then you're able to feast upon the rich, abundance of energy available to you both.

In that space, you can lift each other higher. Out of this exploration, you set up a temple of Love. You prepare the precious body temple for the supreme expression of Love, of two human forms dancing and playing ecstatically for as long as you want.

Throughout, you're watching, breathing and enjoying until you're both complete. Hours or even days after making Love you are charged with its energy. A mere look from the other or a simple kiss brings rushes of ecstasy through you. Foreplay, during play, and after play — another pyramid!

Tantra and Yoga, through Mula Bandha, teach you how to lift your energy out from the genitals, or the basc chakra, and move it up, spreading nourishing energy throughout your entire body. As a man, you can then have multiple orgasms like a woman without ejaculating. It takes cultivating this in your own body first by having a powerful Mula and Uddiyana Bandha. Then it is possible to bring this energy in and up otherwise it is a quick exit out the lingam.

In Tantra, sex is a sacred ritual. When the breath is regulated, softened in unison, merging together, the body absorbs each others energy. They're different energies, and that's why we are drawn to be together. You're attracted to the opposite energy, like a magnet. The lingam deep inside the yoni stimulates her Mula Bandha, since the cervix is the initiation point for women. Also there are reflex points on the lingam which directly sync up with the yoni. For example, there is a reflex point at the head of the lingam which corresponds to the heart. The identical point deep inside the yoni corresponds to the heart as well. All the organs of the body are represented along the lingam and line up identically inside the yoni. Instead of throwing out your energy, you nourish and heal each other. You're no longer losing energy, you're gaining it. You're building energy together, recharging each other.

SETTING THE SPACE FOR SACRED SEX

Entering into this world of sacred sex, it's important to set the atmosphere in a way that you would as if you were entering a sacred temple. When you set the space, it's important to pay attention to the five senses, which are related to the five elements.

255

There's always this symbiotic relationship going on when you're conscious of it. In setting the space, the five elements and senses are nourished. I want to go through each sense and talk about them briefly. It's really for you to discover what resonates for you in creating your own sacred space. I'm only giving you an idea of what is possible. Use your own imagination to creatively set a place of worship.

I spoke of the eyes being the most vital sense organ so obviously, the eyes are very important for the sensual experience. Burning a candle is the best light to accentuate the forms of your bodies. Adorning the room with beautiful colors that resonate with you and your partner through scarves and tapestries is a beautiful way to create an atmosphere conducive for loving each other.

Enhance your sense of smell from the fragrance of flowers along with incense to fill the room with sweetness. Use essential oils that invigorate the sense of smell bringing an elevated feeling of the love you feel for each other. Your personal smell is a way you connect to your partner too. It's important you've cleaned the body, so draw a bath for your lover and bathe them in a ritual of worship. You can put flower petals or essential oils in the water.

Having silk sheets and special oils for massage awakens your sense of touch, which makes the body tingle with joy. Any kind of sensual ways of touching one another heightens the pleasure you have and the connection you feel to your lover. All this raises the sexual energy between you. During the stroking, holding and touching it's important for men to be aware of Mula Bandha so you don't let that built-up energy escape through your lingam (penis) before entering her sacred garden. This energy will move up the spine and spread throughout your body giving you pleasurable waves of an Orgasm without Ejaculating. Each wave gets progressively more intense building the energy to go higher and higher especially when joined together inside the Yoni.

Soft music or the natural sounds of your surrounding environment create an atmosphere of peace and love. You might hear the ocean in the distance or a waterfall nearby. Loving sounds as you caress each other expressing the pleasure you're giving and receiving from your partner creates your own music. Listen to the sounds of each other's breath, for synchronizing the breath is beneficial for merging your energies deeper.

Having sweets or juicy, yummy fruits like mangoes or plums to share with your lover, enhances the sense of taste. Feeding each other your favorite desserts with the eyes closed can be a very exciting sensual experience, which builds up more energy. You can also taste the bodily fluids that are flowing between you.

All of this is happening with a sense of pure pleasure and enjoyment of each other, with the spiritual intention of Love. You're gathering and harnessing this energy. Now what do you do with it? Tantra says pull that energy up, to move it through you. Lifting it up and out of the genitals to the heart where Love resides then up further to the third eye in prayer and gratitude. You are also providing a healing space where you're allowing the energy you've built up for your partner to absorb, and possibly to heal a part of their body. You're setting the atmosphere to create a healing space where each of you can bathe in the other's Love.

You've created the space outside; now it's time to enter the temple within, the temple of two human beings. The meeting of your two divine forms, which Ayurveda, Yoga and Tantra refer to as the Living Temple. You don't have to go to church on Sunday to worship, the living temple is always open and available waiting to be entered.

Once you have created the space, the "fore-play," then it is time to explore each other more intimately. It is time for the "real-play" and then allow time for "after-play" as well. I would like to mention some ways to connect, which will give you some ideas of how you can explore each other and create your own "love story."

Sit upon each other in a cross-legged position in a loving embrace. The woman is on top of the man sitting upright. The lingam is deep inside the yoni. This happens after your beautiful

257

loving foreplay. The woman's legs are wrapped around the man who's sitting beneath her. Being deep inside her, he connects with his own energy by engaging Mula and Uddiyana Bandha, which seals, then stimulates the energy up the spine. The woman can do the same thing by drawing energy up her spine.

You can circulate this energy between the two of you by taking turns. The woman draws the energy from his lingam inside her yoni, then up the spine, to the top of her head. She has the tongue on the roof of her mouth allowing the energy to drop down through the tongue where it loops all the way back to the base of her spine and up again. The man is doing just the opposite by drawing the energy of the woman into him. Pulling it up through his lingam into the base of his spine, then to the top of his head, finally letting it drop down through the tongue to the base of his spine, and up again. This spiral like figure eight links the two of you together at the center point of your lingam and yoni. You can connect this with your breathing as you move the energy together. She pulls the energy up her spine while inhaling he is doing the same. This synchronization of the breath is happening while both of you are looking into each other's eyes and feeling this circulation of male and female energy.

Sex energy used in this way transforms you by celebrating each other in the beautiful dance of rhythmic breathing. In this unison of breath, you nourish each other. You can accumulate this energy to heal each other in whatever way you choose. It is possible to make love for hours on end by keeping the energy moving in various positions. There are thousands of positions described in the Kama Sutra that enhance your ecstatic experience of sex. Exploring in this way with your partner will keep the intention alive and spill over into everything else you do. You will then be using your sexual energy in its highest form.

"I'm not against sex, so don't be in a hurry that you have to drop it. If you want to drop it, how can you understand it? And if you don't understand it, it will never disappear! And when it disappears, it is not

that sex is simply cut off from your being, it is not that you become a non-sexual being. When sex disappears, in fact you become more sensuous than ever, because the whole energy is absorbed by your being. A Buddha is more sensuous than you are. When he smells, he smells more intensely than you smell. When he touches, he touches more totally than you touch. When he looks at the flowers, he sees the flowers more beautiful than you can see – because his whole sexual energy has spread all over his senses. It is no longer localized in the genitals; it has gone all over the body. Hence, Buddha is so beautiful – the grace, the unearthly grace – from where is it coming? It is SEX – transformed, transfigured. It is the same mud that you were decrying and condemning which has become a lotus flower. So never be against sex; it is going to become your lotus flower. And when sex is really transfigured, then you understand what a great gift sex was from God to you. It is your whole life; it is your whole energy. On the lower planes, on the higher planes – it is the only energy you have got. So don't carry any antagonism, otherwise you will become repressive. And a man who represses cannot understand. And a man who cannot understand is never transfigured, never transformed."

— Osho

CONCLUSION

Just as some of the world's greatest spiritual teachers have said that Heaven cannot be accurately described in words, the essence of Tantra cannot be captured in either spoken or written words. To truly understand Tantra, it has to be experienced.

In addition to cosmic, mystical experiences, Tantric masters are also interested in having deeply personal experiences with other people and the world in which they live. When a deep inner-connection is established, the formerly perceived space between any two people or objects becomes filled with the light of Spirit. This spiritual Presence activates and excites the etheric energy within and between the two, joining them as one. That which was contracted and separate is now free to expand and unite. This is true Tantra!

EPILOGUE

I GOT KIN

Plant so that your own heart will grow.
Love so god will think "Ahhhhhh I got kin in that body ! I should
start inviting that soul over for coffee and rolls."
Sing because this is a food our starving world needs.
Laugh because that is the Purest Sound.

— Hafiz

TSUNAMI OF 2004

I would now like to share with you my experience with the Tsunami that destroyed many parts of Asia in 2004. It's a story that demonstrates how a devastating tragedy turns into a miracle of love and generosity. I was in India traveling with my daughter, Shanti. We had just spent the prior month in Sri Lanka where we enjoyed the Grand Opening of my newly built Retreat Center that I had dreamed about for years. This dream came to life from a generous gift given by a dear friend and brother, Fred Lewis. A group of friends and students had gathered to inaugurate and enjoy this beautiful sacred space. I envisioned this being a place for people to live in communion of love and celebration practicing Ashtanga Yoga, Ayurveda and Tantra.

When Shanti and I first got word of the tragedy we thought, how bad can it be? We then were told that 40,000 people died in Sri Lanka alone!!! Immediately we ran to the nearest TV and began watching horrible film clips of the Tsunami ravaging buildings and people in its wake. The media spoke of many locations in Sri Lanka that were devastated, and our Retreat center was in one of these areas. I then ran for a phone and began to call my friend Fred, who was still at the Center. For seven long days I tried and tried to get through but to no avail. I imagined that Fred and everyone there had died.

In the meantime I was overwhelmed with hundreds of emails over those seven days asking, " Are you alive?" Feeling helpless and then hopeless, literally waves of tears flooded my eyes day after day. I began to seriously question my life. I thought, "what is happening here? Is this some sort of sign? A wake up call? A message from God? Am I supposed to be teaching Yoga? Maybe I should be a plumber?" One after another, thoughts and feelings of despair, hopelessness, to the ridiculous. I wanted to stay positive but everywhere I turned the media said there was no way anyone or anything survived in that area. After what seemed to be an eternity, I finally got through to Fred. He told me somewhat calmly, that the Center was untouched and no one we knew was hurt, whereas everything around us was destroyed. (At the time he had no idea of the extent of the damage, since all forms of communication were down for those seven long days.) Saved by a miracle!!! In hearing this I then knew for sure that our Center was meant to be and that it survived for a reason. Once again, a lesson in not listening to the mind. I felt an instant sense of peace. I was back in my heart. Fred told me our Center turned into a temporary shelter and medical complex for the local community.

I knew I had to return soon, and although Shanti wanted to go with me, she had to go back to the States, to school. So by myself, about one month later, I left India and went back to Lanka, as I

now considered this my home. I wanted to go right away, but the media had been describing breakouts of Cholera or other life threatening diseases as an after effect of so many people dying and debris scattered everywhere. When I finally did arrive, what I witnessed was utter devastation. I was not prepared for what I saw on that long ride to our property from the airport. For hours and hours I saw nothing but rubble all along the coastline. People living in cardboard boxes, boats and cars hanging from trees and crashed along the shoreline, piles and piles of garbage with shoes, clothes, tables, etc. The despair in people's eyes as we drove by was heart wrenching. I thought to myself over and over again....
"What can I do?"

It took me a few days to grasp what had happened. It's one thing to see it on TV and another to actually be there. I had heard many horrible personal stories but I can only imagine what actually happened on that frightful day. Once I got over the initial shock I went around the local community and did what I could. I bought a fisherman a boat, a gas burner for another family to cook with, some clothes here and there, but I felt overwhelmed by the immensity of the tragedy. There were so few resources to take care of what seemed like endless needs.

They had no insurance, relatives or friends to help them get back on their feet. Most people relied completely on the help of the government or non-government organizations like the Red Cross, and many other small NGO's around the world, to assist them in some way in order to recover some semblance of their life prior to the Tsunami. The international media informed everyone of this tragedy that took a total of over 300,000 lives worldwide. Millions of dollars were sent to these organizations, but I discovered to my dismay that very little money ended up in the hands of the people who needed it. My immediate concern was how to help as many people as I could and bypass this unfortunate loop. That seemed impossible with my own extremely limited financial resources.

I was then directed to visit a camp that was set up in the village near my home where 29 families were huddled in a large, dark, dingy warehouse with each family being separated from one another only by a flimsy piece of plywood. I listened with tears in my eyes as each one shared their stories of losing family members and all they owned. I was feeling a sense of hopelessness, as they seemed so distraught. I too felt the heaviness of depression covering every mind and heart. However, I noticed how the children, who were so resilient, found ways to make the best of the situation by playing with one another.

I needed to do something fast because I became very close to these people and felt these sweet souls couldn't continue living in these horrible conditions. What they needed were things to get them back on their feet. Suddenly, I was touched with a brilliant idea that lifted my heart. I realized that I had an extensive network of friends and students around the world who I could ask for help. So, I sent an email to everyone on my mailing list, which at the time was about 800 people, asking them to donate whatever money they could spare to help all these families' immediate needs.

What happened next was overwhelming. Money from around the world began to pour into a bank account I set up for the camp. A miraculous out pouring of love right before my eyes. I had met with each family before sending out my message and one by one asked them what they needed to make a difference. I shared with my friends abroad how much each thing cost and what family it would go to. Whether it was a sewing machine at $100, a rice cooker $20, table and chairs, clothes, fishing nets $250, or fishing boats $300 (since most of these people made their living fishing). Each person knew how much to send to help that particular family. Most people just sent money and said that they trusted me to do what was necessary for the people there. Not only was I feeling all this out pouring of love from my generous friends, but I was also receiving so much from the people living in the camp.

264

I felt as if I was a magic "Genie" giving them whatever they wished for, and all they had to do was ask. My heart was bursting with love and thanksgiving. I was a vehicle of love. Never before had I ever felt such an amazing feeling of connection on this scale. My faith in human kindness and resiliency was being transformed daily as I experienced this boundless love in whatever direction I turned. The money kept coming, and the needs of these people were beginning to be met. Most gratifying was the huge difference it made in their spirits as hope finally returned to their fractured lives. They now began to have the ability to work and take care of their families, which empowered them to carry on with their shattered lives once again. They were also touched by how people who didn't even know them would send so much.

Yes, this was a tragedy, but like so many times in life when things seem so wrong, they turn out to be filled with blessings. For me, this certainly was the case. I was so thankful for the opportunity I was given to serve. In that service, I was able to give magnanimously, which changed my life. One of the families I was able to help I adopted as my own. Their names are Saman, his wife Jiva, and five kids, Roshana, Delum, Sanika, Samira and Nilusha. I gave the remaining money that came in to them. They were able to rebuild their lost home and restaurant, which they now call, "Prem Restaurant" in honor of the love that was showered on them by all who contributed.

I share this experience now, because I realized from it more than ever before that we are one human family. It's all about love, and it's about a global love. It can't be just a selfish love anymore.

If we want this planet of humankind to survive, it can't be just about "me." It's one of those crazy paradoxes in life, I've talked about throughout this book. About "being selfish" by loving yourself first, and when you feel so full of love for yourself it overflows, and spills over into helping other people. It's not being stingy and holding on, as I had done in the past, out of fear of not having enough. But when the love is so overwhelmingly flowing inside you, you will not be able to stop it from spilling over into everything you do. Can you see the difference? Like all that is natural and in harmony there is no effort to figure it out or plan. Spontaneously you will be guided to do what is best for all of mankind. I had this opportunity to serve which came my way quite miraculously. I never imagined being involved in anything like this before. I know it doesn't take a shift like this for everyone to wake up, but it did for me.

Up until the experience of the Tsunami, I saw I had been doing intense, disciplined practices for 30 years which enabled me for the first time to share that love with others less fortunate on a global scale. There were many opportunities for me to give over the years but never to this magnitude. What a blessing it was to witness the experience of abundance from all levels showering upon so many.

You must start from this place inside yourself. Then, perhaps, look locally to see how you might serve your neighbors, and then when you're ready, extend that service globally. It is so important to get this simple fact, Be Selfish. This is not what is taught in the Churches or in Society. They all say Love your neighbor first. Give to the needy, help the less fortunate. This is true, but only from a place of fullness and Love of Oneself can you truly make a difference. Otherwise, it will be a giving from guilt, obligation, or egotistical recognition.

OSHO ON LOVE

Love is the radiance, the fragrance of knowing oneself, of being oneself. Love is overflowing joy. Love is when you have seen who you are: then there is nothing left except to share your being with others. Love is when you have seen that you are not separate from existence. Love is when you have felt an organic, orgasmic unity with all that is.

Love is not a relationship, love is a state of being; it has nothing to do with anybody else. One is not "in love," one IS love. And of course when one is love, one is "in love"- but that is an outcome, a byproduct; that is not the source. The source is that one is love.

And who can be love? Certainly, if you are not aware of who you are, you cannot be love. You will be fear. Fear is just the opposite of love. Remember, hate is not the opposite of love as people think. The real opposite of love is fear. In love one expands, in fear one shrinks. In fear one becomes closed, in love one opens. In fear one doubts, in love one trusts. In fear one is left lonely, in love one disappears, hence there is no question of loneliness at all. When one is not, how can one be lonely?

Then these trees and the birds and the clouds and the sun and the stars are still within you. Love is when you have known your inner sky.

The young child is free of fear; children are born without any fear. If the society can help and support them to remain without fear, if they can help them to climb the trees and the mountains, and swim the oceans and the rivers. If the society can help them in every possible way to become adventurers, adventurers of the unknown, and if they can create a great inquiry instead of giving them dead beliefs, then the children will turn into great lovers, lovers of life-and that is true religion. There is no higher religion than Love.

Meditate , dance, sing and go deeper and deeper into yourself. Listen to the birds more attentively. Look at the flowers with awe, wonder. Don't become knowledgeable, don't go on labeling things.   That's what knowledgability is, the great art of labeling everything, categorizing everything. From this age start playing guitar or learn to play the flute. Meet people, mix with people, with as many people as possible, because each person expresses a different face of God. Learn from people. Don't be afraid. This existence is not your enemy. This existence mothers you, this existence is ready to support you in every possible way. Trust and you will start feeling a new upsurge of energy in you; that energy is love. That energy wants to bless the whole existence, because in that energy one feels blessed. And when you feel blessed, what else can you do but bless the whole existence.

Love is a deep desire to bless the whole existence.

* * *

"When the Power of Love overcomes the love of power, the world will know Peace."

— Jimi Hendrix

World peace will follow when it comes from the space of loving ourselves first. This can be the only "real" reason why to practice Ashtanga Yoga, Ayurveda and Tantra. I'm reminded of a quote from the famous Indian philosopher, Krishnamurti, who said, "You are the world and the world is in you."

My sincere wish in writing this book is to stir you to the depths of your Being, encouraging you to go further in your exploration of your Divine self. It has been my humble attempt to give you a glimpse of what these tools have to offer. It is now in your hands to keep the energy alive. Find others in your community to go deeper and know there is always an open invitation for you to visit me wherever I may be, especially at the Shambhala Cove Retreat Center in Sri Lanka, to explore the many aspects which are impossible to experience through a book.

THE ONLY WAY OUT, IS IN!!!

Before I leave you I would like to offer this beautiful expression from India, "Namaste" (Namas-stay), which means, "From the place within me that I know to be Divine, I recognize that within you." Now, I must say goodbye. "Namas-Go."

RECOMMENDED READING

By OSHO:
The Book of Secrets
Sex Matters: From Sex to Super Consciousness
The Mustard Seed: The Gnostic Teachings of Jesus the Mystic
The Path of Yoga: Commentaries of the Yoga Sutras of Patanjali
In Search of the Miraculous Vol. I & II

Yoga Mala
Sri K. Pattabhi Jois

Ashtanga Yoga -The Essential Step-by-Step Guide to Dynamic Yoga
John Scott, www.stillpointyoga.co.nz

Yoga and Ayurveda, Ayurvedic Healing
Dr. David Frawley
*American Institute of Vedic Studies Correspondence Course in Ayurveda - **www.vedanet.com***

Eat- Taste- Heal ... An Ayurvedic Cookbook for Modern Living
Thomas Yarema, Daniel Rhoda, Johnny Brannigan

Ayurveda, The Science of Self-Healing
Dr.Vasant Lad, The Ayurvedic Institute, Albuquerque, NM

Sexual Secrets...The Alchemy of Ecstasy
Nik Douglas, Penny Slinger

RETREAT CENTER

A long time vision has become my reality — a retreat center in Sri Lanka called, Shambhala Cove. On the spectacular coast of Sri Lanka a model community is spontaneously growing. Some visit for a personal retreat to contemplate and go deeper into themselves; for others, it's a social experience to connect with a global family of kindred spirits. It's in your hands to share in the wealth of a daily asana practice, dancing, chanting, workshops/intensives, and eating vibrant delicious tropical fruits and local cuisine, along with enjoying the exotically lush surroundings. All of this taking place in a supportive environment where you are free to grow in whatever way your heart desires. It is in this kind of atmosphere we learn how to nurture ourselves first then nurture each other.

My intention is for this space is to be an Oasis for people to heal on all levels, then in the fullness of what they feel inside, go and spread the Love to others around the world. My invitation to you is come when you can and share in the abundance of this magical paradise.

— Prem

"Home is where you belong, and home is where you can be "at home." Home is where you can relax and be accepted as you are...where nobody tries to change you, nobody expects anything from you and everybody is ready to love you as you are."

— Osho

www.shambhalacove.com

*   *   *   *   *

SIMPLEXITY HEALTH
BLUE GREEN ALGAE NUTRITIONAL PRODUCTS

"Energy for Life"

I have been using these products for over 20 years with incredible results! This organic nutrient-dense Algae is harvested wild from Upper Klamath Lake in Oregon. I consider this Algae to be the most beneficial food on the planet and it is the foundation for this line of products. Unfortunately in this day and age we need nutritional support and this can be your answer as it has been for me.

The power of Blue Green Algae to benefit your health is backed by dozens of scientific studies. It provides full-spectrum micro-nutrition and there is no other single whole food source anywhere that contains as many different and hard-to-find micro-

272

nutrients. It contains vitamins, minerals, trace minerals, all twenty amino acids, phyto-nutrients, anti-oxidants, active enzymes, pigments, essential fatty acids, and much more. These nutritionals totally resonate with my understanding of Ayurveda and modern nutrition. They've increased my immune system function and have enhanced my digestion tremendously. They've personally given me the added strength, stamina, and energy and increased flexibility in my Ashtanga Yoga practice over the years.

They are the perfect compliment to your Asana practice as they are pure Prana foods. I call them "Yoga fuel." When these nutrients find their way into your bloodstream they will nourish every cell of your body. Give them a chance to change your life as they have mine. There is a 90-day money back guarantee, so order now and experience for yourself the miracle of the most potent food on the planet!

If you want to order go to the link:

www.simplexityhealth.com/yogafuel

INDEX

A

A.M.A, 63
Abhyanga, 125
Acidopholis, 119
Acupuncture, 49
Adam, 52, 228
agni, 101, 102, 103, 104, 105, 106,
    108, 209, 249
Agni, 62, 63, 69, 96, 101, 104, 105,
    111, 112
    Jathar, 69
Agra, 14
Ahimsa, 143
AIDS, 118
Air, 59, 61, 62, 63, 65, 70, 83, 92,
    93, 209
Albert Einstein, 169
alchemical, 120, 245
Alchemy, 202, 269
alcohol, 23, 69, 85, 119, 127
Alcohol, 234
algae, 30, 107
Algae
    Micro, 171
Alice in Wonderland, 244
Allah, 146
allergies, 74, 118
Alpert
    Dr. Richard, 7
ama, 63, 71, 94, 96, 101, 102, 103,
    122
Amalaki, 124, 125
Amazing Grace, 162
America, ii, ix, 17, 18, 19, 21, 25,
    26, 28, 35, 36, 97, 119, 169, 205
American, 18, 63, 156, 209, 226,
    236, 269
American Medical Association, 63

anabolic, 91
Anapana-sati, 246
anger, 69, 104, 119
antibiotics, 17, 118
anxiety, 71, 86
anxious, 82
apana, 214
Apana, 176
Apana Vayu, 176
Aparigraha, 143, 144
Arthritic, 71
arthritis, 97, 98
asana, 13, 18, 22, 119, 135, 145,
    147, 148, 150, 151, 172, 178, 187,
    188, 197, 206, 207, 245, 246, 254,
    271
Asana, 19, 27, 87, 112, 135, 147,
    151, 158, 205, 206, 207, 215, 245,
    273
asanas, 9, 14, 18, 134, 135, 147, 148,
    153, 177, 194, 211, 214
asceticism, 241
Asclepius, 200
Ashtanga, i, ix, x, ix, x, xi, xvi, 1, 9,
    10, 11, 13, 14, 22, 26, 27, 28, 41,
    42, 43, 44, 45, 108, 134, 135, 137,
    139, 141, 145, 146, 150, 151, 152,
    155, 157, 158, 159, 160, 162, 165,
    166, 172, 173, 180, 183, 184, 185,
    186, 187, 188, 191, 192, 193, 194,
    195, 198, 205, 206, 207, 208, 211,
    212, 213, 215, 220, 231, 232, 246,
    249, 254, 261, 268, 269, 273
Ashtanga Vinyasa Yoga, 134, 211
Ashtangis, xi
Ashteya, 143, 144
Ashti, 105, 109, 110
ashwaghanda, 124
Asian, 156
Asthi, 109

Astringent, 91
attraction, 116, 148, 202, 231, 233
AUM, 198, 249
aura, 7, 116
Australia, 169
Autonomic Nervous System, 108
Aviyda, 142
Awareness, 54, 202
    Passive, 54
Ayahuasca, 236
AYRI, 14, 137, 194
ayurveda, i
Ayurveda, i, ix, x, xi, xvi, 1, 4, 21,
    27, 28, 29, 35, 38, 39, 41, 44, 45,
    46, 49, 50, 51, 52, 53, 54, 56, 57,
    58, 60, 73, 74, 75, 77, 81, 84, 86,
    91, 94, 96, 97, 98, 101, 105, 110,
    117, 121, 122, 125, 127, 133, 134,
    135, 139, 142, 165, 166, 168, 170,
    177, 209, 211, 213, 220, 230, 235,
    257, 261, 268, 269, 272
Ayurvedic, xii, 27, 57, 75, 78, 83,
    86, 91, 117, 119, 123, 125, 192,
    211, 224, 228, 269

B

Baba, ix, 26, See Das
bacteria, 118, 119
balanced body, 214
Bandha
    Jiva, 197, 254
    Mula, 16, 174, 175, 176, 178,
        179, 180, 181, 182, 186, 189,
        197, 200, 211, 212, 230, 231,
        254, 255, 256
    Uddhiyana, 183
    Uddiyana, 176, 177, 178, 186,
        187, 255, 258
Bandhas, 134, 173, 174, 178, 182,
    184, 202
Basti, 21, 123
Being, i, 3, 10, 31, 40, 42, 51, 75, 84,
    85, 102, 141, 144, 148, 149, 152,
    157, 159, 171, 178, 180, 199, 202,
    224, 228, 233, 245, 247, 248, 253,
    258, 268
belching, 71
Benares, 15, 16
Bhagavad Gita, 141, 164
Bibhitaki, 124
Bible, 38, 52, 136, 164, 210, 249
Bifidus, 119
Bikram, 134, 205
bio-electrical organisms, 200
Bitter, 91, 92
bladder, 69, 150
bloating, 68, 80, 102, 104, 124
Bloating, 71
blood, xi, 19, 62, 69, 70, 95, 106,
    107, 109, 110, 112, 119, 123, 124,
    125, 214
Blood, 105, 106, 107
blood vessels, 70, 106
body
    etheric, 63
bone marrow, 110
Book of Secrets, 245, 269
Born Again, 202
bowels, 71, 76, 150

brahmacharya, 18, 143 224
Brahmin, 224
breast, 102, 173
breath control, 155
breathing, 14, 63, 70, 87, 108, 110,
    134, 141, 145, 152, 153, 154, 155,
    183, 184, 185, 186, 187, 197, 231,
    244, 246, 247, 254, 255, 258
Breathing, 173, 183, 184, 185, 197
Brotherhood
    Global, 194
buckwheat, 171
Buddha, 43, 86, 116, 120, 142, 144,
    154, 161, 162, 209, 210, 246, 247,
    248, 259
Buddhism, 42, 190
Buddhist, 156
buttocks, 116

C

California, 7, 9, 11, 26, 28, 31, 32,
160, 168, 174
  Southern, 11
cancer, 2, 3, 30, 97, 118
Cancer, 97
Capricorn, 75, 202
catabolic, 91
Catholic, 9, 164
celibate, 18, 28, 219
Cell Tech, 171
cereals, 93, 94
cervix, 175, 255
Chakra, 154, 178, 201
Chakras, 57, 134, 195, 197, 203
chanting, 13, 125, 209, 249, 271
charge
  220 volt, 19
Chaturanga, 190
Chi, 49, 57
Chi Gung, 49
Chinese, 57, 177, 195
chitta, 140, 215
Chlorophyll, 107
chocolate, 102, 105, 179, 196
Cholera, 262
Chopra
  Deepak, 34
Christ, 9, 24, 44, 116, 156, 161, 162,
164, 209, 210, 248
Christian, 9, 156, 164, 209, 210
Christianity, 42, 44, 209
chronic, 71, 118, 121, 179
chronic fatigue syndrome, 118
church bells, 249
cigarettes, 85, 97, 119, 179
Clint, ix
Clown Chakra, 153
cobalt, 110
Code
  The Da Vinci, 164
coffee, 14, 85, 127, 179, 261
colon, 20, 70, 71, 110, 123

Colonic, 21
colonics, 71
colors, 78, 82, 83, 87, 88, 125, 196,
201, 215, 256
Conscious, 55, 94, 112, 115, 127,
139, 149, 150, 151, 196, 198, 202
Consciousness, x, 5, 6, 51, 55, 58,
127, 133, 140, 149, 153, 157, 159,
162, 164, 167, 205, 206, 207, 229,
234, 243, 244
Constantine, 210
constipation, 71, 124
copper, 110, 170
cord
  umbilical, 26
cosmic, 11, 43, 58, 65, 98, 146, 153,
154, 228, 235, 259
Cosmic Dance, 170
Cosmic Intelligence, 167
Cosmic Motor, 161
cosmic play, 235
Cosmic Play, 170
Creator, 146
crystalline pineal gland, 201
cymbals, 248

D

Dalai Lama, 219
dance, ix, 111, 232, 239, 241, 258,
267
Dandasana, 190
Dantian, 177
Dark Ages, 210
Darth Vader, 184
Darwin, 199
Das, ix, 26
Dass
  Hari, 27
  Ram, ix, 5, 7
detoxification, 122
Devi, 240
Dharana, 109, 157, 158
Dhatu, 105, 108

Diabetes, 97
diamond, 230
digestive disorders, 118, 124
Divine Insight, 137
Divine observation, 148
Divine pathway, 223
Divine Presence, 253
Divine Union of Sex, 220
DMT, 236
DNA, 64, 98, 99, 198
dosha, 73, 77, 82, 123
Dosha, 77, 213
doshas, 77, 83, 122, 123, 124, 213
Dr. Lad, 27, 28, 29, 75
drashtuh, 141
Drishti, 173, 186, 187, 202
Dristhi, 212
drugs, 6, 8, 10, 23, 33, 64, 71, 85,
  118, 119, 234, 237
  psychedelic, 7
Dukha, 142
Dynamic Mediation, 150

E

Earth, 52, 59, 61, 62, 63, 65, 67, 88,
  92, 93, 133, 156, 168, 198, 203,
  209, 211, 227, 229
Ecstasy, xi, 161, 180, 217, 269
Eden, 52, 228
Egypt, 199
Eiffel Tower, 171
Einstein, xii, xiv, 85, 145, 158, 169,
  226
  Albert, 169
ejaculation
  ordinary, 229
Ejaculating, 256
ejaculation, 112, 181, 229
EKG, 19
Element
  Fire, 60
Encinitas, 11, 28, 160
endocrine, 69, 185, 236

endometrial tissue, 111
enemas, 71
energy
  Mysterious, 170
English, 13, 15, 17, 24, 57, 65, 208
Enzyme, 69
enzymes, 60, 69, 101, 272
Eternal Aliveness, 52
Ether, 59, 63, 83, 92, 249
Eve, 52, 228
E-volve, 199
Existence, 51, 127, 146, 156, 170
Eye of Shiva, 248

F

farting, 71
fasting, 49, 70, 76, 122, 247
Fasts, 215
fat, 55, 102, 104, 108, 109, 116, 124
Fat, 105, 108, 109, 116
feminine side, 175
femininity, 227, 228
Fire, 59, 60, 62, 63, 65, 68, 85, 92,
  93, 209, 224
Flow
  Hatha, 205
  Vinyasa, 205
Folan
  Lilias, 8
Frawley
  David, ix, 269
Freud, 234
frustration, 18, 69, 166, 228
full moon, 214

G

G. U. R. U, 11
Ganges, 16
ganja, 5, 23, 127
Ganja, 19
Garbha, 111
Garbha Utpadana, 111

gas, 71, 80, 102, 104, 124, 263
gaseous molecules, 95
Genesis, 52
Genie, 264
genitals, 175, 228, 255, 257, 259
George Lucas, 190
Gheranda Samhita, 134
GI, 119, 123
ginsengs, 124
Giza, 199
gland
    crystalline pineal, 201
    Pineal, 87, 233, 236, 237
Gland
    Pineal, 233
glands, 67, 69
Global Brotherhood, 194
God, ix, 15, 32, 38, 52, 55, 66, 100,
    138, 143, 144, 146, 147, 154, 159,
    160, 161, 170, 198, 202, 209, 224,
    225, 227, 231, 243, 249, 253, 259,
    262, 267
Goddess, 240
goddesses, 9
Grace, i, 180
    Amazing, 162
Gross to Subtle, 170, 203,195
Gung
    Chi, 49
Guruji, ix, 11, 12, 13, 14, 16, 17, 18,
    19, 20, 22, 25, 41, 42, 135, 137,
    180, 185, 192, 193, 194, 200, 205,
    206, 207, 208, 209, 211

H

Ha, 135, 200
Hafiz, ix, 100, 187, 245, 261
hallucinogenic, 32
happiness, xiii, 148
Hara, 177
Hari, ix, 26, 27, 177, See Das
Haritaki, 124
Harley Davidson, 31, 36

Harvard, 7
Hatha Flow, 134, 205
Healing Systems
    The Mother of all, 46
heart, i, xii, xv, 3, 19, 26, 30, 42, 43,
    61, 63, 66, 71, 95, 96, 97, 98, 104,
    108, 109, 115, 118, 127, 147, 154,
    161, 163, 166, 176, 187, 210, 213,
    225, 228, 230, 237, 240, 255, 257,
    261, 262, 263, 264, 271
Heartbeat, 72
hemoglobin, 107
Hendrix
    Jimi, 268
Himalayan, x, 87
Himalayas, 22, 31
Hippocrates, 200
Hitler, 35, 85, 86, 158
hormone, 87, 236
hormones, 9, 106
hurricane
    Iniki, 198

I

Ida, 200
illusion, xi, 39, 44, 45, 142, 146,
    148, 156
Immortalists, 37
immune system, 23, 68, 69, 74, 98,
    110, 111, 112, 116, 117, 118, 119,
    171, 213, 272
Immunity, 118
India, x, 8, 11, 13, 14, 15, 16, 17, 18,
    19, 20, 22, 23, 25, 27, 42, 43, 51,
    119, 124, 136, 140, 154, 158, 164,
    195, 208, 239, 240, 261, 262, 268
    Mother, 19
Indian, xiii, 2, 14, 15, 16, 17, 24, 26,
    28, 55, 125, 135, 208, 243, 268
inferno
    sexual, 18
insomnia, 71, 81
intercourse

sexual, 229
intestine, 69, 101, 123
intestines, 17, 71, 104
Isvara, 145
Iyengar, 134, 135, 205, 206, 207

J

Jathar, 62, 69, 101, 105, 111
Jathar Agni, 105
jealousy, 69
Jedi, 190
Jehovah, 146
Jen, ix
Jesus. See Christ
Jimi Hendrix, 268
Jiva, 197, 254, 265
Jiva Bandha, 197, 254
Joseph Campbell, 190

K

Kaivaladhama, 19, 154
Kapha, 67, 68, 70, 72, 73, 74, 75, 76,
    77, 78, 81, 82, 83, 84, 85, 87, 91,
    92, 93, 94, 95, 96, 104, 115, 117,
    120, 122, 123, 125, 211, 212, 214,
    228
karma, 24, 58
Karma, 123, 140, 215
    Pancha, 73
karmic, 188
Kashmir, 164
Kazantzakis
    Nikos, 164
kidneys, 110, 213
Klamath Lake, 107, 124, 272
Koan, 180
Koran, 136
Kripalu, 134
Krishna, ix, 161, 209
Krishnamacharya, 135, 209
Krishnamurti, 268
kriya

nauli, 21
Kriya
    Nauli, 20
Kriyas
    Shat, 19, 20
Kundalini, 134, 181, 197, 200, 201,
    202, 205

L

Lad
    Vasant, ix, 27, 269
Ladies Holiday, 214
land of Mu, 227
Lanka, 94, 261, 262, 268, 271
laxative, 71
Leary
    Timothy, 7
Led Ashtanga, 207
Leela, 170, 235
Lemuria, 227
Lennon
    John, 226
Levy, 164
Liberation, 201, 223
lingam, 228, 239, 240, 255, 258, 234
liver, 17, 60, 69
Living Vinyasa, 152
Lonavla, 19
Lotus pose, 18
lotus posture, 150
Love, ix, xv, 43, 80, 96, 101, 106,
    108, 157, 162, 163, 190, 201, 220,
    226, 228, 235, 237, 241, 248, 250,
    254, 257, 261, 266, 267, 268, 271
lover, 157, 235, 240, 256, 257
low back, 118, 214
low back pain, 118
lower belly, 214
LSD, 236
lunatic, 214, 245
lungs, 38, 63, 67, 107, 109, 110,
    150, 160, 161, 184, 185, 213
Lymph, 105, 106

M

macrocosm, 51, 77, 95, 170
macrocosmic, 161
Maha Bharata, 164
Maha Samadhi 160
Maharishi Mahesh Yogi, 205
Majja, 105, 109, 110
Mamsa, 105, 108
Manas, 198
Manda Agni, 104
Mandela
    Nelson, 225
Manifestation, xv, 175, 239, 240, 241,51
Manipura, 201
Mantras, 57, 61
Manual
    Practice, i
Marianna, ix
Marianne Williamson, 225
Marijuana, 5, 6, 23,234
Martial Arts, 183
Masters of the Far East, 8
Matrix, 95, 108, 168, 237, 240, 34, 142, 202
Maya, 55, 142, 156
Meda, 105
Medas, 108, 109, 116
Med-Ass, 116
medicine, 50, 87, 192, 195, 200, 225
    Western, 74
Meditation, 5, 22, 23, 26, 29, 99, 117, 134, 135, 141, 144, 147, 148, 151, 158, 159, 172, 187, 189, 205, 207, 233, 239, 240, 241, 244, 246, 248,19, 32, 64, 72, 86, 117, 141, 144, 151, 158, 164, 248
menstruating, 214
Menstruation, 111
Meridians, 57, 195
Mescaline, 236
microcosm, 51, 77, 95, 161
microorganisms, 119

mind quality, 125
Mira 29, 227
Mohan Brahmachari, 135
Moksha, 123
monks, 18, 35, 219, 225
Mount Kailash, 135, 239, 240
Mudras, 134
Muhammad, 209
Mula, 16, 173, 174, 175, 176, 177, 178, 179, 180, 181, 182, 183, 184, 186, 187, 189, 197, 200, 211, 230, 231, 254, 255, 256, 258
Muladhara, 200, 201
Mulla Nasrudin, 89, 124, 138
Muscle, 63, 70, 106, 108, 111, 125, 175, 179
muscles, 16, 20, 70, 108, 109, 177
Muscular, 108
mushrooms, 32, 33
music, ix, 8, 61, 82, 87, 111, 115, 125, 241, 257
musicians, 83
Mysore, 10, 11, 13, 14, 16, 25, 41, 137, 194, 206, 207, 211
Mysore Style, 206
Mystic Healer, 40
Mystic traditions, 136
Mystic Yogi, 195
Mystics, xiii, 52

N

Nadis, 63, 134, 150, 195, 203
Namaste, 268
Nasya, 123
Native American, 40, 86
natural celibacy, 144
Nature. Blue Green Algae, 107
Nauli, 20,21
Nerve, 105
nervous, 61, 63, 70, 71, 72, 79, 82, 86, 104, 111, 123, 153, 154, 155, 185, 193, 235

nervous system, 61, 63, 70, 71, 72, 111, 123, 154, 155, 185, 193, 235
nervousness, 86
Netri, 248
nirodha, 140, 215
Niyama, 145, 146, 147, 148, 151, 158, 224
noni, 125
nourishment, 86, 87, 94, 101, 105, 108, 110, 112, 174
nutrients, 31, 68, 94, 105, 106, 107, 109, 110, 112, 116, 122, 272, 273

O

Obi-wan Kenobi, 190
Ojas, 57, 105, 115, 116, 117, 118, 120, 124, 179, 213, 232
Old Testament, 52
OM, 6,140, 198, 249
Opposites Balance, 56, 57
ordinary ejacualtion, 229
orgasm, 112, 181, 229, 248
Orgasm, 256
Osho, i, xiv, 42, 43, 44, 150, 161, 205, 231, 235, 245, 248, 259, 272
OTP, 116
oxygen, 107

P

Padmasana, 18, 150, 172
Paine
    Thomas, 209
Pancha Karma, 73, 122, 123, 124, 134, 214
pancreas, 60, 69
Paradise, 52
paranoia, 71, 226
Patanjali, 27, 134, 135, 139, 140, 141, 142, 146, 147, 150, 158, 161, 172, 215, 269
Pattabhi, ix, 11, 41, 134, 135, 187, 193, 194, 269, See Sri

peeing, 71
pelvic floor, 174, 175, 176, 184, 254
pelvis, 177, 188, 211
penis, 228, 239, 253, 256
People Forever, 31, 32, 34
perineum, 174, 175
peristalic, 71
physical, xii, 5, 10, 12, 18, 21, 22, 31, 38, 44, 51, 53, 63, 67, 69, 70, 74, 75, 83, 84, 87, 94, 98, 103, 112, 120, 134, 147, 149, 151, 160, 171, 172, 173, 174, 175, 178, 179, 180, 182, 186, 193, 195, 196, 201, 202, 206, 210, 215, 232, 234, 240, 254
physical immortality, 31
Physics, 61, 168
    Chaos Theory of, 168
Pineal Gland, 185, 201, 233, 235, 237
Pingala, 200
Pitta, 67, 68, 69, 70, 72, 73, 74, 75, 76, 77, 78, 81, 82, 83, 84, 85, 87, 91, 92, 93, 95, 96, 104, 106, 115, 117, 120, 122, 123, 125, 211, 212, 213, 214, 228, 229
plasma, 62, 67, 106, 107
Polyhedral, 168
pooping, 71
postures
    yogic, 9, 239
practitioner, xiii, 27, 78,122, 123, 177, 182, 191, 253
Pradipika, 20, 134, 136
Prakruti, 75, 77, 78, 79, 82, 112, 116, 117, 119, 211, 214
prana, 70, 185, 214
Prana, 57, 87, 110, 115, 116, 117, 118, 120, 176, 199, 232, 273
Pranayama, 18, 19, 22, 27, 87, 151, 152, 153, 155, 157, 158, 244
Pranayamas, 19, 108, 134
pranic, 105
Pranidhana, 145, 146

Pratyahara, 155, 157, 158, 187

prayer, 15, 40, 140, 148, 166, 174,
    225, 257
Prem Restaurant, 265
Prem's Rules, 224
Presence, xv, 44, 45, 51, 52, 54, 55,
    64, 99, 141, 149, 150, 157, 159,
    160, 173, 178, 180, 181, 182, 186,
    187, 196, 202, 220, 244, 247, 253,
    260
    Divine, 51
priests
    Brahmin, 224
Primary Series, 191
prinana, 106
pro-biotic, 118
pro-life, 118
Psilocybin, 236
Pungent, 91
Punjab, 22
Purana, 110
purification, xii, 116, 134, 145, 150,
    178, 193, 209, 246
pyramid
    three-sided, x
Pyramid, 166, 168, 170, 173, 198,
    199, 202
    Double, 168
Pyramids
    Four, 170

Q

Quantum Physics, 168

R

radiant, 49, 70, 73, 84, 116, 171
Raghava, 17, 25
Raja Yoga, 134, 136
Rajas, 85
Rajasic, 85, 185
Rajneesh, 205

Rakta, 105, 106, 107, 123
Rakta Moksha, 123
Rama, 17, 135
Ramayana, 17, 164
Rasa, 105, 106, 107
Rasayana, 124, 125
Rasayanas, 124
Reflexology, 121
reincarnation, 58
Reincarnation, 55
rejuvenation, 73, 122, 124
relax, xiii, 20, 133, 153, 179, 184,
    197, 199, 212, 229, 272
Relaxing, 212
Reproductive tissue, 105
rest days, 213
restless, 54, 81, 96, 103, 148
restless leg syndrome, 81
Retreat Center, 261, 268
ribcage, 184
Rishis, x, 51, 53, 56, 57, 59, 67, 133,
    135, 137, 140, 195
ritual fires, 249
Rue
    Syrian, 236
Rumi, 41, 131, 163, 249

S

S.N. Goenka, 246
sacred sex, 255
sacred temple, 255
sacrum, 172
Sadhus, 19
Sahasrara Chakra, 178
Salty, 91, 93
Sama, 104
samadhi, 229
Samasthiti, 172, 188, 189, 191
samskaras, 142, 178
Sanskrit, 13, 17, 50, 57, 75, 173, 198
Santa Cruz, 26
Santosha, 145
Sati, 240

satsang, 24
Sattva, 85
Sattvic, 85, 86, 185
Satya, 143, 144
Saucha, 145
Savasana, 189, 212
scents, 82, 125, 215
Scorpio, 44, 75
Seasons, 72
Seers, x
self control, 220
self massage, 125
Series
   "Advanced A", 18
   Third and Fourth, 18, 193
SEVEN DHATUS, 105
sex, 8, 18, 23, 35, 55, 70, 118, 127,
   158, 179, 181, 182, 223, 224, 225,
   228, 230, 231, 253, 254, 255, 258,
   259
Sex, 80, 220, 224, 226, 229, 231,
   255, 258, 269
   Divine Union of, 220
sexual intercourse, 229
sexual union, 241
sexuality, 18, 223, 227
Shaman, 32, 40
Shambhala Cove Retreat Center,
   268
Shams-e-Tabrez, 249
Shanti, ix, 28, 29, 102, 227, 261, 262
Shat Karmas, 134
shatavari, 124
Shiva, 134, 135, 239, 240, 241, 243,
   248, 253
Shiva and Shakti, 239, 240, 241,
   253
Shiva Samhita, 134, 135
Shukra, 105, 111, 112,118
Siddhasana, 150
Simplexity Health, 171
Singh
   Charan, 22, 23, 24, 25, 28, 248,
   249

Sirius, 209
Sivananda, 134
six cleansing practices, 134
six tastes, 91, 92, 94
six vital tissues, 112
skin, 11, 35, 57, 61, 62, 69, 70, 75,
   81, 82, 87, 98, 102, 104, 110, 116,
   119, 124, 149, 150, 156, 186, 187
sleep, 38, 71, 72, 76, 81, 82, 127, 146,
   149, 157, 166, 181, 236
sneezing, 71, 97
Son of God, 209
soul, 7, 52, 60, 131, 161, 186, 210,
   231, 240, 261
Sour, 91
Space, 59, 61, 62, 63, 64, 65, 70
Spalding
   Baird T., 8
sperm, 111, 231
spinal cord, 111, 236
spiraling vortexes, 203
spiritual, 7, 16, 18, 19, 22, 29, 35,
   39, 40, 42, 45, 55, 74, 86, 87, 115,
   127, 136, 145, 150, 178, 194, 200,
   201, 207, 219, 229, 241, 253, 257,
   259, 260
spleen, 69
split peas, 94
Sri K. Pattabhi Jois, ix, 11, 269
Sri Lanka, ix, 261, 262, 271
Sri Yantra, 168
ST. FRANCIS, 250
Star Wars, 184, 190
Sthira Bhaga, 193
Sthira sukham asanam, 147
stillness, 10, 38, 178, 198, 215, 247
stomach, 16, 20, 60, 67, 69, 98, 101,
   104, 111, 123
Superconsciousness, 231
Surya Namaskara, 188, 208, 214
sutra, 13, 20, 59, 58,75, 140, 141,
   147, 215,258
sutra neti, 13, 20
Svadisthana, 201

svarupe, 141
Swadhaya, 145
Swami Beyond Ananda, 86
Swami Paramahansa Yogananda, 160
Swami Vivekananda, 205
Swastika, 158
Swatmarama, 134
sweat, xi, 11, 62, 69, 102, 123, 184, 212
Sweet, 91, 92, 102
sweetie, 102
synergy, x, 220
Synovial, 68

T

T.K.V. Desikachar, 135
Tamas, 85
Tamasic, 85, 86, 185
Tantra, i, ix, x, xi, xvi, 1, 44, 45, 54, 56, 57, 58, 87, 112, 127, 142, 168, 177, 181, 216, 220, 223, 224, 225, 227, 228, 230, 233, 235, 237, 239, 241, 243, 244, 245, 253, 254, 255, 257, 259, 260, 261, 268
Tantric, xii, 168, 220, 244, 253, 259
tantrika, 253
Tapas, 145, 150
taste, 60, 91, 92, 93, 94, 101, 102, 106, 131, 156, 171, 196, 257
Tejas, 57, 115, 116, 117, 118, 120, 232
tetrahedron, x, 221
Tetrahedron, 168, 172, 173, 188, 195, 198
Tetrahedrons, 168
Tha, 135, 200
The Aquarian Gospel of Christ, 164
The Bible, 31, 209, 210
The DaVinci Code, 164
The Last Temptation of Christ, 164

THE PYRAMID CODE, x, 168
The Spirit of the Age, 210
therapeutic, 123, 150
Third Eye Technique, 248
thirst, 62, 71
Tibet, 135, 164
Tibetan, 168
Tikshna Agni, 104
Tower
    Eiffel, 172
toxins, 11, 63, 71, 94, 101, 110, 123, 148, 150, 151, 215
Toxins, 178
Tree of Knowledge, 52
Tree of Life, 52
Tridoshic, 124
TSUNAMI, 261
TSUNAMI of 2004, 261

U

Uddiyana, 176, 177, 178, 184, 186, 187, 230, 255, 258
Ujjayi, 173, 183, 184, 186, 187, 197, 244
ulcers, 69, 124
umbilical cord, 26
Universe, xii, 51, 125, 140, 144, 146, 168, 169
Upanishads, 17
urination
    excess, 69
Utpadana, 111

V

Vader
    Darth, 184
vagina, 111, 175, 240, 253
Vamana Rishi, 135, 136, 207
vasthanam, 141
Vata, 67, 70, 71, 72, 73, 74, 75, 76, 77, 78, 81, 82, 83, 84, 85, 86, 87,

88, 91, 92, 93, 94, 95, 96, 102, 104, 115, 117, 118, 120, 122, 123, 125, 211, 212, 213, 214, 229
vayu, 176
  Samana, 176
  Udana, 176
  Apana, 176
  Vyana, 177
Vedas, 17, 136, 140
Vedic, 58, 139, 158, 269
vedic astrology, 125
vegetarian, 7, 23, 86, 96, 158
vegetarianism, 5, 10
vibrant, xiii, 21, 50, 55, 73, 86, 87, 96, 105, 112, 119, 171, 179, 192, 207, 215, 225, 271
vibration, 57, 140, 161, 178, 181
Vigyan Bhairav Tantra, 243
Vikruti, 75, 76, 77, 112, 115, 211
village, 15, 23, 240, 263
Viniyoga, 135
Vinyasa Flow, 134
Virechana, 123
Vishama, 104
Vissudha, 201
Vivekananda
  Swami, 205
VPK, 77, 81, 82, 83, 87, 88, 92, 115, 117, 123
vritti, 140, 215

W

warrior, 2, 19, 177, 183, 228
Water, 59, 60, 62, 63, 65, 67, 68, 92, 93, 209
Wizard Yogi, 173, 188, 198, 200
womb, 46, 102, 175
World
  Ashtanga, 41

Y

Yama, 143, 146, 148, 151, 158, 224

Yamas, 143, 144, 147
Yang, 57
yawning, 71
yeast infections, 118
Yin, 57
Yoda, 190
Yoga, i, x, ix, x, xi, xvi, 1, 4, 5, 7, 8, 9, 10, 11, 13, 14, 17, 18, 19, 20, 21, 22, 23, 24, 26, 27, 28, 29, 31, 32, 37, 38, 39, 41, 42, 43, 44, 45, 49, 50, 54, 55, 56, 57, 58, 64, 69, 70, 72, 76, 82, 86, 87, 96, 99, 104, 106, 112, 117, 125, 127, 133, 134, 135, 136, 137, 139, 140, 141, 142, 144, 145, 146, 147, 148, 149, 150, 151, 152, 153, 155, 157, 158, 159, 160, 162, 164, 165, 166, 168, 172, 173, 175, 177, 180, 181, 182, 183, 184, 185, 187, 188, 189, 191, 193, 194, 195, 197, 198, 200, 205, 206, 207, 209, 211, 212, 213, 215, 220, 223, 224, 227, 228, 230, 231, 233, 235, 236, 237, 241, 243, 244, 245, 249, 254, 255, 257, 261, 262, 268, 269, 273
  Ashtanga, xi, 12, 22, 27, 134, 137, 191, 194, 205, 206, 211
  Ashtanga Vinyasa, 134
  Asthanga, 23
  Hatha, xi, 20, 134, 135, 136, 147, 200, 205, 209
  Power, 134
  Raja, 134, 136
  Vinyasa, 205
Yoga Chikitsa, 191
Yoga Journal, 26
Yoga Korunta, 135
Yoga Mala, 136, 211
Yoga Sutras, 135, 147, 150
Yoga Therapy, 191
Yogananda
  Swami Paramahansa, 160
Yogi
  Maharishi Mahesh, 205
  Mystic, 195

Yogic, xii, 20, 21, 31, 94, 117, 156,
  165, 176, 190, 199, 205
Yogis, i, x, 19, 20, 208, 220
yoni, 234, 240, 253, 255, 258

Z

Zen, 26, 42, 180, 182
Zietgeist, 210
zodiac, 202